# JOURNEYS
## WITH A TIN CAN PILGRIM

from corporate lawyer to Airstream nomad
finding joy in everyday life

## LYNDA ROZELL

st. john's press

*Nihil Obstat:* + Michael F. Burbidge
Bishop of Arlington
August 23, 2021

The *Nihil Obstat* is an official declaration that a book or pamphlet is free of doctrinal or moral error. No implication is contained therein that those who have granted the *Nihil Obstat* agree with the contents, opinions, or statements expressed.

Published by st. john's press
www.stjohnspress.com

All rights reserved. No part of this book may be reproduced in any form by any electronic or mechanical means (including photocopying, recording, or information storage and retrieval) without permission in writing from the publisher.

For more information and bulk sales, please email info@stjohnspress.com.

©2021 by Lynda Rozell

Library of Congress Cataloging-in-Publication Data
Rozell, Lynda
Journeys with a Tin Can Pilgrim: from corporate attorney to Airstream nomad, finding joy in everyday life

ISBN 978-1-955027-02-1 (paperback)
ISBN 978-1-955027-03-8 (e-book)
Library of Congress Control Number:
2021913800

Cover design and book illustrations: Hege Terese Fjæra, Olle Bolle Design
Design: INgrid Design
Editor-in-Chief: Torund Bryhn
Editor: Richard Willett
Photographs inside book: Lynda Rozell
Back cover photograph: Renata Grzan Wieczorek, FortheLoveofBeauty.com

Printed and bound in the United States of America by IngramSpark

Unless otherwise noted, biblical quotations are from the New American Bible (Revised Edition).

This is a work of non-fiction. In nearly all instances, only the first names of persons described in this book are used. In some cases the first name or details have been changed to protect the individual's privacy.

Two percent of proceeds from the sale of the book will go to the Homes On Wheels Alliance, Inc., a nonprofit 501(c)(3) public charity dedicated to assisting seniors and the working poor with securing unconventional housing as shelter, www.homesonwheelsalliance.org.

# DEDICATION

This book is dedicated with thanks and love to my friend Deirdre McQuade, a sister in Christ with a smile that lights up every place she goes. Her courage, faith, and joy in the face of adversity continue to inspire me in my journeys.

# CONTENTS

| | |
|---|---|
| **INTRODUCTION** | **1** |
| **Part One: Uncovering My Identity** | **6** |
| 1. All Things Work Together | 7 |
| 2. The Antitrust Lawyer | 9 |
| 3. Whatever Happened to Gloria Steinem? | 15 |
| 4. Surviving the Dark Night | 27 |
| 5. Finding My True Self | 33 |
| 6. A Bolt of Silver | 44 |
| 7. Go and Fear Nothing | 51 |
| 8. Buying the Airstream | 54 |
| 9. Signposts on the Journey Part One | 72 |
| **Part Two: Getting on the Road** | **76** |
| 10. First Trip | 77 |
| 11. Familiarizing Myself with the Dashboard | 84 |
| 12. Weighing It All Again | 97 |
| 13. Signposts on the Journey Part Two | 110 |
| **Part Three: Living on the Road** | **114** |
| 14. Driving Lessons | 115 |
| 15. Disaster Strikes | 133 |
| 16. Witness | 146 |
| 17. The Importance of Water | 158 |
| 18. The Restorative Power of Meals | 170 |
| 19. Seeds | 177 |
| 20. Being Present | 184 |
| 21. Finding Community | 192 |
| 22. Church Communities While Traveling | 205 |
| 23. Travel Plans and Road Maps | 211 |
| 24. Traveling during a Pandemic | 225 |

| | | |
|---|---|---|
| 25. | Fuel Stops | 231 |
| 26. | Breakdowns and Repairs | 236 |
| 27. | Signposts on the Journey Part Three | 245 |

**Part Four: Renewal on the Road** — **250**

| | | |
|---|---|---|
| 28. | Creativity | 251 |
| 29. | Becoming Your True Self | 263 |
| 30. | Signposts on the Journey Part Four | 272 |

**CONCLUSION: Around the Next Corner, Over the Next Hill** — **277**

| | |
|---|---|
| RV Translation Aid for Beginners (Glossary) | 281 |
| Resources | 286 |
| Thanks | 289 |

**Shortcuts, Detours, and Sidebars**

| | |
|---|---|
| Reflections on the Trees at Memorial Falls Poem | 14 |
| Psalm of My Heart (Conversion) Poem | 43 |
| Why an Airstream? | 50 |
| Five Things to Look for in a Tow Vehicle | 58 |
| How to Shop for an RV | 62 |
| Campground Etiquette | 83 |
| Electricity | 90 |
| Twelve Towing Tips | 120 |
| Seven Steps to Backing In | 124 |
| Arrival and Departure Tips | 128 |
| Weather Tips | 132 |
| Favorite Gizmos and Gadgets to Pack | 142 |
| Saints | 157 |
| Water Tips | 160 |
| Introduction to Religious Terms | 168 |
| Making Friends on the Road | 190 |
| Spiritual Childhood Poem | 248 |

# INTRODUCTION

Welcome to the journey!

This book is for you if you are thinking about living in a different way, if you have some level of dissatisfaction with your current circumstances.

It may mean that you are considering purchasing an RV, travel trailer, van or school bus, or an Airstream in particular.

It may mean that you are inspired or disturbed by the book or movie *Nomadland* and want to know more about modern day nomads.

It may mean that you are looking for beauty and the divine in life.

It may mean that you are suffering loss and yearn for healing.

It may mean that you feel apathetic about any kind of faith.

It may mean that you want to grow in your relationship with God.

It may mean that you yearn to become more fully Catholic in all aspects of your everyday life.

At various points in my life, I've been in all those places. I'd like to invite you to accompany me for a bit and then for you freely to discover your own path amid these circles. Your path may differ, but mine may help you find yours. This book is about how I came to live in an Airstream full-time, my adventures and lessons learned from nearly three years of travel, and the hope and joy I found that you too can have in your life.

At the end of each part of this book, you'll find an interactive religious reflection in a "Signposts" chapter. You can read them, discuss them with others, or choose not to look at them at all. Fair warning, though, that my faith shines within everything I write, whether you see it or not. Through my stories of life on the road, I lead you on a journey of self-discovery to find yourself as God made you to be. If you are overtly hostile to the idea of a God who personally loves the amazing, unique you, this book may challenge you to consider something new.

It's not just a spiritual memoir and devotional though! You'll also learn a lot of practical stuff and experience some adventures with me along the way, living the nomadic life in an Airstream RV.

Part One, "Uncovering My Identity," explains how I went from corporate lawyer to Airstream nomad. My husband and I were both busy professionals caught up in a whirlwind pace of work and entertainment. People change over time, however, and we grew apart, not together. I rediscovered my religious faith, but he felt left behind. Being wined and dined and admired lost its appeal for me as I focused more on the interior instead of the exterior. My baffled husband protested that "I married Gloria Steinem but woke up with Jerry Falwell." In the wake of our divorce, illness also forced me to detach from my work and the rewards that had been so important to me in my youth.

Part Two of the book, "Getting on the Road," addresses the practical aspects of getting on the road—from purchasing a tow vehicle and trailer, to downsizing to the Airstream, to weighing it all again before embarking on my journey. That said, this book is not for someone looking for a comprehensive technical manual on how to buy, maintain, and live in an Airstream or other RV. There are other books for that. Instead, the stories share what I learned about Airstreaming and RV life based on my personal experience as a woman in her late fifties camping in a travel trailer for the first time. You may also like the sidebars which summarize tips for nomads, and the glossaries that define terms for new RVers and those unfamiliar with religious references. I've also included a directory of resources for more in-depth exploration on your own.

Part Three, "Life on the Road," chronicles my adventures and growth while traveling. You might view it as the brighter side of *Nomadland*, the movie about a fictional woman's journey into healing and freedom on the road. Or as one friend remarked, if you remember *Zen and the Art of Motorcycle Maintenance*, you might relate to my story as a variation on that theme, as "Christianity and the Art of Airstream Travel." As in Part Two, the practical and spiritual are interwoven through storytelling, with sidebars providing a summary of tips for RV life.

All these paths and themes come together in Part Four, "Renewal on the Road," as I reflect upon creativity and identity and the fruits of my travels. I let go of everything to find joy. God is never outdone in generosity. What I gave up from my past life has been repaid many times over with what really matters. Every day I wake up in my Airstream, I experience it all as a gift —birds chirping, rain pattering on the shiny curved roof, or soft pink light glowing as the sunrise paints the sides of my tiny silver home with brief swaths of color. Peace in my heart as I gaze at my campfire on a starry night inspires me to share the reasons for my joy with others.

Journey with me as I experience the beauty of God in creation and community on the road. Let's go!

# Part One

# UNCOVERING MY IDENTITY

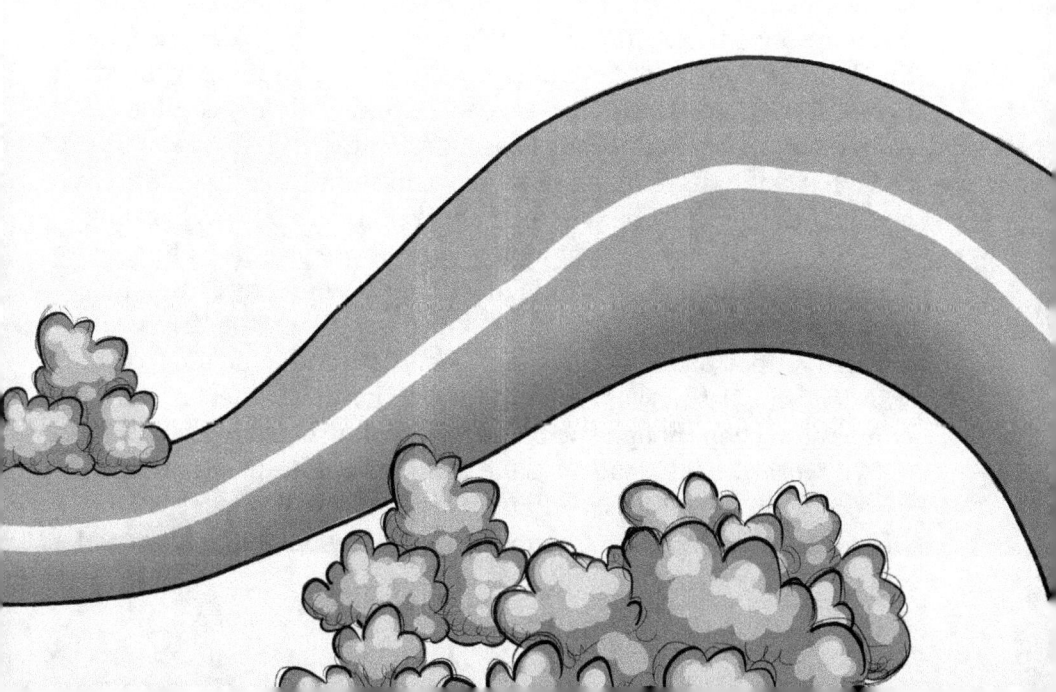

CHAPTER ONE

# ALL THINGS WORK TOGETHER

*"Toto, I've a feeling we're not in Kansas anymore."*
—Dorothy in *The Wizard of Oz*

Lightning flashed, illuminating the wildly waving branches that lined the narrow road. I couldn't see far in front of me. My hazard lights kept me company with a steady blink, while my copilot was passed out on the floor of the passenger seat.

"What was I thinking?" I thought to myself. "Next time, if there is a next time, I will change my plans if there are storms brewing. And I definitely won't tow at night." With those promises, I prayed silently for safety in the Florida downpour. Penny, my Chihuahua, was supremely confident. She looked up from the floor and yawned, unperturbed by the sharp peals of thunder. So long as she was near me, Penny was content, making her the perfect traveling companion even though she couldn't take a turn driving.

We were on the road to Lake Talquin to camp in a friend's yard as we traveled west. I'd just picked up my first-ever RV—an Airstream travel trailer. It happily tracked my big green truck as I peered through the storm, looking for taillights ahead of me. My fear of the weather didn't dampen the warm glow I felt seeing my tiny silver home behind me. Still, I fervently prayed as daggers of lightning briefly illuminated the roiling black sky above through the nearly solid wall of water streaming down my windshield. The frantically waving wipers barely kept it clear enough to see the edges of the road. I didn't dare pull over, because the narrow road had drainage ditches on each side and my visibility was so limited. I drove slowly, hazards flashing, not another car in sight.

Gradually, the storm passed. Through the disintegrating wisps of clouds, stars became visible. Soon, I found a place to pull off the road and call my friend. An hour later I'd arrived and parked in her yard. We walked and fed Penny, who'd remained blissfully asleep through the worst of the storm. Together, we sat on my friend's porch with her dogs while we ate dinner and caught up.

I didn't bother to unhitch or connect to power, but simply opened my Airstream's windows and slept. The soft light of the sunrise woke me and the world smelled new. The open road beckoned. As I drove away later that morning, newly refreshed, I thought about how all paths in my past had converged to bring me to this freedom and peace.

CHAPTER TWO

# THE ANTITRUST LAWYER

*"I feel thin, sort of stretched, like butter scraped over too much bread."*
—Bilbo Baggins in *The Fellowship of the Ring* by J. R. R. Tolkien

## Wined and Dined and on the Fast Track

Forty years ago I worked every day for nine months in a row, except one Sunday afternoon. Married young, I whizzed through my college, master's, and law school degrees at the University of Virginia while my husband completed his Ph.D. and worked at a nearby college. At the tail end of the 1980s, as a summer associate attending a prestigious law school, I was wined and dined by firms seeking fresh talent. Outings in hot air balloons, Kennedy Center performances, fine restaurants, private tours of the Supreme Court, and more were the norm for the lucky few being wooed by top-tier law firms.

I even met my namesake—Lynda Bird Johnson Robb—at a small cocktail party at her home when her husband, Chuck Robb, the former governor of Virginia, joined the firm I was working at for the summer. Upon being introduced, I told Lynda that I owed the "y" in my name to her. When my mother sent out christening invitations for the name "Linda," an aunt had sent back a gift for "Lynda." My mom liked the spelling so much that she chose it (thankfully so, since there were many Lindas in my classes in elementary school!). My aunt, I explained to Lynda Robb, spelled my name with a "y" because she, as Vice President Johnson's daughter, spelled her name that way.

At that revelation, the elegant Mrs. Robb arched her eyebrows and said "I'm horrified to be old enough to have a summer associate named after me." I think she was kidding, but was not entirely sure, since she abruptly turned away to enter a different conversation.

That ended up not being a career-limiting gesture, however, as I did receive a generous offer from and ultimately joined the same firm as her husband. My first job out of law school was working for that well-known firm in Washington, DC, with around seven hundred lawyers in seven different offices. I joined the antitrust team, working for one of the finest lawyers and human beings I've ever known—Bill, the partner in charge of the DC branch of that team. Armored with my tailored suits, black steel-reinforced briefcase, and high heels, I plunged into busy days of intense work.

Meanwhile, my husband took care of the house in Virginia and meals, while enjoying with me the fine dining, entertainment, and exotic vacations that my work made possible. Of course, FedEx packages could find me even at a tropical beach, and documents reviewed could be sent back by overnight delivery whenever the law firm needed me.

Even exercise was at a gym near work. All my thoughts and energies were focused on doing the best possible, highest quality work. When we were on tight deadlines, the firm even arranged a hotel room overnight in DC so I did not have to waste time commuting back home to sleep. Meals were brought in for us in crisis-type situations. The camaraderie and quality of the people I worked with made this lifestyle enjoyable. And my natural yearning for approval and praise was amply fed.

That pace will burn out even the most enthusiastic young lawyer, however. While not as intense as the first nine months working in a relatively new area of law for the firm, my next several years were chock-full of interesting research, advocacy, and writing projects as I honed my skills and reputation. I loved working on some creative volunteer projects, called pro bono work, expected of all lawyers as part of their professional responsibility and particularly encouraged for those on a partnership track. I had the chance then to help individuals rather than corporations. A theory I advanced even became new law in a copyright case that went to the Supreme Court.

When you overreach and push yourself, out of pride instead of for service, you can go astray. Doing things well is a virtue. Nonetheless, when it slips into intemperance, the perfect becomes the enemy of the good. Eventually, my pride caused me to stumble. I didn't see that at the time, because I had no religious faith back then. I hadn't developed my relationship with God and I lacked a supernatural perspective, or any other means of insight. Like the people who built the tower of Babel, I was completely focused on what I could do, not on the meaning of it. The pace of life kept me from stepping back and looking at things more deeply.

## Looking Back with Perspective

As I continued my drive west with Penny and my new Airstream, I realized that now everything was about the deeper meaning. My journey was spiritual as well as physical. The clear blue sky, freed from all the remnants of yesterday's storm, contrasted with the dark and frightening scene Penny and I had traversed last night. The roots of my journey to the present, I realized, were in a difficult past now redeemed by the grace of God.

Back in the late 1980s and early 1990s, one valuable asset I brought to my team at the law firm was the ability to be the person on the ground when others were out in the field. My mentor and other senior attorneys traveled to clients through all sorts of time zones, and even if they were three or eight hours later than DC, I'd often get an email or a voicemail message that they needed an issue researched or documents gathered and sent to them. Thus, they could go to dinner with clients or go to sleep after a long day in their time zone, confident I'd have the answer ready for them the next morning or sooner.

Because every moment I worked was accounted for in billable increments, it made no sense for me to spend time on tasks like copying or faxing that my staff could do for me. My mentor and I shared a phenomenal secretary named Susan. Her duties went far beyond calls, scheduling, filing, and reconciling our time sheets and expenses. She'd order food delivered when we would otherwise be too busy to eat. She'd let me know when it was time to triage my overflowing purse or take my pile of shoes out from under my desk because the carpet was going to be cleaned. Because I was a perfectionist and worked extremely hard, my legal work was very good and people relied on me. Fortunately, my mentor, although sharing those work traits, also had a great sense of humor. I took myself too seriously to develop one until later in life. Both technology and my ability to laugh at myself have advanced greatly since those days.

Late one afternoon, I received a message from Bill that some documents and analysis were needed by the next day. I stayed until about 11 p.m. and did not want to simply drop off the fifty or so pages in the inbox for the night staff to fax after they finished other urgent projects for other attorneys. I wanted to be sure they reached Bill on time. In my zeal, I used a fax machine on our floor myself, leaving secure in the knowledge that I'd accomplished my task and could drive the hour home to sleep.

The next morning, I received a phone call bright and early. Bill thanked me for my hard work and said he just had one question. What was on the other side of the blank pages delivered to his hotel room?

The fax had arrived perfectly, in time for the meeting for which he needed it. However, I'd placed the document in the machine facing the wrong direction. Fortunately, Susan had come into the office early before I arrived. She saw the copy I'd left her on her desk, so she was able to resend it to Bill as soon as he noticed the glitch.

I was horrified, but Bill laughed until he was practically crying and said he was glad to know I was human. It gave him a great story to tell for many years—even in retirement, where he now makes short videos about butterflies.

All this happened long before I began to address my hidden mental health issues. Under the facade of the brilliant, ambitious, and effective lawyer, I was a lost soul. Despite my accomplishments, I felt anxious and insecure, as if I were an imposter playing a part in a show. I didn't let people get too close, in the fear they'd see who I really was and reject me. During this time, my husband was the sun around which my universe revolved. But he too reveled in my professional success, which unfortunately only reinforced my tendency to value myself for what I did rather than who I was. I didn't realize how unhealthy both my professional and personal lives were until I began my long journey to faith in God, who loves me for who I am.

Today, I still have to check my tendencies to exhaust myself by overdoing things. Even so, I'm able to tolerate my limits and failures with affection and good humor, knowing how God views them. Keeping that in mind, I pulled over at a highway rest stop with my Airstream. After a couple of hours of towing, it was time to walk Penny and get a fresh cup of coffee. I poured some water into her bowl and set it on the ground near a bench. I might not get to my destination when I'd planned, but the sun and a small breeze refreshed us both as we relaxed before continuing our journey. I said a small prayer in thanksgiving for the beautiful day and asked for continued protection on the road. As I sipped my coffee and Penny rolled in the grass, I smiled thinking about how I'd arrived at peace from my former anxiety to get everything right, to be always in control. I felt quite fond of my past self, as if she were a child of mine rather than myself, because in accepting my flaws and turning them over to God, I had allowed Him to help me grow—still an ongoing process!

MEMORIAL FALLS, MT

## REFLECTIONS ON THE TREES AT MEMORIAL FALLS

*Are we wrapped around stones too?*

*The tree roots emerge like carvings, twisted, sinuous*

*Where does the rock end and the roots begin?*

*The crown of green reaches up exploding brilliantly against the blue sky*

*But these unseen roots intertwined deep within the foundations*

*are what makes it possible*

by Lynda Rozell © 2021

CHAPTER THREE

# WHATEVER HAPPENED TO GLORIA STEINEM?

*"When we are no longer able to change a situation, we are challenged to change ourselves."*
—Viktor Frankl

## Conversion

Before I started to rediscover faith in God, my life revolved around work and my husband. The law firm expected work to be my top priority. Hungry for praise and appreciation, the monetary rewards and excellent reviews I received motivated me to put my work first. My husband was a workaholic too, so we did not think this whirlwind was odd. We enjoyed fantastic expensive vacations, frequent meals out, opera and concerts—all the trappings of the yuppie life. Having to upend personal plans and accept phone calls and drop everything when needed by the firm seemed a small price.

This merry-go-round paused when I broke a finger horseback riding.

With our busy schedules, my husband and I decided to spend time together taking riding lessons on Sundays. Since neither of us practiced any religion, Sunday seemed the perfect day. Admittedly, form-fitting jodhpurs and fancy black leather riding boots were part of the appeal for me at that stage in my life. English riding seemed quite elegant and an appropriate vehicle for an urbanite couple to get exercise together without going to a sweaty gym.

My horse was called Bambi—a deceptively charming name for an evil horse that seemed to delight in stopping short before jumps and in wandering off the path to eat anything that attracted his seemingly insatiable appetite. In retrospect, I'm sure my inexperience and tension played a large part in Bambi's attitude. However, one morning I broke my ring finger simply pulling myself up into the saddle. Bambi had nothing to do with it, although I'd had several falls from that horse on other occasions.

Fortunately, I took my rings off right away. Then, I ignored the pain until after we returned home and my finger swelled up in shades of deep purple. My husband and I had planned to wallpaper a bedroom together, so I took some ibuprofen and continued full steam ahead. Once we finished, he glanced at my finger again and told me, "I think you'd better go to the emergency room," so I did.

One thing you never want to hear after getting an X-ray and meeting with an emergency room doctor is "I've never seen anything like this before!" My ring finger bone between the knuckle and first joint contained an alarmingly large bone tumor. Thankfully, it turned out to be benign.

There was a famous hand surgeon who happened to be in the hospital, so the emergency room physician called him in for a consult. The surgeon's eyes glistened with happiness as he told me that this was a remarkable enchondroma, and he would be glad to have me as a patient. His plan was to remove the tumor and replace the gap that would be left with bone tissue taken from my hip. The expert hand surgeon even ended up asking my permission to photograph the surgery and write about it. First, though, my broken finger had to heal. Essentially, the bone was a hollowed-out eggshell supported by the tumor inside. That seemingly strong facade had hidden debilitating disease within.

This medical event stopped my fast-paced lawyer life short in its tracks. I had to take time off from work. Due to the demands of physical therapy, and the fogginess of pain medication, I went on short-term disability using the excellent benefits provided by the firm.

This period gave me time to think and reflect. Without work, I felt empty, useless, and unfulfilled. Yet, I suspected that work was really not the answer.

I began doing a lot of self-help and spiritual reading. I remembered occasions over the years when I had felt prompted to go back to church and to pray, but set those feelings aside as not my main concern then or even now, during my recuperation. I ignored a sign in front of a church I drove by often on my way to physical therapy that read "Inactive Catholics, Rediscover Your Church: We Welcome You Home!"

Instead, I used my unaccustomed free time for rest, making meals with my husband, spending time with our dogs, and reading. In thinking about my career, I realized the most fulfilling work I'd done involved helping other people, not the highly lucrative and mentally absorbing complexities of antitrust law. I considered changing my field of practice. I also worried about whether I might have later physical complications and whether the stress of my work would impact my health in other ways. My husband had settled into a good job, and we discussed how I really didn't need to make as much money. On the other hand, I loved the people I worked with and the great assignments I received. I started researching alternative career possibilities even as I started back into the rhythm of working at the firm.

As I gradually transitioned back to work, doing physical therapy for my hand, I became closer to David, a friend of mine from law school who worked at the same firm. He was a year ahead of me in a different practice area. My husband and I had gotten to know him well due to a shared interest in politics. We lived near one another and always sought him out at firm events. We were happy for him when we heard that he'd gotten engaged.

David began regularly stopping by my office to remind me to take the time to do my physical therapy exercises. Years ago, he'd had a similar benign bone tumor in his pinky, but slacked off on therapy. He still could not bend it very much. David persisted in reminding me to stick to my therapy exercises even during the business of daily work.

Then, in February, everything changed.

I returned from lunch one day to find many empty offices and a few sobbing secretaries on my floor. News had arrived that David, whose gentle nature and humor made him popular with many of our colleagues, was not coming back. He had died of a heart attack climbing a mountain in Argentina while on vacation. His body could not be retrieved immediately due to weather conditions. David was only thirty-three, just two years older than me.

Shocked at the news, I closed the door to my office and sat at my desk trying to understand how such a good person could die so young. I was devastated by David's loss and couldn't believe I'd never see his cheerful smile again. Anger and grief like a tumultuous wave crashed over me in what I thought was the safety of my carefully constructed full life. Where was God, if there was a God, in this?

I heard a voice in my heart gently say "go to church and pray for him." I realized that all the other times I previously had heard quiet promptings to return to church I had shut out that voice. This time, I listened within my grief.

I found a nearby church, Saint Stephen the Martyr in Georgetown. Sitting in one of the wooden pews, I sobbed. I talked to God for the first time in many years. I promised Him to start going to church again and asked him to take care of David and David's family. I was ashamed that God apparently had to hit me over the head with a two-by-four because I'd ignored His earlier promptings. Of course, David's death wasn't about me, but God allowed that loss to produce good fruit in turning me back to Him.

David's death marked the start of a radical metanoia, or conversion, for me. For the first time in decades, I began feebly to pray, trying to remember prayers from my childhood. I started occasionally attending Mass on Sunday at the church with the welcoming sign I previously had ignored. It slowly dawned on me that a less hectic pace of life, one that allowed time for introspection and for helping other people, might be something God wanted me to do and might be a healthier way to live. My husband thought it would be good for the two of us to spend more time together, provided I could maintain a certain income, not simply work for legal services or a clinic for the poor as I initially contemplated. With his qualified support, I spoke with my mentor at the firm and began applying for government jobs.

I quickly landed a staff position in consumer protection at the Federal Trade Commission, for a much lower salary than I'd been making in private legal practice. The work expectations were far different from those of the firm. I could expect to enjoy most weekends and holidays off and would not have billable hour expectations to fulfill. As I gained more time with a slightly slower pace of life, I began praying from my heart, not just by set formal prayers. Before I knew it, I was attending church every Sunday. The Gospel readings I heard there made me want to know Christ more. I realized I was hungry for God and that I'd been missing something crucial in my life for a very long time.

As I finished my coffee at the highway rest stop, I smiled again, remembering how my younger self had stumbled into a longing for truth. Penny already was tugging on the leash, clearly ready to walk more before getting back in our truck and continuing our journey. I dumped out her remaining water and we resumed our stroll.

We headed back to the parking lot, detouring around trees and bushes that caught Penny's attention. She jumped and barked when a small breeze rolled an empty paper cup toward her. She cautiously approached it and pushed it with her paw, darting back when it moved. Then she grabbed it in her mouth and dropped it, looking at me expectantly. I absentmindedly rolled it on the ground for her to chase as my thoughts turned again to the year I returned to the Catholic Church. Penny's surprise and then acceptance of something new reminded me of how often I was startled as I found out and cautiously tested what Catholics actually believe.

One of the first Sundays I attended Mass as an adult, I was shocked to my core when the priest preached about the Real Presence—that the piece of unleavened bread and the wine consecrated by the priest and received in Communion literally were the body, blood, soul, and divinity of Jesus Christ. How was this possible? How did I never hear this in years of catechism class as a child?

I related to the disciples who felt shocked and turned away in the Gospels in disgust at the idea of consuming human flesh. They left Jesus behind because this teaching was too hard to accept, but in my heart I knew it was true. Like the fisherman Simon who became the apostle Peter, I believed Jesus Christ so where else was I to go? Plus, being concealed in the outer appearances of bread and wine made the idea of actually consuming my Lord one of awe and wonder rather than disgust. If this could be true, maybe more things I'd rejected in my childhood and never thought about again also were true. I finally understood why Catholics kneel on one knee when entering a Church. Jesus was physically present, waiting for us—waiting for me!—in the tabernacle. The God of the Universe voluntarily made Himself small and vulnerable so that He could be united with us. A deep joy began to fill me as I realized that this God was a person who loved me, the real me, and I loved Him back.

I began to long to receive Jesus in Holy Communion, so much so that I decided I would go to confession. I'd learned through the homilies I heard that receiving the consecrated bread or wine means that you are in communion with Christ and the Church; I didn't want to receive Him burdened by sins that separated me from Him. Despite my terror at going to confession for the first time in eighteen years, I gathered my resolve, praying for courage since the last time I'd gone was when I was only thirteen. I had a lot to confess, and I had yet to understand that confession was not about punishment and humiliation, but rather about God's healing mercy and the gift of grace to help avoid sin in the future.

The Saturday afternoon that I entered Saint Leo the Great Catholic Church in Fairfax for confession I literally trembled. "Do I really want to do this?' I asked myself. "Maybe I should wait until I've studied more." But my heart was drawn to the tabernacle. I longed for Him, to be fully united with Him in love. Fighting the urge to turn around and run, I took my place in line. Inadvertently, I cut ahead of some young children whom I had assumed were waiting for their parents. I was so nervous that I didn't remember that children go to confession as young as age seven or eight.

When it was my turn, I entered the dim confessional, a tiny room separated from another tiny room by a screen. I could make out the outline of the priest's face through the little holes in the screen and realized it was Father Daly, an elderly, no-nonsense priest whom I'd heard preach several times.

"Bless me, Father, for I have sinned. It's been eighteen years since my last confession and I don't really know how to do this," I whispered.

"Alleluia! Welcome back!" he boomed. "It's wonderful that you are here. I'll walk you through it." He did, and it wasn't as hard as I'd thought it would be. After he absolved me and I left the confessional to pray some prayers as penance, I felt so full of joy that I might have just floated up to the ceiling. It was like I was looking back at the church, the town, and the world from a distance, in the arms of my Father God. It didn't dampen my exhilaration at all when a man approached me in the pew rather apologetically to tell me that his kids were upset that I'd cut in front of them in line. I just smiled at him. "Oh, I'm so sorry! I just went to confession for the first time in years and didn't realize they were old enough to be in line. I thought they were waiting for you! Please let them know that I'm sorry."

During confession, Father Daly had suggested I sign up for the annual inquiry course for converts so I could learn more about my faith. The class led me to deepen my intellectual knowledge, but the really significant thing for me at the time was the lightness and happiness I finally felt at being home in the Church. This "reversion"—as some refer to the renewed conversion of adults who return to the Church after a period of absence—changed my life, slowly but surely.

As I placed Penny back in the truck, I felt amazed that I was actually here in the present towing a shiny Airstream with a beautiful green Dodge Ram 1500. If someone had told me all those years ago that I would one day be traveling the country full-time trusting God to let me know how to serve Him in the moment, I would have laughed out loud at them. Yet now I was laughing inside with joy, thanking God for changing my life and freeing me to leave the past behind to follow Him.

It didn't happen overnight, I thought, as I started my truck and watched the lights on the trailer glow. Conversion takes a moment, but sanctification is the work of a lifetime, as one saint has stated. Like yeast, the Holy Spirit changes the substance of who you are, transforming you into something else. Such metamorphosis sometimes leads to conflict.

## From Gloria Steinem to Jerry Falwell

Everyone knows when they get married that they and their spouse will change. We imagine we will grow together like two trees leaning into each other from different roots, branches intertwining over the years. Unfortunately, sometimes changes happen that draw us apart instead of together.

At first, my husband supported my new interest in faith. He could tell that I was happier and excited about reading and learning more. When my relationship with Jesus began to change me, though, and impact more than a few hours on Sunday mornings, faults in our marriage that had always been there deepened. I no longer was content to keep busy with travel, opera, fine wines and food, but was focused more on the interior life. I tried to engage him in it as well, but failed. Not only was he not interested in a personal relationship with God, he was baffled and upset by the time and attention I was devoting to prayer and worship. He thought my faith would be just one in a series of diverting hobbies I pursued for a while before dropping each of them and doing something else, like horseback riding or acrylic painting. When that didn't happen, he became unhappy. "I married Gloria Steinem," he complained, "and I woke up with Jerry Falwell."

Actually, I really never was Gloria Steinem; it was just a facade. My husband and I met at college, when he was the resident advisor for my dormitory. I was unsure of my own self, and had no interest at all in religion then. Just before I met him, I switched majors when I discovered that my talent for art was rather pedestrian when compared to others enrolled in the art program. My perfectionist self wouldn't accept less than excellence. In my mind I could hear echoes of my father's voice whenever I failed to get the highest grade. "What happened to the other 5 percent?" my father (and later I) would ask, rather than being content with my effort and a score of 95 percent. That hypercritical interior voice motivated much of my hard work in school and professionally.

By contrast, my future husband thought I was amazing and frequently praised me. He adored me and pampered me with gifts and flowers and romantic gestures. I fell deeply in love and we got engaged just six weeks after our first date. I enthusiastically joined in his interests, happy to be so involved with him and have no conflict at all. We took classes together, studied together, and after moving to Charlottesville, Virginia, we made new friends together. Our social life and hobbies revolved exclusively around each other. For the first five years of our marriage, we never even had an argument, mainly because I thought he walked on water.

We stayed on the same trajectory for many years, even after we each pursued our own professional careers. But I began to realize that something was missing and felt increasingly anxious and sad. If I disagreed with my husband about something, he became cold and distant until I figured out what was wrong and changed my behavior or opinions to stay close to him. I felt increasingly hollow on the inside, like I wasn't a real person, but just an outline of one.

When my friend David suddenly died and I finally opened a door to God's persistent seeking, everything changed. God filled the emptiness in my spirit with love and happiness. I would wake up thanking Him for the day. Throughout the day, I'd make time to try to get to know Him better through prayer and reading the Bible and other spiritual books. Once I started taking the inquiry class, my eyes were opened. I would learn something and then try to tell my husband about it. I attempted to engage him with explanations of how the Old Testament prefigured the coming of Christ and how God was not distant but intimately concerned with every detail of our lives. Earnestly, I tried to convince him with logical lawyerly arguments based on history and philosophy. I remember when I proclaimed to him that "Jesus really is the way, the truth, and the life! It's all true. God is a real person who loves us and wants us to be happy by living in harmony with Him, now and forever." I begged my husband to be open to accepting this gift so we could grow together in love with the Lord. This did not go well.

"You've lost your mind," he responded. "If you want to go to church, fine, but leave me out of it."

As I grew in faith, I realized my own dignity and became more independent. I began to try to live consistently with my beliefs and to love my husband in a more genuine way, not simply by agreeing with him on everything. I became friends with Catholic mothers in a mom's group and joined a prayer circle. I struggled to be kind and loving, and to let my husband see that I was a better wife for having found God. However, I wouldn't back down on what I saw as fundamental to being a faithful daughter of my Father God, like regular prayer, volunteer work, teaching our children the faith, and trying to follow the Ten Commandments and the teachings of the Church as best I could in daily life.

It was a long journey from those years to the present, I mused, as I drove over to the gas pumps to top off my tank before getting back on the road. While I waited my turn, I leaned over to scratch Penny's upturned belly, smiling at how her tongue hung slightly askew out of her small mouth.

My oldest daughter called me right before I left the gas station. She wanted to confirm the date I expected to be near her home in Virginia, as she was trying to arrange a visit with her father. He had stopped talking to me a few years ago, so she wanted to be sure she wasn't inviting us both for a visit at the same time. We compared schedules and I continued on my way. I thanked God for the present and how everything had turned out. The sunny open highway ahead of me was quite a contrast to the dark road I had traveled when my children were small and my marriage died.

How I changed when I found God—or rather allowed Him to find me—threatened the way my marriage had been. My husband never bargained for a fundamental transformation in his wife. He longed for my old self, the twenty-year-old that he had married, or at least the still immature go-getter attorney pursuing a plush lifestyle with him. He missed the young woman who adored him above anything or anyone else.

Our differences led to arguments. Admittedly, I didn't respond well to conflict and often reacted with fear and distance. I began to realize the possible cost of my conversion while stubbornly clinging to the possibility that we could stay together. "You are trying to be holier than the Pope,' he complained. "Ninety-six percent of Catholics don't believe everything the Church teaches." I struggled intellectually and spiritually to try to compromise where possible, but I couldn't turn away from what I knew to be true.

After years of counseling and trying to make things work, I finally realized the marriage was over the day my husband told me he was divorcing me. "Lynda, let's go get some Indian food, just the two of us," he suggested. A neighbor agreed to babysit our small children, and we drove to a favorite Indian restaurant making small talk.

"This is so nice," I said, reaching for his hand at the table.

He pulled his hand back and put down the menu. "I asked you here to let you know I want a divorce," he said. "This isn't going to work. You want things I don't want. It's like you joined a cult," he told me. "I don't even know who you are anymore. I thought you'd come around over time, but instead you now have something you share with the children that excludes me."

"You don't have to be excluded," I argued. "I thought we were getting along better."

"No," he said, "I stopped trying and saved myself the aggravation. I'm not arguing with you anymore. I'm just done."

I never forgot that day or the pain that followed. It haunted me for years, and the repercussions exceeded anything I thought I could bear. But with God all things are possible, and God was true to His promises to me, His prodigal daughter.

At the time, however, I felt like the bottom had dropped out of my world. I choked down the food with my stomach churning. My husband calmly enjoyed his meal, chatting with the waiter, relieved to have implemented the decision that would in his estimation make him much happier than staying with the person I'd become.

I became distraught. Even through the worst of our arguments, I had thought we would manage to stay together and eventually work things out. I hadn't realized that I might be called to live the scriptural exhortation that following Christ would lead to conflict. "Do you think that I have come to establish peace on the earth?" Jesus asks his disciples, "No, I tell you, but rather division. From now on a household of five will be divided, three against two and two against three; a father will be divided against his son and a son against his father, a mother against her daughter and a daughter against her mother, a mother-in-law against her daughter-in-law and a daughter-in-law against her mother-in-law." (Luke 12:51–53). Earlier, he told them that "I have come to set the earth on fire, and how I wish it were already blazing!" (Luke 12:49) The fire lit in my spirit by the Word of God burned—but also generated new life.

CHAPTER FOUR

# SURVIVING THE DARK NIGHT

*"Desolation is a file and the endurance of darkness is preparation for great light."*
—Saint John of the Cross

Ironically, while my marriage was slowly falling apart, success in my work as a staff member at my agency had led to promotion to the highest level I could achieve there without being a member of the Senior Executive Service. I served as an attorney advisor on the personal staff of two sequential commissioners at the Federal Trade Commission.

With greater responsibility, however, and the professional accolades that affected me like a drug, came greater stress at work. As daily conflict with my husband worsened, I kept thinking about my marriage problems. Worrying and grief took up my mental energy. I became bogged down in the details of projects, finding that I could only do one thing at a time instead of juggling multiple assignments at once with ease. Sleep was almost always elusive, and I constantly felt tense and on guard, not knowing what other catastrophe would spring up. My faith wasn't very deep at this point, so I had not learned to trust God in all things. Instead, I struggled to do it all and ignored my feelings, burying my anguish under layers of hard work and keeping busy, a method that had worked for me in my youth and my professional life to date.

"Thankfully, Penny," I remarked to my always understanding dog as we stopped in a traffic jam, "I don't do that anymore. It really doesn't work; it just conceals the real problems." She looked back up at me earnestly, probably wondering if I were going to give her a treat. When traffic started to move again, I turned my eyes back to the road and saw that the slowdown was due to an accident. As we passed a car with a shattered windshield and crushed hood, I said a prayer for those involved and the first responders helping them. The broken glass reminded me of how I crashed mentally and emotionally when my husband told me he was divorcing me. Like the pressure of ice coating tree branches in layers during a winter storm, the weight of the layers I was hiding behind then became overwhelming and I shattered.

In my grief, I could barely get out of bed in the morning, much less take good care of my children. They learned to make their own lunches and wash their own clothes—or not—until I hired a nanny. I struggled to perform at work. Others who cared about me there tried helping by assuming some of my responsibilities during what they thought was a temporary hard time. Weeks stretched into months with no improvement in sight.

Although I tried to find spiritual and psychiatric help, I could not escape the darkness. I didn't accept my suffering; I fought against it, but I didn't invite God into that struggle. I kept focusing on what I could do to fix the unfixable and became sadder and more exhausted as I failed again and again. Various courses of medication did not help what was diagnosed as clinical depression. Like a swimmer caught in a whirlpool, the harder I fought the deeper I sank. I pictured in my mind's eye clinging desperately to Jesus's outstretched hands in this storm or pulling myself up onto a thin tightrope stretching across the turbulent chasm. Saints and my loved ones encouraged me while I kept slipping precariously close to the depths.

After twenty-one years of marriage, where I depended upon my husband for my sense of self-worth and for many practical details of life, like managing money and paying bills, I was on my own. I hadn't yet learned to rely on God peacefully in the storm. Like Peter, I jumped out of the boat in faith to run toward Jesus. Unlike Peter, when I started to sink, I didn't let Jesus catch me but unsuccessfully went back to my old habits of pretending I could handle it myself. The waves of darkness that battered me weren't just from the loss of my marriage. All the barriers I'd carefully erected against trauma from my past also collapsed, sweeping me away in a tsunami.

My husband and I became enmeshed in a struggle over custody of the children. Eventually we agreed upon a shared custody arrangement: the children alternated a week with me and a week with their father. A few years after our divorce, he remarried. Once our children were grown and we no longer shared any responsibility for them under the divorce settlement, he cut off all contact with me.

In the immediate aftermath of our separation, however, my mental health continued to deteriorate. I couldn't understand why God would let this happen when I was trying to be faithful. Yet, like Job, I kept praising Him even in my misery. I struggled not to give in to despair, not to listen to the lie that kept popping into my head—that He too had left me, because I was unworthy of love. This was such a struggle because I was still a baby Catholic. I had not yet reached the point where faith was so real that I knew God would never change, never hurt me gratuitously, and never abandon me, no matter what other people did.

In retrospect, I know now that the suffering I experienced then freed me from a deep-rooted dependency on others for affirmation. What I thought was love from the most important persons in my life was instead many times a desire to control me based on their own wounds. This painful process actually cauterized my own unhealed injuries from childhood and my pre-conversion adult years. It eventually allowed me to become fully alive in God's love. It lanced a boil of poison that lay deep within my soul and allowed the pus to drain so I could become whole and healthy, as the person God created me to be.

At the time, though, I was miserable. I desperately tried to reassert my own control over circumstances beyond it. In an attempt to stabilize my work situation, and at my commissioner's kind but firm suggestion, I transferred to a less demanding staff attorney position instead of continuing to try to work as an attorney advisor at the commission level. Even then, I still struggled with simple tasks. Writing complex analyses or legal briefs or even a simple speech was way beyond my abilities. My brain was in a fog. There were days I could not remember where I had parked my car or what I was supposed to do next, and I'd burst into tears of frustration at work. A kind paralegal once helped me collect my belongings from my office and walked with me to locate my car. All the sadness, darkness, and pain of the past seemed to drown out any progress I'd made.

My condition kept getting worse. Often as I walked to work after parking, I would stand on the side of the street fighting the impulse to throw myself under a bus. Every moment of the day was an exhausting struggle not to give into the blackness that constantly surrounded me and threatened to overwhelm me. I prayed not to hurt myself or leave my children without a mother.

Worst of all, I felt far away from God. He didn't seem to answer my prayers. The warm feelings and consolations He had provided to me when I first came back to the Church and in difficult times during my marriage were gone. Most times I went to church, I cried silently in the pew. There was no peace in my heart, and I felt my thoughts going around and around like mice trapped in a maze. I gradually slipped into prayer by rote rather than an exchange from the heart.

Since then, I've learned that God always hears our prayers, but does not always give us what we think we want. God heard Jesus's prayer in the Garden of Gethsemane that He be spared from the extreme suffering and death He was about to undergo. That wasn't the full prayer, however. By recognizing and embracing God's complete knowledge and desire for our happiness, Jesus qualified his request: "Father, if you are willing, take this cup away from me; still, not my will but yours be done." (Luke 22:42).

I fervently prayed that God would preserve and strengthen my marriage. When that prayer was not answered, I did not accept it. Even though I was trying to be a good daughter of God, my efforts did not produce the reward I requested. What we desire is only given to us by our Father who loves us if it truly is best for us.

Often, we don't understand the answer we receive to prayer, but even more often—at least for me back then—we reject His answer when He doesn't do what we ask.

My failures in my marriage and work destroyed the self-esteem and confidence I had in my intellectual talents and professional achievements. My direct supervisor for my new staff attorney position gave me a stinging assessment in which he pointed out that no one was willing to work with me anymore because I was now a detriment rather than as asset to team assignments. He felt I was somehow doing this on purpose to make him look bad, and years later he apologized to me for not understanding the extent of my mental health issues at the time. It really wasn't his fault that he was confused. I could still pretend on occasion that everything was all right, even when I felt dead or in pain on the inside.

My depression eroded my ability to be present emotionally for my children and to care for them during subsequent struggles with my ex-husband regarding their upbringing. I cried a lot during Mass and in other public places; so much so that a grandmotherly lady I knew only by sight at daily Mass came up to me one day and just hugged me and told me it would be all right. My newfound joy in becoming fully Catholic seemed to vanish as I struggled not to despair over God's refusal to answer my prayer the way I expected. I battled a persistent false thought that perhaps He didn't love me as much as I thought He did.

My mental and spiritual health also affected my physical health. I developed a stomach hernia, and I thought I was having a heart attack one day when returning the license plates from the family car and picking up new ones for a vehicle registered in my name at the Department of Motor Vehicles. I broke out into a sweat and had severe chest pains. As the EMTs wheeled me out, a concerned clerk placed my new plates on the blanket wrapped around me. It turned out to have been a panic attack.

Family members visited to help and encourage me. Despite all the help, I couldn't get back on my feet. I stared listlessly at the patterns of wallpaper, trying to distract myself by reading junky novels or watching mindless television. I soon used up all my leave as well as leave donated to me by coworkers and friends at my agency. Even once I was home instead of at the office, I needed the nanny to help me take care of the kids. If anyone was upset, I just retreated to the stillness and safety of my room. I ran up debts to avoid defaulting on my mortgage.

Although I could not feel it, through grace and the help of good priests and friends, I somehow kept faith in God. Only His love got me through this time, even though I could not feel that either. On the advice of a priest and faithful girlfriends, I stopped listening to the lie that I wasn't good enough to be loved and began very consciously offering my suffering to God in union with Jesus's suffering. I began to pray again regularly, in desperation. Occasionally, God sent me small signal graces, concrete signs that reminded me that He was with me. A call from a friend, a peaceful moment watching my youngest daughter sleep, the gift of a prayer card appearing right when I most needed it. Trying to keep dark thoughts at bay, I meditated on Jesus's agony in the Garden and on being a small child cradled in His arms or in Mary's lap. I found some relief in prayer before the Blessed Sacrament, but it seemed to vanish as soon as I left the physical boundaries of the church.

My mental health continued to deteriorate. If I could hold things together for a bit, like butter being scraped too thinly on bread, as Bilbo Baggins would say, I then paid for it with complete collapse. With enormous grief, I began to accept that I could no longer do the things I'd worked so hard all my life to achieve. Everything, even the ability to care for my children, was slipping away. The words and images of prayer seemed to vanish. Only faith remained, because even in the dark and even during His silence, God gave me enough grace for me to know He still was there and that He loved me.

At the urging of my supervisors at the staff attorney position from which I'd now been absent for months, I applied for and eventually received disability retirement. The lowest point was the day I wrote to the Virginia State Bar voluntarily inactivating my law license, because I no longer was capable of working as a lawyer. In fact, surrendering my old life as well as my new one was what saved it. Despite struggling against that surrender, dragging my feet, I stumbled forward to the future, entrusting everything— including my mental health—to God's embrace.

CHAPTER FIVE

# FINDING MY TRUE SELF

*"Let nothing disturb you. Let nothing frighten you.
Everything passes away except God. God alone is sufficient."*
—Saint Teresa of Avila

## Recovery and Reset

Although I've never returned to the same level of intellectual and multitasking abilities I had during my law firm and government careers, over the years I found happiness and peace. With intensive therapy, rest, the right combination of medication, and a gradual maturing in spiritual life, I slowly improved. Since my analytic left-brain talents were frozen and atrophied, I explored my creative and intuitive aspects. I enrolled in a massage therapy school and opened my own small business performing pregnancy massage. The physical labor helped my mental state as well as my spiritual one as I learned to offer this work to God.

Emotional, physical, and spiritual healing was a process that took years of trying, failing, and trying again. Eventually, I started working for Tepeyac Family Center, a nonprofit obstetrics and gynecology practice. I'd delivered my children with these doctors, and many of my massage therapy patients used them as well. Here, I found further healing as I started with simple office tasks. Through the intervention and encouragement of the practice administrator, I gradually resumed more challenging work. Over time my spiritual life deepened and improved as I prayed with patients and colleagues and offered to God what I did at home and in the office. Regular prayer—both my own and that of others who prayed for me—was key to this growth and healing.

As my children grew older, conflict with my ex-husband diminished. While I fell down often mentally and spiritually, I kept getting up with the love and help of my Father God. Rather than berate myself for my failures, I offered them to Him and trusted His mercy. It is easy to write this in a few words. It was not so easy to do it, day after day. I don't take it for granted even now. Nonetheless, I wouldn't rewrite my past even if I could. These experiences gave me great empathy and love for those who struggle and a desire to help them find the source of all life—God's intense, passionate, personal, and unconditional love for them. God has a plan for everyone and His plan is for our happiness.

That plan wasn't what I'd expected, but I'm confident in faith that it was the one I needed and the best for me. The fulfillment I find today in being a Tin Can Pilgrim for God is immeasurable. He began to reveal this to me in small steps that began with what seemed to be a misstep. Seven years after I started working at Tepeyac Family Center, I accepted an invitation to join a hiking group on a Saturday. I looked forward to getting exercise and to praying with other members of the group.

I'd just crossed a creek, stepping on wet gray stones and scrambling up a vine-covered embankment. The group was keeping a fast pace to complete a seven-mile circular trail. A flat area where we could walk alongside one another and talk, instead of breathing hard in a single file, was my undoing. I let my attention wander and stepped on a stick that rolled in the small smooth river stones. My feet shot out from under me and I landed hard on the gravel alongside the riverbed.

Since I was a bit older than the other hikers, and the terrain was so easy at that point, I was embarrassed. They helped me up and I dusted off my jeans. I knew I'd twisted my ankle under me when I fell. Not wanting to admit I was hurt, I put on a brave face and announced that I was heading back to the parking lot, so I didn't delay the rest of the group. "Are you sure?" they asked. "Absolutely! I'm fine, but I need to take it slower," I lied. There were lots of other hikers straggling along in small groups on the popular trail, so I wasn't concerned about getting back on my own.

As my companions went ahead at my insistence, I sipped some water. When I started walking back, however, I realized that even at a slow pace, my ankle was hurting a lot. I found a sturdy branch, stripped off the smaller shoots, and leaned on it as I walked. Things got progressively worse. I stopped several times to rest.

When I reached my car, I took off the hiking boot and sock. The purple-and-red swelling on my foot and ankle didn't look good. I grabbed some Ibuprofen from my first aid kit and asked a group of tailgaters for some ice from their cooler. By then, the first of my group had finished the round-trip trail and came over to check on me.

Another friend drove my car to an urgent care. As it turned out, I had a severe sprain. Rest and therapy over the next few months gave me time to realize I might not want to wait until I was a lot older to visit places like the Grand Canyon and Yosemite.

I'd put off such vacations in the outdoors for too long, but the real lesson I should have taken from my fall was not to be so proud. It didn't make sense to try to keep the pace of people twenty years younger than me. In fact, I realized I didn't particularly like zooming by the scenery because I missed the small details of nature that are so beautiful: buds and shells, tree branches framing the sky when viewed from beneath their green canopy, small birds that scurried away in the underbrush at our approach. Exercise outdoors wasn't meant to substitute for a treadmill. It was to be experienced and lived, as an encounter with God through His Creation. I resolved to slow down (and be more careful!) once I regained conditioning after my recovery.

Still, the pace of work prevented me from spending much time outdoors. Although I was not billing hours, my old workaholic habits died hard. I found myself spending more and more time working at the nonprofit center, because there always was something pressing to do. I knew that I needed to make a change, but I was having trouble breaking out of my self-imposed poor habits.

By winter 2018, I found myself at another crossroads. I was on the verge of becoming an empty nester. One daughter was out of the home, and another was nearing departure. I began to contemplate the next stage of life. By this time my mental health had improved through extensive therapy, and with it, my physical health. I knew the work I did had value by helping other people, but the more I did at work, the less emotional energy I had for other relationships, including those with my daughters.

Although I was going through the motions, the joy that accompanied my return to faith in God decades ago had dimmed. I was trusting in what I could do, rather than in who I was as a daughter of God.

I began to get back to basics. I started to pray more regularly again, setting aside time just for that purpose and no other. I began attending a prayer circle again and went on a retreat. Despite being very busy with work, I made a special effort to get to church more often.

This quiet time I gave back in reflection to God let me hear Him more clearly. I started to listen more and just sit in comfortable silence with Him, rather than ask Him for things or complain. I still brought up requests and told him about what had gone wrong or what was hurting me, but now I returned to conversation rather than monopolizing the prayer time with my list.

As I pondered the past during my drive west, I realized, with the benefit of hindsight, that my life had been a series of downsizings, of stumbling and falling back, then getting up again. Downsizing didn't just mean going from a large house to a condo and then to an Airstream trailer. Although I remained close with my daughters—and, of course, Penny—my relationships with my parents and my ex-husband, for better or worse, were resolved with separation.

Growing up I'd had an unusually close extended family. Throughout our childhood, my siblings and I enjoyed the attention of many doting relatives, as well as the freedom to play around the cove bordering my parents' large bayside property on the East Coast. When we got tar on our feet playing on my parents' dock, my mom would patiently rub it off with soft butter. Our father blew cigar smoke on us when we fished off the dock in the evening, to keep away the mosquitos. We spent hours in the water at a nearby beach until our fingertips wrinkled like prunes from the salt water.

Nearly every Sunday, my mom's relatives had family barbecues, often under the towering chestnut trees that sloped down to the cove from my parents' yard. While the grown-ups sat in lawn chairs complaining about politics and tourists, we gorged on sweet tiny scallops that my uncles had dredged from the bay and wolfed down charred hot dogs, ice cream, and watermelon. As we got older, each of us children took turns working in the summer at my grandma's old-fashioned movie theater, helping out at the popcorn stand or taking tickets. It wasn't really her theater, but she'd worked there as the manager for so many years, we thought it was.

My grandma believed in God and went to church every Sunday. I loved her dearly, but I didn't have her faith. Somewhere between childhood and my teen years it evaporated. Before confirmation, typically received at age thirteen or fourteen, I told my mother that I wasn't sure I even believed in God.

Confirmation is a sacrament in which the Holy Spirit comes into the believer's soul more fully, empowering the recipient with the gifts of wisdom, understanding, counsel (right judgment), fortitude (courage), knowledge, piety (reverence), and wonder and awe (or fear of God, in the sense of loving Him so much that we fear being separated from Him, as distinct from a fear of punishment). It is a big deal. Confirmation is not a graduation from religious education, but a step into a new stage of spiritual adulthood. I don't remember if I understood this when I was preparing to receive the sacrament of confirmation, but I knew that I'd have to answer "Yes" to a series of questions about whether I believed in God.

I asked my mother, "How can I answer yes to the questions that are part of the ceremony when I'm not sure I mean it?"

"It doesn't matter," she explained. "My mother will kill me if you don't get confirmed. Just say yes to all the questions about belief in

God and the Church and you don't have to go to church after this if you don't want to."

I felt crushed. My reservations didn't matter, but neither did the bigger question of whether there was a God. I dutifully went through with the confirmation to please my mother, despite knowing I was lying. For years, I sporadically went to church at Christmas, Easter, and other big occasions, usually with my father, at a different church where he was an usher.

My relationship with my father was anxiety-ridden. He was a giant I worshipped as a child and sought to please, but I never felt I succeeded. He would boast to colleagues about his children's accomplishments. Sometimes, at dinner parties in the formal living room in which children were not normally allowed, he'd invite us in to recite poetry, play music, or display artwork we'd created, before dismissing us. He had high expectations and little tolerance for having his directions not followed. Families are complicated, though, and everyone has their own wounds. I love my parents, through God and with Him and in Him, as the wounded children they no doubt were.

Despite some very rocky periods during my teens, even after I moved away and my grandma passed away, I maintained a relationship with my parents. During law school and my busy law career, we found time for regular phone calls and the occasional visit. My husband loved the free summer vacations at my parents' home in what had become a sought-after, tony resort town. During my darkest days after my divorce, my parents' home became a refuge of sorts for me and my children. They also visited me in Virginia and provided financial help at a time when everything else seemed to be falling apart.

Later, a family tragedy destroyed our relationship. My mother and I disagreed on how to handle it. She did not accept my actions to stand up for what I believed and what was best for my family. My parents stopped speaking to me. The details are not what matters here, as many families sadly have deep divisions. I hoped that time would heal wounds, but it didn't.

Finally, the year before I quit my job, sold my home, and embarked on the road with my Airstream, I accepted that my ties with my birth family had been severed beyond human repair. During that time, a dear friend and sister in Christ gave me the support I hadn't even known I needed.

## One Door Closes, Another Opens

Everyone needs a friend who sees doves in the shape of clouds. For me, that's my friend Laura. She invited herself on a trip I took seeking reconciliation with my parents. As we drove north, we prayed together and lessened the monotony of the highway by sharing what we saw in the shifting sky. I saw dragons; Laura saw doves.

After years of leaving unreturned phone messages, I had decided to reach out to my parents in person. Perhaps high walls reinforced with pride could not be breached remotely. As a daughter, I felt I should take the initiative to honor my father and mother by making the first move toward reconciliation. As part of my faith journey, I forgave the hurts I'd experienced and wanted to let my parents know that I still loved them and was sorry for their pain.

Yet forgiveness is not the same as reconciliation. The consequences of wrongdoing still remain regardless of whether we forgive the person who committed an injustice. But what does happen is that the sorrowful past loses its power over the one who forgives. Forgiveness heals the forgiver, if not the forgiven.

Keeping this in mind, I had told Laura what I planned to do even though I thought it had little chance of success, and she'd insisted on coming with me. Her humor and prayerful presence on the long drive up I-95 was just what I needed, although I hadn't known that in advance.

After navigating through New Jersey and New York, we arrived at my mother's house in that familiar seaside resort area. We parked in the dusty turnaround on the dead-end street bordering her cottage. I hadn't been there in years. The bushes had grown and branches had fallen from trees. An anchor that used to be in the front yard was missing.

As Laura and I looked at the quiet cove, I recalled climbing the twisted oak tree overlooking the shore when I was young. I used to seek refuge in the embrace of branches and rough bark, watered by tears of frustration and unexpressed anger.

Laura asked if I wanted her to come with me. I told her no, and asked her to pray. I walked through the weathered gray fence, up a couple of brick steps to the small roofed porch where wind chimes and hanging baskets of bright flowers still swayed. I knocked on the door. Through the glass panels on either side, I could see a walker with rubber balls shielding the glowing hardwood floors from the metal struts. I recognized the riot of plants and carousel figures along the edge of the picture window. The furniture was new. I waited for what seemed like a long time and then heard footsteps.

My mother opened the door and looked back at me. "Lynda? Why are you here?" she asked.

"Mom, I want you to know that I love you and forgive you. You're still my mom and neither one of us is getting any younger."

She looked at me with stony gray eyes and pursed lips. She was thinner than I remembered.

"I don't understand," she said tersely. "What do you want?"

"Isn't it possible to forgive one another and have some sort of relationship going forward?"

"No. That's not possible," she flatly stated. "Don't come back here." She closed the door.

I turned away and walked slowly back to my car. I'd known it wasn't likely this would work, but I felt at peace that at least I'd done everything in my power to heal past wounds. I couldn't control her reaction, only my own actions.

Laura looked hopeful and said she'd prayed about a hundred Hail Marys. I told her what had happened, my eyes filling up with emotion. She hugged me and told me I'd done the right thing. "I know" I said. "Thank you for being here with me. Let's go."

I took one last look back at my childhood home, then drove to the Airbnb we'd rented for the weekend. The next day I visited my grandma's grave, cleaning up some weeds and placing fresh flowers on it. I walked around the small town with Laura. We visited the church where I was baptized and married. We swam at the beach where I'd spent much of my childhood playing. Efforts to find other relatives—all of whom had shut me out of their lives when the rift occurred with my parents—were unsuccessful. Yet, I was at peace.

I continue to love and honor my parents by praying for them. Occasionally I'll leave a message on their answering machine that is never returned. I remind them that I still love them on occasions like birthdays and Christmas.

This loss is a hurt that never goes away, but God transformed it into a beautiful gift to Him. Like a dove, my sorrow flies away with soft fluttering wings and one day, at least in eternity, may rest peacefully in olive branches.

This tremendous gift of loss and suffering lets me love others more. I can be there for them and walk with them, knowing that neither they nor I will ever be alone, but always within God's gentle hands. A companion, like Laura, literally is "someone who suffers with" in the root meaning of the word. Just as Laura did for me, I can listen to others' anger and be present for their tears. I can pray with and for them, with certain hope that one day God will heal their grief and pain, glorify their wounds, and comfort them with the peace only He can give.

## Discovering My True Self

As my long drive with Penny drew closer to our next campsite, we exited the highway and passed a large intersection where multiple roads crossed one another. We all come to crossroads in life, I mused, but may not always recognize them at the time. In 2018, my work—like my stage in life—was at such a crossroads. I'd worked hard for years at Tepeyac, devoting my skills in writing and project management to help the practice administrator improve systems and design and implement new programs. Eventually, I healed enough to reactivate my law license and to occasionally assist with basic contracts and legal advice for the practice. Working with outside attorneys when needed, I eventually secured Tepeyac's transition to a beautiful location with a long-term lease.

By spring 2018, there were literally no major projects left for me to do. Just like my children, Tepeyac had grown and didn't need me as much. It didn't make sense for the always struggling nonprofit to pay me to answer phones or meet with persons seeking financial assistance, when they could pay others less to do those tasks. My skills were underutilized, yet I had to make a certain salary to live in the very expensive location in which I'd raised my children.

Perhaps another ministry or charity just starting out would be an appropriate alternative. I thought about networking and updating my LinkedIn account, but was always too busy. I also considered whether I should move to a less expensive area to find work, but I'd lived for nearly my entire adult life in Northern Virginia and had no idea where to go. I began researching tiny homes online to see whether I could downsize and cut my expenses while remaining in Northern Virginia, where I had many friends and contacts.

I decided to place all the possibilities in God's hands. The painful losses I'd experienced, yet also the peace I'd gained, led me to a space where I could more freely and fully give myself to whatever God wanted. I'd had to get to this point before I could fully surrender my life to Him. In that surrender, I found real freedom.

"I am Yours," I prayed, "give me the grace to follow Your will in all things, to take small steps toward what You will for me, even if I don't understand it."

Telling God you are willing to do whatever He asks is a dangerous prayer! God replied to my surrender in a surprising way I describe in the next chapter—through a flash of reflected light on the side of the highway on a drive to Richmond. His inspiration to simply go on the road and trust Him has led to the happiest and most fulfilling work of my life. I could have remained where I was, or worked at another nonprofit. Instead, He called me to become a Tin Can Pilgrim and to use all the talents, skills, and life experiences He gave me to love Him more intensely and love others through Him.

## PSALM OF MY HEART (CONVERSION)
*by Lynda Rozell ©2021*

*In the quiet I hear you...In the stillness I seek you*
*Beneath the leaves find you in the whispers of grass*

*Still soft voice calling...My stumbling feet falling*
*You catch me again and again*

*Wandering pilgrim, awestruck child, faithless yet faith filled*
*My errors redeeming*

*Oh Lord I love you*
*I seek you to know you, to follow, adore you*
*and share you with others*

*Suddenly fearless*
*Song fills my throat*
*Bursting and bubbling like the springs in the stream*

*No longer clinging to the roots on the banks*
*Casting myself out into the deep*
*Arms outstretched lifted by your grace sifted*
*I become wheat*

*No longer choked*
*by weeds and by sorrow*
*But now uplifted*
*Raised to my feet*

*The better to praise you*
*To call your sweet Name, Lord*
*To be your servant, even your friend*

*Open hands gifting*
*All that I am Lord*
*To you only, finally trusting*
*Your child's now home*

CHAPTER SIX

# A BOLT OF SILVER

*"She was so much surprised that for the moment
she quite forgot how to speak good English"*
—Lewis Carroll, *Alice's Adventures in Wonderland*

## The Airstream Moment

After placing everything in God's hands, I continued with my daily work and prayer life. In May 2018, as I drove to Richmond for a business meeting, a bright bolt of reflected sun on silver caught my eye. At the side of the highway, there appeared to be a fleet of shiny airplanes parked in a row sparkling in the bright sunlight. I wondered if there were a sci-fi convention nearby, with models of spaceships. Intrigued, I noted the exit so I could check it out later on my way back home.

In fact, it was an Airstream dealership. I'd never seen these smooth, rounded trailers before, nor did I have any particular interest in any kind of mobile home. Undeterred by my proclaimed disinterest, the dealer invited me to look inside one. Skeptical, but not wanting to be rude, I opened the door, stepped in, and entered a new world. I stared at the sleek modern tiny home I found inside.

The refracted light from the many windows made the pale wooden cabinets glow and the soft silver ceiling and walls shine. Patterns of light fell on the floor from the skylight and vents. The design was harmonious, with a round whimsical sink and soft cream cushions. The curved ceiling made the Airstream feel like a delightful submarine from a child's imagination. Everything had a function and united beauty with utility.

"This is it! I could live here," I realized. Peace flooded my weariness, soothing it away like a perfect spring day. I thanked God, hearing a soft yes in the happiness I experienced as I explored every nook and cranny of the Airstream, then walked around the outside of it once more.

This wasn't a logical, left brain decision. It was an epiphany. As I left the dealership and drove home with a handful of brochures, I realized that the Airstream fit my current needs like it had been made for them.

First, I didn't have to pick one area of the country to live in without experiencing it first. If I changed my mind or events intervened, I could always reverse course, resell the Airstream, and do something else. I hadn't yet realized that this was a part of the vocation God gradually revealed to me. Instead, I was gathering rationales in strands around me to make my inspiration stronger, like a bird strengthening her nest by interweaving bits of yarn with twigs and feathers.

Airstreams are the oldest brand of travel trailer made in the United States. They are sleek, futuristic yet classic, and beautiful inside and out. Every inch of space is used wisely and aesthetically. Airstream trailers look essentially the same as they did in the 1930s. The Airstream factory in Jackson Center, Ohio, fondly called "the mothership" by Airstream aficionados, is the sole source of new Airstreams. They are still primarily assembled by hand, including the many rivets that dot the aluminum shell, which is evocative of an airplane or spaceship. The differences within a particular line, such as the Flying Cloud model, are in the optional features, location of the bedroom, and the colors of upholstery and countertops.

## Reflections

After my Airstream moment, I voraciously absorbed the dealer's brochures in detail surrounded by the trees shading my urban balcony. The leaves stirred with the breeze and fluttered the pages I had spread out before me. That evening, I began avidly watching online videos and reading blogs of full-time RVers.

Although I'd fallen in love with Airstreams, over the course of the next few weeks I researched all the alternatives and considered a van or drivable RV so I would not have to hitch and unhitch a trailer. Nevertheless, the advantages of being able to park my tiny home, then unhitch and drive around in my truck were compelling. Before purchasing an Airstream, I looked at Some Other Brand (SOB) travel trailers.

To be completely honest, the aesthetics of the Airstream, with its sleek, uncluttered modern look, drew me. The light wood cabinets and floors and panoramic windows made me feel as if I were in a spa overlooking a beautiful vista. It felt like a home, a place of quiet refuge for me to reenergize and emerge refreshed to carry out my daily tasks. Airstreams bring the outside inside with their windows and skylights.

Additionally, Airstreams are a piece of living history. As one of the earliest trailers made in the United States, they represent a unique form of Americana. Founded in 1931, the company survived many changes without fundamentally changing their product. The sleek aerodynamic design of Airstream trailers allows wind to flow around them more easily. This saves on gas and makes towing less stressful.

I loved the story of Wally Byam, the founder of Airstream, and his philosophy of "See More, Do More, Live More." It appealed to my sense of adventure and desire to be more comfortable with not knowing what lies ahead around the next corner in the road. The community of Airstream owners provided an instant "tribe" of persons eager to share their enthusiasm and expertise with a new owner. Later in my travels, this community played a key role in continuing my journeys. At the outset, however, it was another strong incentive to stick with the brand that first caught my eye on the side of the road to Richmond.

Aphorisms Wally popularized in the Airstream culture also resonated with me. "Let's not make changes, let's make only improvements." "Don't stop. Keep right on going. Hitch up your trailer and go . . . see what's over the next hill, and the one after that, and the one after that." Even his motto that "adventure is where you find it, any place, every place, except at home in the rocking chair" inspired me. I wasn't ready for a rocking chair. It was only later that I realized I could take people in rocking chairs along with me virtually in my travels as a Tin Can Pilgrim!

After discovering Airstreams, I began to follow various Airstream bloggers. The Long, Long Honeymoon was particularly entertaining. I learned about various populations of nomads who, by choice or necessity, had opted out of "sticks and bricks" houses and lived on the road, some on public land, some in RV parks for short- or long-term stays, and some constantly traveling.

In this process, I also watched many how-to YouTube videos about Airstream maintenance and repair. I'd always enjoyed working with my hands, whether drawing, gardening, or remodeling parts of my home. The need to acquire new skills specific to an RV seemed a welcome opportunity to expand my knowledge and keep very physically active. Being active was a key part of maintaining my mental health, so this seemed a good fit on many levels.

Since my trailer would be my home, I wanted one that would last, with a good record for maintenance and repairs. Many lovingly renovated older Airstreams are still on the road. They hold their value more than most other brands. If I became too old or feeble one day to live in my Airstream, I reasoned, I'd likely be able to get a deposit on a "sticks and bricks" home by selling my trailer.

Very quickly, the idea that I could do this took root in my heart. I realized that the nomadic population, like the rest of our post-Christian society, had many people in it who had never experienced God's love for them, who didn't know their true identity as beloved children of God, or had no relationship at all with their Divine Father. Could I witness to them through friendship, assist with problems they might experience in their lives, and care for those who needed someone to listen? Could I manage financially to simply go and then figure out later how to sustain this over time? And what of my own grown children, one of whom still needed financial support to finish college and the other who wanted to continue living with me until she could go to graduate school? How did I carry out my responsibilities to them if I embarked on this adventure?

During these weeks of discernment, many of the Mass readings were about trust and being summoned to do God's will. I placed the idea before God and asked Him that if it was His will that I just trust Him and go and wander wherever He led me. He answered yes, in many quiet ways, working through others and through the words of Scripture and my favorite saints. By letting go of all the things I was holding on to, I could discover the person God meant me to be.

AIRSTREAMS IN LINE AT FACTORY

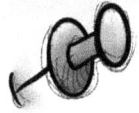

## WHY AN AIRSTREAM?

- Best snacks — fellow Airstreamers know how to enjoy life
- Lasts longer and depreciates less than other trailers
- Instant community
- History as an American icon
- Tows well due to aerodynamic shape and relatively low center of gravity
- Craftsmanship and quality materials
- Excellent use of space
- Panoramic windows and lots of light inside

And... BEAUTY

GO TO WEBSITE

CHAPTER SEVEN

# GO AND FEAR NOTHING

*Go and fear nothing, I will help you"*
—Blessed Mother to Sister Adele
Champion, Wisconsin, c. 1859

### Discerning the Call

After my Airstream epiphany, I pondered what it all meant and how to embark on this journey. Being practical, I researched the costs of living full-time on the road. I'd always been prudent with spending and lived below my means, so effectively retiring early was not impossible. I love the outdoors and camping, and I like to drive. Even though I'd never traveled in a trailer, it seemed a feasible way to live in relative comfort and go to many places I'd never seen. I'd never driven a truck, but that was easily remedied. Nothing was set in stone. If I needed to return to work, find work I could do on the road, or settle down in one location, that could happen. Best of all, by bringing my own little home with me, I could visit my grown children easily no matter where they ended up.

Now that I thought I had an idea of what God wanted me to do, I placed it back before Him to see if I was hearing His call correctly. I prayed, "If You want me to do this, please remove all the obstacles. If I'm not hearing You correctly, then please make it clear that I should not do this.' I felt an incredible sense of peace and happiness at being free to choose to follow whatever God had in mind for me.

He answered as things fell rapidly into place. My children were supportive. So were my friends at work. But most definitively, many small signs pointed to not looking behind, not coming up with things I had to do first, but simply answering His call.

## Vocation

My life experiences shaped me, but God as a divine sculptor used them to uncover my true self. The challenges and joys, the losses and sorrows, all opened space for me to turn to Him and invite Him to let me see who I was meant to be.

This is an ongoing process, like an onion shedding layers of skin, or a gem surrounded by rock that eventually emerges as erosion or the strike of the miner's pick breaks it free.

We all have a particular vocation in our lives to which God calls us for our happiness. Sometimes this call is very subtle, and sometimes more direct. We find it in the circumstances of our ordinary lives, but He may transform the ordinary into the extraordinary.

In 1859, Mary the Mother of God appeared to Adele Brise, a young Belgian immigrant, who settled with her family on farmland in the Green Bay area of Wisconsin. Mary's message and the miracles that followed testify to the power of faith and the willingness to follow God's call.

In October 1859, Adele was carrying grain to a grist mill, when a lady in white appeared to her between two trees. The following Sunday, the lady appeared again. She instructed Adele with a simple direct message: "I am the Queen of Heaven . . . Gather the children in this wild country and teach them what they should know for salvation . . . Teach them their catechism, how to sign themselves with the sign of the cross, and how to approach the sacraments; that is what I wish you to do. Go and fear nothing. I will help you."

Simply, Adele did just that. She devoted her life to the mission given to her by the Blessed Virgin Mary. Adele traveled on foot up and down the peninsula, instructing children. As Sister Adele she founded a red brick convent and school with the community of sisters she attracted. The convent and school buildings remain there today along with the fourth generation of the original chapel. Pilgrims visit from all over the world.

The shrine's simplicity in the middle of farmland in rural Wisconsin contrasts starkly with the grandeur and size of many other shrines. Yet, somehow, it seems a fitting homage to Mary, her simple message, and Sister Adele's quiet obedience through her daily work. What seems a simple and ordinary charge—to teach children to make the sign of the cross, know their faith, and obtain the sacraments—veils the great supernatural reality and eternal impact of those actions.

Moreover, the power of the faith that makes this place a pilgrimage site today is tangible within its quiet. In 1871, an intense fire destroyed much of the surrounding area, yet went around the grounds of Sister Adele's mission. More than 325 persons were killed locally, while the blaze known as the Great Peshtigo Fire killed more than 1200 persons overall and destroyed many acres of farmland and homes. As Sister Adele and her community, students, and neighbors sheltered within the chapel and prayed, the fire stopped, extinguished by sudden rain. The intense flames merely charred the outside of the chapel fence. All those inside were unharmed. Since then, many healings have occurred through prayers offered at the shrine.

I find Adele's story inspiring. What I do is not grand. There are no startling miracles or instant healings involved (as far as I know!). Instead, it is a small, simple apostolate expressed in my daily life as a nomad. God asked me to be present to others with the intention of helping them see God's love for them. He didn't provide an instruction manual, but asked me to trust Him to lead me where He wanted me to go.

CHAPTER EIGHT

# BUYING THE AIRSTREAM

*"See More, Do More, Live More"*
—Wally Byam, founder of Airstream

### The Right Vehicle

Once I heard clearly what God wanted of me, it was my turn to answer that call. First, I needed to learn how to drive a truck and find the right size truck based on the size of the Airstream I would tow. Initially, I looked at twenty-foot Airstreams, but they seemed a little too small for my only living space. I settled on a twenty-five-foot double axel Airstream trailer amusingly called a "Flying Cloud."

Based on the Airstream's size and weight, and other requirements for towing, I began to research what trucks to consider. At this point, I wasn't planning to embark on my journey for another year. Nonetheless, I decided to move ahead with obtaining a truck since I'd never driven one. That way I could get used to handling a much larger vehicle well before I'd need to tow anything with it.

My friend Karen generously let me drive her truck for practice, since I felt intimidated to even test drive a truck after driving a small car for years. Driving a truck proved quite different from zipping around in the cute little Mazda 3 I'd had for the past five years. I had to turn wide at corners to avoid hitting the curb. Parking in narrow spots designed for cars presented a challenge.

Next, Karen and other friends then took turns accompanying me as I test-drove used and new trucks over the course of a few weeks. The road feel and comfort of the RAM and the GMC trucks appealed to me. I made a list of the towing and safety features I wanted: extended mirrors, a towing package with a hitch receiver, plus handles and step rails to help get in and out of the truck.

The smell of the truck was a key factor. If I were a dog, I'd be a bloodhound. I'm very sensitive to smells and loathe the smell of cigarette smoke. Finding a truck not previously owned by a smoker wasn't that easy. Fortunately, I had no particular preference on color, other than wanting to avoid black so the vehicle would be more visible.

Little did I know how little visibility was going to be an issue.

On my fifth trip to CarMax, a bright green truck with a big black racing strip caught my eye. It was hard to look away even though it seemed a bit much. Since the window sticker indicated low mileage and the necessary towing features, I opened the door and cautiously took a breath. Success! This one actually smelled like a new vehicle, without a hint of smoke. Plus, it already had every towing feature I wanted, even items that I thought I'd have to add myself, like convenient handles and step rails.

I took some photos and sent them to my daughters. My youngest texted back "Mom, that is a tricked-out truck [referring to the oversized black tires and rims, black stripe on the hood, and the sunroof]. Buy it!" My oldest texted "You can't buy that. It is too green and too big . . . it's the Hulk!"

The green RAM drove like it was made for me. It was only a year old, with nearly forty thousand miles left on the original warranty. The color started to grow on me as I sat in the truck for a while. Inspired by both my daughters' comments, I bought the green truck and named it Bruce (for Bruce Banner, the scientist in the Marvel Universe that turns into the Incredible Hulk).

At this point, I figured I'd drive Bruce around for about a year and gradually start thinning out my belongings, as my daughter who still lived with me was a year away from leaving for graduate school. Also, it might take quite a while to purchase the Airstream trailer now that I'd narrowed down the size and features appropriate for my camping plans.

## God's Timetable, Not Mine

Again, God had something else in mind.

One Friday night in late June, I talked with my neighbors Joanne and Hank about what I was considering doing and why. I'd run into them in the parking lot when I'd arrived home quite late from work after a very long day. Joanne and Hank were very encouraging and excited for me. They thought the green truck was great.

The next day, after morning Mass, I came home to find a beautiful bouquet of red, white, and blue roses waiting in a vase at my door. There was a card, but I assumed the flowers were for my daughter from her boyfriend. I called her and she looked at the card and laughed, saying "Mom, this is for you!"

The cover of the card was a photo of a winding open road with a blue sky and mountains. Inside, my neighbors had written that they sent the flowers to celebrate my independence and courage in following what they felt sure was a call from God for me to travel and minister to others on the road. My daughter was touched by the card and flowers. She urged me to go right over to thank them in person because it was so sweet. I did.

I asked Joanne how she had managed to find the perfect card and flowers on such short notice, since we'd only talked last night. She said, "Well, yesterday morning I was at the Dollar Store and this card caught my eye. I decided I should buy it and just have it to give the right person at the right time. Then, we talked to you and thought of picking up the roses and I realized I had the right card for you."

During my conversation with Joanne, I mentioned that I wished I could go sooner, but I did not want to disappoint my daughter. She was counting on living with me until the following summer,

BRUCE AT SHRINE OF THE MOST BLESSED SACRAMENT

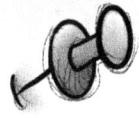

# FIVE THINGS TO LOOK FOR IN A TOW VEHICLE

1. **Towing capacity** — compare to the weight of the trailer you will tow; use the VIN to get this information from the manufacturer as it varies considerably and the dealer is not the best source of information
2. **Hitch receiver** — necessary, but doesn't guarantee you also have the towing package
3. **Towing package** — factory installed integrated brake controller and tow/haul mode
4. **Towing mirrors** — you can add these later easily but they usually come with towing package
5. **Comfortable seat** — essential for long distance driving

GO TO WEBSITE

when she planned to leave for graduate school. Joanne suggested that I talk with my daughter about moving up the timeline.

When I returned home, I told my daughter about the conversation and asked her if she wanted to live with me for another year. "Mom, I've only been staying with you because I thought you'd be too lonely if I moved out too," she said. "A few weeks ago I had the chance to move in with one of my friends from work, but I don't know if that's still available." I suggested she call her friend right away.

Surprisingly, her friend picked up immediately. An answered phone call was a small miracle in itself in a world where text messaging is the norm. The shared apartment was still available. In one phone call, my daughter had a place to live and a move-in scheduled for when we returned from a long-planned vacation coming up soon.

Next, I consulted my financial advisor and we went over figures to see if I could effectively retire. He suggested that I not wait a year, as I originally had planned. My projected expenses would be so much less than my current expenses that it would work out better to do it sooner rather than later. My health was stable, and I could continue to provide some help to my daughters as they transitioned to independence.

Similarly, my Realtor was confident I could sell my townhouse condo for the price I needed this year, but if I waited it was harder to predict. I'd been lucky several years before to purchase a 2500-square-foot, two-level home with many updates, in a location walkable to George Mason University and charming historic Old Town Fairfax City. My quiet, lovely neighborhood was highly desirable.

Finally, I talked with my supervisor at work. She asked me to stay long enough to train my replacements and finish some ongoing minor projects. Better yet, she wanted to contract with me to do some limited consulting on the road.

Just like that, there were no obstacles to moving forward, or to doing so far sooner than I had planned. Unlike those in Luke's Gospel who offered excuses not to follow Christ's call to come away with Him, I had no one to bury and no fields to plow. Instead, I leapt into the future He wanted for me.

## My Home on Wheels

Eager to start my journey, I started calling Airstream dealerships to find the particular model and features I thought would work best for me in a full-time rolling home. Even here, God kindly continued to encourage me that I was moving in the right direction.

I'd spent time shopping online and locally to select the right model Airstream for me, before buying my truck Bruce. However, now that I had a truck capable of towing the Airstream I preferred, and the impetus to go forward immediately, I could not find one in stock with the features and colors I liked best. I called Airstream dealerships up and down the East Coast. It looked like I'd have a four- to six-month wait while one of them ordered it from the factory.

Finally, I called the last dealership on my list, Airstream of South Florida, in Fort Myers. A very helpful salesperson took my call. "Your Airstream just came on our lot last week," he exclaimed after I read my list of must-haves. I explained that I couldn't pick it up any sooner than the end of September, because I needed to train my replacement at work and sell my home. "No problem," he offered. "If this is the one you want, we can do all the paperwork now and then we'll store it for you here until you can pick it up." I obtained a quote and asked for his name. It was . . . Bruce! If I needed another gentle sign that I was on the right path, this was it. I flew down to Fort Myers, checked out the Airstream, and put down a deposit.

The important task of naming my Airstream required consultation with friends. Fortunately, I was part of a group on Facebook that followed the Marvel Universe stories intently. Betty (Bruce Banner's first romantic interest), Natasha (the "Black Widow" ex-agent who follows the Hulk around for a while), and Veronica (the satellite-launched shiny metal hull designed to contain the Hulk if he gets too unruly) were suggested. Betty and variations like Tin Lizzie were relatively common names for Airstreams. Natasha sounded too Russian for an American icon.

One of my non-Marvel fan friends pointed out that Veronica means "True Icon" in Latin. That made the choice clear, on several levels. The Airstream is iconic in terms of its history and mystique. But also, for me it symbolizes what God is asking of me.

VERONICA THE AIRSTREAM AT LAKE COCHITI, NM

# HOW TO SHOP FOR AN RV

- Don't pick the first one you see without checking out others — walk around, sit inside, move (or turn) from the kitchen stove and sink to the refrigerator and meal prep storage, lie down on the bed, stand in the shower or wet bath. Can you see yourself in this RV?

- Decide what your needs are before looking at all. Do you want to leave your RV at a campsite and drive your tow vehicle to explore nearby areas? Do you want to tow a small car behind a drivable RV? Will you be a full-time, occasional part-time, or frequent part-time RVer? How many people and pets will travel with you?

- Consider the differences between a large or small drivable RV, trailer, 5th wheel, van or popup camper. How do they match your needs?

- Consider purchasing used. RVs depreciate (Airstreams, not so much). Avoiding a loan payment on the RV and/or tow vehicle helps with budgeting for your RV life.

- Have an RV inspector check out the one you select, just like you'd take a used car to a mechanic before purchase — even a new RV needs to be inspected before you drive it away. Either educate yourself or hire a professional.

GO TO WEBSITE

It represents in its beauty and novelty trust in an unfolding future, where I follow His lead wherever it takes me without knowing each step ahead of time. A home on wheels is the literal and figurative icon of my mission.

Later, I found that Veronica and her successor, Alvie, were great conversation starters. People will often approach me to say they haven't seen an Airstream on the road in years, or that a relative used to have one. Every once in a while, they ask if they can take a peek inside. Usually, I'm happy to oblige, provided the circumstances are safe and in public.

People automatically assume one is wealthy when one owns an Airstream. Airstreams are costly, even though they hold their value well. Perhaps a less expensive trailer, even if I had to replace it more frequently, might be better for making me seem more approachable. Ultimately, I decided to trust God's initial inspiration from when I first spotted those Airstreams at the side of the road in Virginia.

## Downsizing and Downshifting

In just a couple of months, I literally went from a 2500-square-foot condo full of belongings to a 25-foot Airstream and 5x5 storage unit. The fact that it happened at all was yet another sign I was on the right track.

I had three weeks to get my house ready to sell before leaving with my daughter on our previously planned vacation in Spain. The Realtor felt the best time to put my house on the market would be while no one was home. Before I returned from vacation, it sold to a buyer who wanted to move in as quickly as possible. With only one month until closing, I used the time to literally give away nearly everything in the house. I kept only what I needed for a space less than one tenth the size, plus some family mementos and heirlooms.

Like many parents, I held on to concrete reminders of my children's infancy and childhood: a big pink-and-white dollhouse with tiny delicate furniture and curtains, American Girl dolls and accoutrements, artwork, crafts, and baby clothes. Besides those mementos, my town home's closets and cabinets were full of Grandma's china, lovely red glasses from an aunt's estate, and all sorts of clothes.

Some of the arts and crafts went into storage. Others I photographed and put the pictures on a flash drive. From a collection of fifty or so cups and saucers that Grandma had started, to which I had added, I selected ten and wrapped them for long-term storage. The rest went to a consignment shop, along with a beautiful olive-wood nativity set, assorted tchotchkes, many Christmas ornaments, vases, and artworks. A friend who lived alone happily received my garden statues of Mary and an angel.

During this process I came face-to-face with memories of my old life. I got lost for a few hours going through old papers and piles of old photographs. It started when I picked up a photograph of me wearing a red polka-dot bikini on a beach in Hawaii. The young Lynda was holding half a coconut with some icy drink in it, a yellow straw, and a tiny paper umbrella. She smiled at the camera. In the next photo, my ex-husband and I looked out from behind Ray-Ban sunglasses, with our fluffy 1980s hair blowing in the breeze. A pang of sorrow passed through me as I saw how young and happy we were. We still were very much in love then. I carefully placed these and other photographs of us together in a plastic box for storage.

Next, I found letters we'd written to each other in college and graduate school, some old *Brides* magazines, and legal papers from our divorce. Glancing at these items, I became distracted. I wondered if I had handled things differently, if we might have managed to stay together. Yet as words leapt off the pages drafted by our lawyers, I recalled again the bitterness and anger I felt at the time and the darkness that consumed me. How frightened I was then that my mental health would cause me to lose my children to someone who had turned from loving me to hating me, who had a secure job, who like me had spent time away from a career to care for them as infants, and who—unlike me then—was together, charming, and very persuasive. He seemed to have it all, while I was losing everything, including my mind. But actually, he didn't have it all, because he chose not to. He didn't want God in his life.

He felt betrayed that his wife had taken a path he rejected, and so he didn't want me either.

My old anguish seemed to ooze from the sheaves of paper. I placed them firmly in a shred bag and prayed in thanks for the love of God that had set me free from fear and led me to healing. I prayed for my ex-husband, that he too would find peace and happiness. I stopped for the day, done with the stack of paper and photographs.

The next morning I turned back to going through works of art. I kept a few carefully selected favorites, including a replica of Saint Luke's icon of Mary and an original oil painting I'd picked up in the Virgin Islands. The shimmering light and reflections of a church steeple captured the waves, tropical trees and flowers that represented my love of nature.

Did I really need three or four long gowns for formal events? I concluded I needed none of them. What about several drawers full of sweaters, sweatshirts, warm pants, hats and gloves? I planned to follow good weather, but decided to keep two of each warm weather clothing item stored in a bin in my truck in case I ended up in cool weather. I was giddy with giving things away.

The linen closet quickly emptied, to leave me with one set of sheets and a change, plus one set of sheets for any guest. My trailer had a collapsible dinette table that together with the rounded cushions from the dinette seats made an extra bed.

Towels from my linen closet went to a thrift store as well. Soft lush cotton towels would take too long to dry, and the bulk could quickly use up my limited storage space. Instead, I purchased a couple of microfiber towels that would dry quickly and roll up into small cylinders for storage.

For dishes, all I really needed was two plates and two bowls. A set of lightweight cutlery for four would suffice. Campers tend to bring their own utensils and dishes to shared meals, and I could always supplement with paper plates and plastic cutlery. My fancy glass flutes, red wine goblets, slender white wineglasses, and even my everyday drinking glasses threatened to shatter from the motion of the trailer. Instead, I gifted some, stored some, and purchased two plastic wineglasses, two plastic juice glasses, and two plastic drinking glasses.

As I shed the layers of my previous life, I smiled at how much I'd accumulated and how freeing it was to let go of it. I enjoyed knowing that one friend could use my dining room table, another a bedroom set, and that silk scarves from work could have a new life with yet another friend. Because my daughters needed furniture and kitchen items for their apartments, I grieved only a little that I was giving up a beautiful everyday china set in soft yellow and green pastels. I'd treated myself to it just a year ago and enjoyed the variegated cheery patterns that seemed to make every meal taste extra good.

My goal was to sell as much as possible, give away the rest, and only if needed toss it in the trash. "Sell it, gift it, toss it" was my motto.

"Sell it" involved consignment shops. I preferred that to Craigslist as I didn't have the time to meet with strangers, although I did post a few large pieces of furniture that would have been too hard to bring to a consignment shop or dump. Frankly, I was happy to sell them for a fraction of their theoretical worth just so I didn't have to move them myself. I got rid of my mattress and bedroom set this way.

"Gift it" meant posting pictures on my Facebook news feed for friends to let me know what they'd like. From a quilted wall hanging to vases to small end tables, everything needed to go. This process culminated in a "house parting" party (the opposite of a housewarming party). I took delight in seeing friends leave with my former belongings!

"Toss it" meant filling up thirty-six large garbage bags. I was amazed at what was in the back of my closets and pantry. I found lots of outdated medicine and expired food staples, as well as some prom dresses and shoes in boxes that dated back to high school.

How large my house looked after these giveaways! Stripping it down to the walls and bare wooden floors mirrored stripping away my attachment to all sorts of items, physical and otherwise. As the house slimmed down, I enjoyed the space more.

Books were hard. I love to read and had quite a library. Fortunately, I could donate many religious books to a local Catholic school. Others I gave away at my house parting party. I ended up carrying quite a few in my Airstream at first, and kept a couple boxes in storage. Over time, that changed. I now use Kindle primarily. If I do buy a book now, I give away another book. Lending libraries at RV parks help, because I can drop off books there, sometimes with a prayer card and my blog card tucked inside.

## Moving into the Airstream

Three weeks later, I stared at the pile dominating my nearly empty living room. I'd selected a frying pan, a stovetop casserole dish, and a saucepot, along with minimal cooking utensils, including a ladle, a slotted spoon, and a spatula. Out of some fifty pairs of assorted footwear, from slippers to snow boots, I'd narrowed it down to ten. My crockpot and toaster and small coffeemaker topped off the pile, resting on top of my toolbox.

As a project manager, of course, I had researched what other campers recommended. Some suggestions were invaluable, like a lantern that could be recharged by a car charger or the USB ports in my trailer. I purchased spare fuses and tools to keep my 7-point connections free from rust, plus a spray to help keep the rubber seals flexible and protected. Living in the DC area, I'd long had an emergency kit, with food and water supplies for three days. That went into the pile, as did my camping tent, tarp, stakes, backpack, portable stove and water filter, and assorted paraphernalia for cooking outdoors; art supplies, some family photos, a statue of Saint Joseph and one of Mary, books and more books that I just didn't want to part with, toiletries and the contents of my medicine cabinet; towels and sheets and pillows, a couple of blankets and sleeping bags. And, of course, Penny's crate, dishes, dog food, grooming and care items, plus her favorite toys.

I pulled out the bathroom scale. Based on the carrying capacity of my trailer and truck, I started refining that pile further.

This may sound painful, but actually once you get started detaching from your belongings, it is very satisfying. Still, I have to admit that when I later misplaced a favorite bracelet that most likely slipped off my wrist while hiking, I cried. My attachment to it was to the givers—my daughters—so the loss of the bracelet was more than the loss of the item. I looked into replacing it and then decided that the memory of the bracelet and the fact that they'd given it to me was enough.

Not only did I shift my perspective so that my things didn't own me, I also learned the value of repairing rather than discarding. I learned to mend rather than discard clothing with torn seams.

I'd always considered myself relatively handy, but moving into a home on wheels called on me to up my game considerably. Back when I was first out of work on mental health disability, I spent weeks renovating my floors, cabinets, and molding, doing a good part of the work myself. I thought I knew my way around a toolbox, but systems in an RV are different. I had to learn about electricity and plumbing, even if I didn't necessarily do the work myself. Also, small, easy-to-fix items, like a range hood that came loose, or latches that broke on a cabinet, were not worth the trouble of using the warranty unless I needed some more complicated repairs.

One of the reasons I bought a new rather than used Airstream was the three-year warranty. Just learning how to live in a trailer full-time was enough of a learning curve, I figured. I discovered, however, that even a warranty is only as good as your ability to make use of it. During the COVID pandemic, many dealership service departments closed or restricted appointments to those who recently had purchased their Airstream at that dealership. I ended up traveling hundreds of miles to the Airstream factory when I had a leak I couldn't repair.

Honestly, transitioning into full-time life as a nomad was easier than I had imagined. I spend about the same amount of time I used to on home maintenance, but the tasks differ. Moreover, being able to move my home easily to follow good weather or see what lies beyond the next curve in the road makes keeping my rig in tip-top shape a pleasure.

## You're Doing What?

I started living full-time in my Airstream and camp hosting while I was still transitioning from my work at Tepeyac, the nonprofit ob/gyn practice. When you work for a nonprofit, you promote everywhere you go. Divine Mercy Care, Tepeyac's parent, raised funds to support the center's services to the poor and underserved. I regularly attended Divine Mercy Care fundraisers and other events to connect with prospective donors and existing supporters.

At one such reception, after I'd started living in my trailer, the communications director introduced me to some donors who had contributed to the build-out of Tepeyac's new offices. I'd directed that project the previous year and could answer questions about the new chapel and design choices. As is usual, conversation went to little personal details, seeking common experiences.

"Have you worked here long?" a well-dressed lady with silver hair and understated jewelry asked me.

"Yes, I've been a patient and volunteer for many years, then joined Tepeyac as an employee about eight years ago," I answered, taking a sip from my wineglass.

"I actually met Lynda because she was a neighbor down the street, and she introduced me to Tepeyac," said the communications director cheerfully.

"Oh, we live out in Great Falls," said the silver-haired lady. "I don't actually come here for care, but we love what you do."

"I know Great Falls well," I said. "I used to go swing dancing out there."

"Oh, do you live nearby?" she asked.

"No, I just moved into my trailer out in Manassas."

She cocked her head as if I were joking and laughed.

The communications director gracefully extricated me from the conversation by introducing the donor to one of the doctors standing nearby. She grabbed my arm and leaned in close. "You can't say that!" she hissed. "Come up with some alternative, like you live in the country. Or, at least, that you live in your Airstream."

I definitely received mixed reactions from friends and work colleagues when I embarked on my marvelous adventure. "Maybe you should just rent out your house for a bit," one Realtor friend cautioned. "It's hard to get into the neighborhood you've been living in." Another couple wondered if I were having a midlife crisis. "It would be a lot cheaper to keep your day job and get a boat or new car," the husband suggested.

Still others were concerned for my safety. "Isn't it dangerous to travel by yourself?" asked my friend Carol. "Won't you get lonely and depressed? What if you get hurt?"

Fortunately, the Holy Spirit had answers for those concerns. They were things I'd asked myself in prayer during my discernment process. Here's where my analytic, left-brain skills, which I'd been slowly improving during my time with Tepeyac, came in handy. I did a lot of planning. My insurance was good all over the U.S., and I arranged with several friends to keep contact with me every few days. I sent a planned itinerary to my daughters, in case cell service was poor and they needed to contact a park or campground to find me. With regard to personal safety, I researched tips online from others, particularly women, who traveled by themselves. What seemed doable and comfortable for me to prepare, I did.

There also were those that understood me perfectly. "I'm so thrilled for you," said Laura. "You are just the kind of person who can do something like this, because you trust God. I got goose bumps hearing about how the Lord worked through your neighbors to encourage you."

"Thanks for not thinking I'm crazy," I laughed.

"Still, you'd better call me every couple of days," she responded firmly. "I need to hear from you, and don't hesitate to reach out if you're in a situation."

I've maintained that community with old friends. I also found instant community by choosing to purchase the brand of trailer that first caught my eye. Airstream owners tend to gravitate toward other Airstream owners, by virtue of the somewhat unique and historic character of the Airstream, and the charismatic nature of Airstream's founder, Wally Byam. His legacy even today colors the private Airstream club that organizes rallies and caravans, like those he promoted back in the mid-twentieth century.

SAINT JOSEPH'S ABBEY CHURCH

CHAPTER NINE

# SIGNPOSTS ON THE JOURNEY PART ONE

*"When we are lost in the woods, the sight
of a signpost is a great matter."*

—C. S. Lewis

During any journey, it is worthwhile to take stock of where you have been, where you are now, and where you are going. When we scale a mountain on a switchback trail that wanders back and forth, up and down, we may not realize how far we've gone. When we look ahead, the trail may vanish into mist or be hard to discern.

God gives us signposts in our life. We don't always see them ahead of us, but they may become clearer in retrospect. One of my favorite saints reminisces about tall signposts usually painted red that marked the trails in the mountains near his childhood home:

> *"When the snow fell, covering up everything, paths, seeded fields and pasture thickets, boulders and ravines, the poles stood out as sure reference points, so that everyone would always know where the road went."*
> —Saint Josemaria Escriva, *Friends of God*

Every journey, whether in the natural world or spiritual life, needs signposts. At the end of each part in this account of my pilgrimage, I'll offer a few simple signposts in the form of thoughts and questions that may help mark the road for your own journey.

 Look back over your life. Where there were challenges, what came out of them that changed you? Did the results help you with a future challenge or new direction?

 How have friends and mentors impacted your journey? Who has been a companion on the way for you? How can you be a companion to others?

 What is your relationship with the Divine? Do you know God? Who is He to you? Do you fear Him or see Him as a loving parent? Is He uninvolved and far away or deeply interested in every detail of your life?

 What would a close relationship with God look like to you? Does that cause you to be anxious or peaceful? Why?

 Ask God for insight. Ask Him to help you pray and create quiet time to listen. In the presence of God, reflect that you are loved as a precious son or daughter. What are the implications for your life?

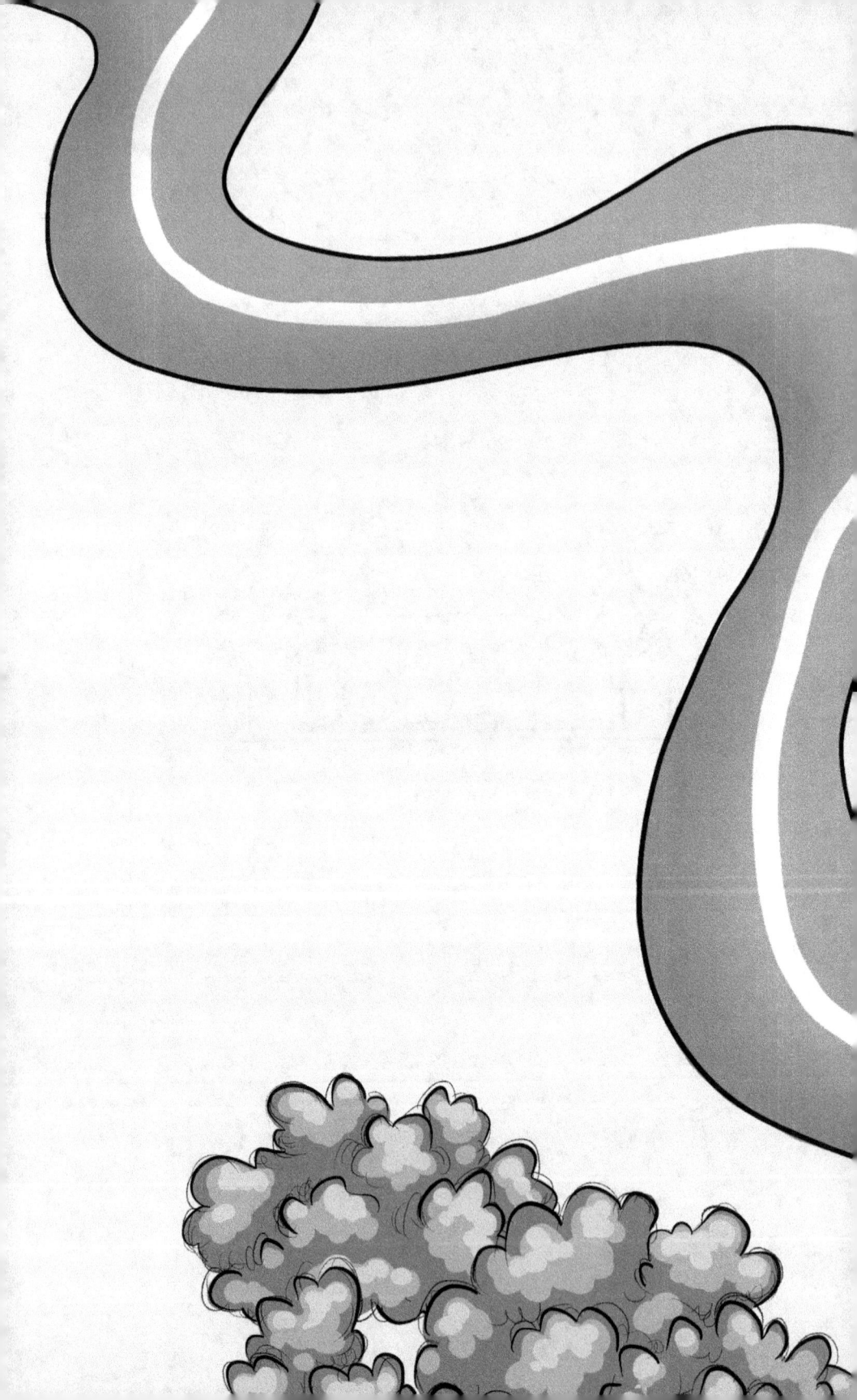

# Part Two

---

# GETTING ON THE ROAD

CHAPTER TEN

# FIRST TRIP

*"Happy are those who find refuge in you,
whose hearts are set on pilgrim roads."*

—Psalm 84:6

## Beyond the Dealer's Lot

As I drove to Florida to pick up my Airstream, I reflected on how I had traded in my house and life in a busy urban area for something with much less certainty. Whatever the challenges and adventures looming ahead, I needed to keep my eyes on the road in front of me. Focusing on the present, on the tasks of every day, helps me live in the presence of God and see the supernatural in the natural. This is true even in the most prosaic details of how to adapt to living in a travel trailer.

As I drove away from the dealership, towing my Airstream for the first time, I was glad it was only a short distance to an RV resort for my first overnight stay. The dealership had comped one night and I purchased another. This initial campsite would give me a chance to absorb the lessons I'd been given about how my Airstream worked. I had my owner's manual and an incredibly helpful book, *The Newbies Guide to Airstreaming* by Rich Luhr, that the dealership had provided with my purchase.

Best of all, the salesman, Bruce, and his wife both lived in the same RV park in which I'd be staying. They'd been full-time Airstreamers for years. Bruce kindly gave me his cell phone number and explained I could call him if I ever had questions or needed help. That was a big relief.

Even so, towing on I-75 for my first trip, I wondered, "What have I gotten myself into?" I kept being startled when I looked in my rearview mirror and saw the Airstream's gleaming windows right behind my truck. "Who's tailgating me like that?" was my first, instinctive reaction. I soon acclimated to using my backup camera to see behind me. I very cautiously signaled way in advance, and checked my extended towing mirrors before pulling into traffic. Since the Airstream towed easily, I relaxed incrementally while retaining my newbie's white-knuckled grip on the steering wheel.

At the dealership, I'd obsessively videotaped every step of my three-hour walk-through and orientation. One of the reasons I had picked this dealership was that it committed to making sure you understood how your trailer worked before you left the lot. I'd sat in the passenger seat of my truck while the technician showed me how to set the brake controller and tested it by stopping short using the trailer brakes.

Still, I was mentally exhausted after the long day and the excitement of picking up my trailer. When I arrived at the RV park, I was thrilled to learn my first spot was a pull-through. I'd never backed up my new Airstream (or any trailer, for that matter) and planned to find a big empty parking lot the next day to practice.

## Setting Up the Campsite

Guided by a friendly camp host in a golf cart, I positioned my shiny new Airstream in the correct spot. Thankfully, the site was level, so I didn't need to experiment with the leveling blocks. Next, I tackled setting up the surge suppressor and electric cord at the power pedestal. That was relatively easy. I didn't bother with water or sewer hookups the first day, since so much else was new. I'd left the dealership with a full fresh-water tank and empty black and gray tanks.

Taking deep breaths and trying to look confident so I'd feel that way, I placed the wheel chocks under the trailer tires. Chocks are graduated blocks that prevent the trailer from rolling away if someone bumps it or, more likely, when you jack up the front of the trailer to hitch and unhitch. I gingerly used the electric jack to raise the Airstream and loosen the tension on my heavy metal weight-distribution and sway-control bars. I even remembered to bend my knees and lift with my legs to take off the bars. After tucking the bars under the trailer, I lowered the jack and released the hitch lock so I could begin the unhitching process. Essentially, I needed to raise my trailer once for removing the bars, take them off, lower the trailer, then unlock the hitch lock and raise the trailer once more to release the ball from the receiver.

I think I took half an hour to do this as I kept reviewing my video on the phone, angling it so I could see in the bright tropical Florida sunshine. Perspiration rolled down my face and my hair kept sticking to it, so I put my hair up into my cute white Airstream baseball cap that I'd purchased at the dealership.

Properly attired, I finished unhitching by pulling my truck forward a few inches away from my trailer. Next, I lowered the jack and checked again to be sure the trailer was level. Beneath the Airstream are little square feet that tuck up while traveling but act as stabilizers when cranked down to the ground at a campsite. Stabilizers on an Airstream do not bear any weight, but lessen the degree of "bounce" that occurs when the trailer is balanced on the front jack and tires. I extended my stabilizers and stairs, and unlatched the outdoor cover on the vent for the kitchen exhaust fan. Finally, I brought Penny and her crate into our new home and began unpacking things from the truck to set up inside.

My sense of happiness at how pretty the Airstream looked inside refreshed me, along with a cool bottle of water. I put Penny on her leash. We walked around my bright green truck and admired my silver home. My windows looked out onto palm trees, a creek, and a small bridge. Penny and I walked past rows of other trailers as we followed signs to a footpath over the bridge. There was a circular dog walk through woods and tangles of underbrush. Palm fronds, spiky green succulents, and tropical flowers punctuated the trail with lush foliage encroaching on the dirt path. I avoided going anywhere near the creek, as small dogs are alligator snacks in Florida.

As we walked, several friendly ladies waved at me from their campsite near the water. They were setting up a picnic table and grills. It all looked rather elaborate, but I said to myself "one step at a time." I was only staying there for a short while, so it didn't seem worthwhile to put out my outdoor equipment and awning. I looked forward to an upcoming longer stay when I planned to set things up as an extra room outdoors to easily socialize with other campers just as those friendly ladies were doing.

## First Night in the Airstream

Penny and I returned to the Airstream, and I pulled out some food to heat up on the stove. Following instructions, I turned the burner on and twisted the ignite switch then waited three clicks for it to ignite. Nothing happened. After several attempts, I turned everything off and called the dealership.

"Is the propane on?" the service person asked.

"Yes, I'm turning the switch," I answered.

"Go outside and open the cover to the propane tanks," he instructed patiently. "What color is showing on the display?"

"Red," I answered.

"OK, then turn the knobs, and when the display is green you should be able to go light your stove."

"Oh . . . thanks," I said, feeling rather stupid.

"There's a lot to learn when you haven't camped before," he responded cheerfully. "You'll get it!"

I have to admit I felt a certain sense of accomplishment once Penny and I had dinner. As I blessed the food, looking out through my Airstream's panoramic windows at the campground and the riot of green tropical foliage, I thanked God again for bringing me here. Since I felt oddly reluctant to baptize my brand-new black tank, I used the campsite facilities for toileting and showering that evening. Back in the Airstream, I made my bed and swept sand from the floor. As I put Penny's leash on to take her back out for one more walk, I thought, "This isn't that hard."

The door wouldn't open.

I looked at the latch and didn't see anything wrong. I tried it again, but I could not get out. It was about ten thirty in the evening by then. Fortunately, I had my salesman's cell phone number. I called him and he said he'd be right over. He pulled on the door from the outside while I turned the handle and pushed from inside to open it. Gratefully, I stepped outside.

"Is this normal?" I asked. "Do I need to take it back to the dealership?"

"It's just new," he said. He demonstrated how to close the door and then push it again firmly to make sure it aligned. He also mentioned the importance of leveling. "After you do this a few times, it will be fine," he said. "You can always get out through the fire escape window or in through the outside storage compartment under the bed if you are locked out." I looked dubiously at the small entrance to the storage compartment and resolved to make sure I tested that fire escape in the morning.

"How do I avoid getting locked out . . . ever?" I asked.

"We keep an extra set of keys in our truck and hidden in a magnetic compartment outside the trailer," he said. "Some people wear their keys on a lanyard and hook it by the door so they have to touch it to go outside."

I liked that idea and picked up a lanyard the next morning. It has an additional advantage. When I hike, my keys jingle, making it less likely I'll surprise wildlife. I also put a screamer alarm on the lanyard. In bear country, I carry bear spray as well, keeping in mind the cartoons of bears spitting out bells as they complain about the pits in their meal.

## Getting Familiar with the Stinky Slinky

The next morning, I enjoyed a quick swim in the resort's pool and went back to reviewing my notes and figuring out where I wanted to store things in the Airstream. I looked again at my videos demonstrating water and sewer use, then set up my fresh-water hose and my "stinky slinky," the black sewer hose that connects my black and gray tank outlet to the RV park's sewer inlet in the ground at my site. Bruce had promised to return that afternoon to see if I had more questions. Meanwhile, I asked a man walking his dog if he could take a look at my setup as I wanted to be sure that if I used it, I would not send water or worse spraying everywhere.

The whole black tank and dumping experience really isn't that difficult. Still, everyone has disaster stories that they are all too willing to share. There's even a humorous e-book, *Tales from the Black Tank* available from the Virtual Campground, that chronicles a few. I really didn't want to have any of those experiences—and so far have not.

Penny and I have come a long way since our early days as full-time RVers. My reveries of the past on our drive west didn't end when we arrived at our campsite and settled in for a stay. Instead, I began to journal our adventures and to write about the spiritual aspects of my journey from the past into the present. Let's look next at the basics of full-time RVing and what they can reveal when you look beyond the surface.

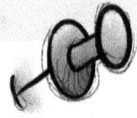

## CAMPGROUND ETIQUETTE

<u>SITE</u>—DON'T cross someone else's site. Treat it as if it has invisible walls. DON'T leave without dousing your fire or coals in the firepit or grill. It should be cool to the touch. DO keep your site clean while camping and dispose of trash immediately to avoid unwanted animal visitors. DO leave your site cleaner than you found it, in particular if it is public land or park land. This preserves it for others.

<u>SOUND</u>—DON'T run your generator during quiet hours (or if boondocking unless it is very quiet and you don't have anyone near you). DON'T play music or TV so loudly that people can hear it full blast next door (unless they want to hear it!). DO realize that if you can hear your neighbors, they can hear you. DO knock verbally not by pounding the door.

<u>STUFF</u>—DON'T unpack your outdoor furniture or roll out your awning in an overnight parking lot stay. DON'T leave your dog tethered or in a cage outside when you are not also outside. DO turn off your outside lights overnight (especially the "neighbor-hater" round light at window level outside your Airstream's door!).

GO TO WEBSITE

CHAPTER ELEVEN

# FAMILIARIZING MYSELF WITH THE DASHBOARD

*"And it occurred to me there is no manual that deals with the real business of motorcycle maintenance, the most important aspect of all. Caring about what you are doing is considered either unimportant or taken for granted."*
—Robert M. Pirsig, *Zen and the Art of Motorcycle Maintenance*

## A Different Dashboard

When you first learn how to drive, you familiarize yourself with your dashboard. Each function is something you may use every day or only in an emergency, but you'd better know how to turn the radio on and where to find the hazard lights.

Life in a trailer has its own kind of dashboard. From getting mail to using water, everything is different when you change lanes in life and move from the on ramp to the highway.

My truck already had a tire pressure monitoring system (TPMS) on its dashboard for the truck wheels. This system automatically alerts the driver if tire pressure falls. As you'll read a bit later, I eventually added another TPMS for my Airstream's wheels. The truck dashboard also contained a sliding lever to activate the trailer brakes if more braking power were needed for the trailer itself than that provided by integration with the truck brakes.

Within the Airstream itself, there are various devices that form a dashboard of sorts, albeit scattered about in different locations. The dealer showed me how to read the gauges monitoring the battery charge, fresh water remaining, plus the space remaining in the gray and black tanks. The control panel for the furnace, heat pump, and air conditioner displayed the current and desired temperature. I added a hygrometer to measure humidity inside my tiny home, as well as a thermometer for inside my refrigerator.

A dashboard in a broader sense is anything that keeps track of what you need to keep your rig running. For a nomad, that includes mail, energy usage, water, and even the most basic items that we take for granted in a "sticks and bricks" home, such as a toilet. As I learned to navigate life as a nomad, I became more familiar with my small environment and the tools I needed to keep it safe and comfortable. Sometimes they seemed to take on a supernatural aspect, while other times they were simply humorous. Since God has a sense of humor, even the most prosaic things that made me smile in this learning process were a gift from Him.

## Mail

"How do you get your mail?" is often the first question people ask when I tell them I live everywhere. Actually, mail is one of the simplest aspects of transitioning to full-time travel. Several services exist to help people who live in boats and RVs establish an address for receipt of mail and for documentation purposes.

My favorite YouTube channel when I was preparing to hit the road was the Long, Long Honeymoon. They recommended a mail service located in Green Cove Springs, Florida, called Saint Brendan's Isle (SBI).

The name caught my attention. Saint Brendan the Navigator was an Irish priest and monk believed to have sailed to many islands. As the patron saint of sailors, mariners, travelers, elderly adventurers, and whales, Saint Brendan is a good intercessor for nomads.

Essentially, SBI acts as my postal agent. For a modest monthly fee, they receive mail for me as well as deliveries requiring a physical address. When mail arrives, the outside of each envelope is scanned to my unique secure account and I receive an email alert. I can then select to have SBI hold or forward the mail or, for an additional charge per item, open it and scan the contents. Once scanned, the mail can be archived if I choose or held for me to pick up.

When I'm in the area, I pick up my mail in person. Otherwise, for a small handling charge plus shipping, SBI sends the mail to me upon request, at the local address I specify (typically my current campground or a local friend's home). If I use USPS to send the packet of mail, then I can even have it sent to General Delivery at my current local post office. This works well if I'm staying off grid or at a campground that does not accept mail for campers. For the amount I use SBI's basic and additional services, I estimate I spend about $50 per month.

SBI also walks its customers through the process of establishing Florida residency and domicile. Other popular options providing similar mail and residency services include Escapees RV Club and Good Sam Mail Service.

I have to admit that the legends of Saint Brendan influenced me to pick the service named after him. He too was a nomad. The saint traveled in a small boat through parts of the Atlantic, to Scotland and Wales, but perhaps even as far as Greenland and Newfoundland. A whimsical legend has the saint and his companions putting in with his small boat on a bare island in the middle of the sea. They begin to celebrate Easter Mass, which starts with a bonfire. Suddenly the island moves. It is a whale, which playfully slides the boat and its sailors back into the deeps to continue their journey.

Saint Brendan's beautiful prayer for travelers also struck a chord with me as a new nomad:

*Help me to journey beyond the familiar*
*and into the unknown.*
*Give me the faith to leave old ways*
*and break fresh ground with You.*
*Christ of the mysteries, I trust You*
*to be stronger than each storm within me.*
*I will trust in the darkness and know*
*that my times, even now, are in Your hand.*
*Tune my spirit to the music of heaven,*
*and somehow, make my obedience count for You.*

## Energy

You don't realize how much energy you use until you have to be conscious of it. In an Airstream, or other RV, power isn't as easy to take for granted. Sometimes you'll plug in something and everything will stop working, because you are drawing too much power at once. You wind up being conscious of how many amps different appliances use, so you don't overload your circuits. This information usually is on a label on the appliance (blow dryers and portable dehumidifiers both use a lot of electrical energy, for example).

When I first started traveling, I had one day at a campsite where no matter what I did or what I turned off my power kept cutting out. It was a blistering hot day, and I wondered if there were a general problem in the campsite or if I had miscalculated by running a portable microwave and my air-conditioning at the same time. After I'd made several frustrating trips back outside to flip the switch on and off, a camp host cruising around the site in a golf cart noticed my dilemma. He called the office for help. It turned out not to be anything to do with my use. The power pedestal had a wiring problem.

After this I upgraded my simple surge protector to an Electrical Monitoring System, or EMS. This handy device diagnoses problems in addition to protecting your rig from voltage that is too high or too low. Although an EMS is expensive, RV electrical system repairs—especially in an Airstream, where the wires run between inner and outer aluminum panels—are far more costly. You may burn out your EMS if it is triggered, but you will save your electrical system.

Knowing what the electrical problem is has other benefits. You feel very authoritative when you can casually tell the office that the polarity is reversed or the pedestal is not properly grounded. Armed with diagnostic information, you'll generally be given a different site or permission to use an adjacent pedestal with little hassle, rather than being told the problem is with your rig because no one else complained. This leads to another important tip: check your pedestal power before you unhitch, in case you need to move!

Another helpful item is an EZ-Start for air-conditioning. This device lowers the amps needed when the air conditioner first starts or cycles on. If you use too many amps at once, you will blow a circuit either within your RV or at the pedestal or other power source to which you are connected.

Now it is second nature for me to always be aware of my power storage and usage capacities and adjust my use to stay within the limits of my energy. Power comes in two flavors: AC from pedestals, generators, and outlets, and DC from batteries. Newer Airstreams have a battery monitor that tells you how much charge remains in the RV batteries. The monitor is easy to see and understand, not subtle like the methods we may use to monitor our personal stores of physical and spiritual energy. For a deeper dive into how electricity and batteries work in an RV, see the sidebar at the end of this chapter.

It is vital to respect the power of electricity. Like the Sons of Thunder in the Gospel of Mark, we really don't fully appreciate what we are risking in calling down fire from Heaven. James and John looked at the power Jesus promised them as a tool without fully appreciating its destructive nature. The impact of the lightning they suggested be targeted to sinners was more devastating than they'd appreciated; it would have deprived those sinners of the ability to repent before they died.

Once I tried to unplug my power cord from the pedestal after a weeklong stay, only to find that I couldn't budge it. I had to ask for help, but even my burly neighbor could not remove it. The campground office sent a maintenance person who managed to detach my cord, only to find that one of the prongs on the plug was black and gunky. The plastic surrounding it actually had melted a bit, then resolidified, essentially gluing the cord to the pedestal.

The maintenance guy told me that if water gets in between the outlet and the plug, as may happen in a heavy rain, especially if you accidentally don't push in the plug all the way, electricity arcs and burns the prong. He suggested using a bit of dielectric grease that repels moisture between electrical connections. I use that periodically and also double-check that my connections are firm. I've seen other campers even rig up some sort of waterproof cover for the pedestal in bad weather, even if just a plastic bag or jug.

Subsequently, I realized just how important this is. An arc can actually cause a fire. A fellow Airstreamer posted a photo on Facebook of a scorched outlet and panel from this very issue. Once again, I learned how what I don't know can get me in a lot of trouble—especially when it comes to power.

Like our RVs, if our spirits and minds are flooded with too much energy or starved by too little, we become disoriented and disconnected, overcome or weak. We can short-circuit and trip our own breakers, necessitating a reset, rest, and refueling.

Just as we carry adapters and surge protectors for our RVs, we need to carry spiritual and mental tools to convert power up or down as needed. We may use meditation, prayer, silence, or deep breathing to slow down. To increase our energy, extroverts may spend time with other people, while introverts need their alone time. Stimulants like inspiring music, fresh air or scents, praise and worship, exercise, or volunteering to help others also have their place for powering up. Solo stargazing soothes, as does the occasional bottle of beer or glass of wine enjoyed over campfire conversation.

Power comes from within and without, but always is a gift from God as the source of everything. He may energize us through His indwelling within our souls or through the external graces He imparts to us.

External graces may work through other people or events or objects. This can be subtle or dramatic. For example, when my neighbors gave me the perfect card to encourage me with a picture

# ELECTRICITY

Like most RVs, Airstreams have two types of power: alternating current (AC) at 120 volts and direct current (DC) at 12 volts. The two systems are different but complementary. Power needs to be transferred from sources outside the RV for current use or stored in the RV for later use. There are several ways to do this.

A power pedestal at a campsite has AC power outlets at 30 amp or 50 amp, sometimes both. To get that power to your RV, you use the corresponding 30- or 50-amp power cord that plugs into the RV. I carry an adapter to change 50 amp to 30 amp, because my Airstream operates on 30-amp power.

AC power also can come from a generator or a residential home's 120-volt outlet. A 120-volt outlet starts at 20 or 15 amps depending on its fuse, but loses some power depending on the distance and gauge of the extension cord, adapter if any, and power cord that carries that power from the outlet to the RV. For instance, when I connect to 15-amp power from a friend's home electric system while camping in their yard, I'll use a 15-to-30-amp adapter along with a heavy-gauge extension cord. (I carry a 10-gauge cord. The lower the number of the gauge, the less power is lost in transition.)

Your tow vehicle alternator sends DC power to your RV through the seven-pin connector plug. Solar panels also generate power stored in the RV batteries.

After entering the RV, AC power goes to a distribution panel to then run outlets for a microwave, coffeemaker, and other AC appliances. A converter changes AC power into DC power to be used or stored in the 12-volt batteries carried in or outside of the RV. DC power runs lights, fans and vents, the furnace, and the water pump in an Airstream. An inverter converts stored DC power from the batteries to AC power when needed.

of the open road winding toward mountains, which they had purchased the day before, not knowing to whom they might give it, that was an external grace. Many months later, in an incident I describe further along in this book, when I was feeling doubtful about continuing my journey after an accident, the cantor at church the next morning sang a song that perfectly expressed why I was traveling. That very welcome external grace was a direct answer to prayer, because I'd expressed my fears to God and asked Him if He really wanted me to continue on the road.

Internal grace is the indwelling of divine love and mercy. It comes to us from God as a gift, through prayer and the sacraments, such as baptism. Sacraments are visible signs and efficacious channels of God's love and mercy into the souls of all who receive them with proper disposition. Through spiritual nourishment, internal grace helps us recognize the workings of God in our lives and transforms us to become more like Him.

If we don't have the right adapters, we can't use these sources of love and mercy to power our actions. If we don't have the correct extension cords or fail to maintain our batteries, we have less energy available. When we tap into the grace of God, we are filled with joy that others can see, and we are able in turn to share the power of grace to benefit and energize others. Thus, in RV lingo, we are simultaneously inverters and converters.

For the RV, energy comes from gasoline or diesel, propane or electricity to fuel its needs. For us, grace provides spiritual and emotional energy, while food and water give us nourishment and hydration to generate bodily and mental energy. All types of fuel are necessary. In fact, keeping you and your rig properly fueled is so important, it has a whole chapter later in this book.

## The Black Tank

Perhaps the most common questions about RV life quickly progress from fuel to waste.

"What do you do for, you know, going to the bathroom?" asked Miriam. I'd met her at a fundraiser when I was living in my

Airstream in Northern Virginia while I trained my replacements at the nonprofit. This was a conversation I'd had many times with different people. Those not familiar with RV travel seem very concerned about toileting, even when we meet over a meal or at a fancy cocktail reception.

"I have a toilet that receives fresh water from my fresh-water tank when I press on a lever to flush it," I explained. "What goes into the toilet bowl is pushed by water and gravity down a valve that opens into a holding tank when I flush."

"But then what, how do you get rid of it?" She cocked her head. "Surely you don't just leave it on the road!"

"Of course not," I said cheerfully. "There are three tanks: a fresh-water tank to supply water if you aren't hooked up to an outside water source, a gray water holding tank for shower and sink water, and a black water holding tank for everything that goes down the toilet," I elaborated. "You refill your fresh-water tank when needed, and you dump the gray water and black water holding tanks either at your own full-hookup campsite with an individual sewer outlet or at a dump station with an outlet that everyone in the campground uses. Sometimes if I'm on the road I'll use a dump station at a gas station or water district. It's basically a hole in the ground covered by a lid that you open for dumping."

"But, how do you get it from the holding tank to the dump station in the ground?" she asked. "Isn't that messy and, well, unhealthy?"

"Not when done correctly!" I answered. "I've heard many disaster stories told around campfires, where people forgot to check that a hose was secure or where a hose broke in the process of dumping. One person told me that he was in rush and forgot to unhook the hose before pulling away, which created a mess."

A lot of people base their vague fear of sewage in an RV on movies like Robin Williams's *RV* where a brown geyser erupts. Or they've seen the meme of Randy Quaid as Cousin Eddie in *National Lampoon's Christmas Vacation*, drinking a beer while emptying a detached sewer hose into the storm drain. Don't do this.

Fortunately, the mysteries of the black tank are not that mysterious and mishaps are far less dramatic. I store my "stinky slinky" (the accordion-style black plastic sewer hose) in the outside storage compartment on my trailer's bumper. I also have a rarely used spare carried in a round tube with a lid under the trailer.

When your tank is about three quarters full, it's time to dump. You can gauge how full the black tank is either with sensors built into the tank that send a signal to a monitor or simply by looking down the toilet when flushing. While you can't see the gray tank level, I find the sensors and just the experience of knowing how much water I can use before dumping suffices. The gray tank does not contain solids, so it is not as critical as it is for the black tank to know how full the tank is before dumping.

"Why does it matter how full the black tank is?" Miriam asked with a shudder. "Wouldn't you want to get rid of that sewage as fast as you can?"

"Not if you want to avoid the dreaded poop mountain," I answered, enjoying her clearly fascinated but disgusted reaction. "If solids accumulate without liquid, they can dry out and cause problems. Gravity is your friend. If you don't have enough liquid to dissolve and flush out solids, the solids pile up right under where they enter the tank from the toilet. This literally builds a pile of dried poop. It's really not making a mountain out of a molehill to call it a poop mountain, because it is not easy to correct."

"Great," she gasped. "What else?"

"If you don't have enough liquid, poop and toilet paper can get stuck in the valves or inside your stinky slinky. If you leave the dumping outlet valves on your trailer open, with the sewer hose connected to the campground's sewer outlet, you create this problem by continually draining the liquid out, leaving the solids in your tank or hose. I've seen people have water come shooting back up their sewer hose because it was blocked. Not a fun cleanup! Not to mention, if you leave the valves to the sewer hose open, odors and other things such as insects can migrate up from the underground campground holding tank into your holding tank. I heard about someone who was trying to unclog their tank following such a mistake and saw something moving inside the tank. It was a mud puppy."

"I don't know what that is, but it can't be good," Miriam said, shaking her head. She waved off the waiter offering us pate on crackers.

"It's like a salamander," I said. "Not common at all! Little tiny sewer flies are usually the first sign that something is amiss if you forget to close the valves."

She grimaced. "So, you leave the hose hooked up into the sewer outlet, but close the dump valve on your trailer?" she confirmed.

"Many people do. For me, just being one person, I tend not to leave the sewer hose hooked up at all, but take it out when I need to dump. Every time I dump, I dump the black tank first then the gray to flush out any nasty debris still in the stinky slinky."

"I see," she said.

"But," I went on, thoroughly warming to the topic now, "if I have a source of water where I'm dumping, which is usually the case, I hook up a special water hose only used for cleaning the black tank and rinse the black tank once I've dumped. My trailer also has sprayers that will spray the inside of the black tank. If for some reason I don't have access from the outside of the trailer to run water into the black tank, then I'll dump water down the toilet inside by filling and flushing the toilet with fresh water."

She shook her head again and took another sip of wine as the string quartet played in the background.

"Isn't this a really disgusting job?" she said. "Don't you get water and worse on you?"

"Well, step one is to put on disposable vinyl or latex gloves." I laughed. "You'd be surprised how many times I've seen people do this without gloves! That's really gross. I throw out the gloves when I'm done, taking them off one at a time so I never touch the outside with an ungloved hand. Even then, I always either wash or hand sanitize my hands afterwards."

"Honestly," she thoughtfully remarked, "diapering babies is far worse."

"Things can go wrong" I admitted. "I once tried to rinse out the inside of my stinky slinky with a hose after I detached the slinky from the trailer so it would still drain into the dump inlet. The water sprayed harder than I realized and I lost my grip. I had to change my clothes before getting back in the truck," I noted, watching her carefully. "Used bleach on that load of laundry!"

"OK, then," she said. "That doesn't sound pleasant."

"No," I acknowledged. "At least now that I've made that mistake, I haven't tried it again."

I swirled the ice in my drink, looking down reflectively. "Ice is very nice though."

"How much have you had to drink?" Miriam laughed.

"Not much, but the conversation reminded me of a trick that RVers use when they can't clean out the black tank with water after dumping."

"Please, don't hold back now," she said. "What does ice have to do with it?"

"If you're in a bind, you can put ice cubes down your toilet before towing. The motion of towing shakes the ice and breaks up whatever is in there, the ice melts, and you can hopefully flush out any lingering debris at the next dump site."

"Not quite what I think of when I hear 'shaken not stirred,'" she retorted.

"Exactly, now you're getting into the spirit," I said. "You know you really are an RVer when you get excited about receiving a drain valve cover with a handle."

"I have to ask, but I think I'll regret it," she said.

"The valve on the RV that the black and gray tanks drain through sometimes gets stuck when dust and dirt kick up on the road," I answered, "so you'll get to your campsite, put one end of the sewer hose in the sewer inlet, squat down to open your dump valve to connect the other end of your sewer hose, then find you cannot turn the cover to open the valve. I've learned to splash some water over it to loosen it, but it sometimes is still quite tight for me to turn." I paused, taking a sip of my drink.

"So when a friend I met on the road posted a photo of a valve with a handle, I hopped on Amazon and ordered it. So did about fifty other nomads, judging from the post comments!" I chuckled. "The handle won't help if the valve is frozen shut—that requires warming it with a hair dryer or parking where sun can shine directly on the valve. But it's great if you just need better leverage. It's kind of embarrassing if your new neighbor's first introduction involves you falling on the ground because you slipped trying to turn a valve that won't move. This handled valve promises to save me from repeating that experience."

"I see why you'd be pretty happy about that," Miriam wryly commented, "but I think we've aired out all the black tank issues pretty thoroughly now. You've reminded me I need to make an appointment with my therapist and maybe do a cleanse before the next party I attend."

CHAPTER TWELVE

# WEIGHING IT ALL AGAIN

*"Which of you wishing to construct a tower does not first sit down and calculate the cost to see if there is enough for its completion?"*
—Luke 14:28

## Keeping It Steady

Having a sense of humor really helps when living full-time in an RV. Some things are deadly serious, however.

Anyone who's driven much on highways probably has seen a truck or trailer swaying. The back of the vehicle being towed starts to fishtail, moving from side to side. This can quickly get out of hand. With each oscillation back and forth, the movement increases, resulting in the trailer yanking the tow vehicle sideways or off the road.

A YouTube video using toys vividly demonstrates how the distribution of weight affects sway. When a weight is placed near the hitch of a toy truck and trailer, and an external force pushes the trailer sideways, it self-corrects. When the weight is near the back of the trailer, the same push results in the trailer turning over.

Reality is a bit more complicated, but that's the basic concept. Sway can quickly turn into disaster, as I share later in this book. Properly distributing weight on your trailer and using safety devices like anti-sway bars and a tire pressure monitoring system are key parts of getting ready to travel. It sounds dry, but I'm including an explanation here because I later learned how critical it is to get this right.

## Weight Limits and Weight Distribution

Weight has several dimensions for the aspiring travel-trailer operator. First, there's the dry weight of your tow vehicle. This is the weight as you find it on the lot, without anything added by the dealer or any water. Not to be confused with this measurement, there also is the actual Gross Vehicle Weight or GVR. This includes all the fluids, cargo, and passengers, as well as any dealer-installed items such as a tonneau cover to keep rain out of your truck bed and cargo out of sight. Last, there is the Gross Vehicle Weight Rating or GVWR. This rating is the maximum weight your vehicle frame is built to carry.

Tongue weight is how much weight sits on the ball of your tow vehicle's hitch when you hitch up your trailer. Normally this should be 10–15 percent of GVWR. You can use a tongue weight scale on a level surface without the stabilizers down to check this weight.

A weight distribution hitch is like a wheelbarrow. It lifts the back of your tow vehicle by moving some of the trailer's weight forward onto the front axle of the truck. That way the back of the truck doesn't fall like a seesaw from the trailer's weight and lift the truck's front wheels off the ground. While that is a bit of an exaggeration for the sake of understanding, basically you are redistributing weight between the two axles of your tow vehicle to keep it steady and on the road. The Gross Axle Weight Rating or GAWR for your tow vehicle is the maximum weight for each axle. You'll find it in your owner's manual or on a label inside the driver's door. In older trucks, it may be under the truck near the hitch receiver.

Sway distribution bars compensate for the sideways motion and lever effect that a blast of wind or a quick lane change can have on the trailer. Some hitches have separate anti-sway bars; others incorporate both anti-sway and weight distribution into one set of bars or other feature of the hitch. Your dealer can help you select and can set up the weight distribution hitch and/or anti-sway bars for you, but as I'll explain later you should understand what they do, so you can check that it was done correctly.

This all sounds like a lot to take in for the towing novice. Making a visit to a truck stop with a CAT scale makes it a lot easier. Load up your truck with everything and everyone you plan to carry in it (or equivalent weight in the same positions). Fill up your fuel tank, then find the scales and read the instructions. The scales are flat panels that you drive onto, placing each set of wheels on a separate panel. A post contains a button you push to get weighed. The disembodied voice of a CAT scale operator will ask you for some identifying information about your vehicle so they can give you the correct data when you're done.

The first time I did this I mistakenly put both sets of my truck wheels on the same panel. Instead, position your axles on two separate panels to get the weight carried by each axle.

The weight for each axle should be well within that axle's rating, and the total weight for all axles should not exceed the GVWR (gross vehicle weight rating) of your tow vehicle. If not, you need to decrease what you are carrying. Like the pioneers in covered wagon trains going west and tossing out pianos and fine china at the side of the road, you'll have to choose what (or who!) to leave behind. You may decide you need a bigger truck for everything and everyone that you want to carry.

Next, if all is well with the truck, add your trailer loaded with everything you'd want to carry including a full tank of fresh water. You'll find out if your trailer is overloaded or if it is too heavy for your truck. The trailer weight should never exceed the maximum weight rating of the trailer. If your loaded trailer weighs too much, you'll have to discard some of your cargo.

Remember, each axle on your trailer needs to be below its maximum axle weight rating. If you have two axles, you may be able to solve a weight excess on one axle by redistributing your cargo so both axles are below the GAWR. Don't stop there, though. Even if both axles are below the GAWR, check whether one axle is carrying a lot more weight than the other. Do this by subtracting the baseline weight of each axle from the actual loaded weight of that axle. If there's a large disparity between the results, you'll want to fix that as well, likely by getting your hitch adjusted.

This sounds intimidating. At least, it was for me! I didn't actually visit a CAT scale until after I'd had an accident involving uncontrollable sway. One of the generous women who helped me after my accident taught me how to check my tongue weight and other weights. Now I do this several times a year, especially if I change out the cargo I'm carrying. I always leave a safety margin well below the total weight rating.

I imagine Joseph carefully positioning Mary on top of their donkey, with packs of food, water, and camping supplies on the sides of the animal. No doubt, he learned what he would need to carry his precious cargo safely to Bethlehem. His plans may not have turned out the way he thought (they didn't). Nonetheless, he still had to make sure he had enough food and water, the right equipment, and the tools he needed to travel.

The process of figuring out whether your fully loaded trailer and tow vehicle are within maximum weight and component weight allowances may seem confusing and dry. Yet it is critical knowledge for safe travel towing a trailer, just as safe driving in a car requires you to know how much to inflate your tires, at what interval to change your oil, what type of oil to use, and what octane gasoline to put in your gas tank.

## Budgeting

I remember when I was seven months pregnant. Complete strangers would come up and want to feel my belly and ask detailed questions about the baby. For whatever reason, the same lack of boundaries seems to exist for people curious about full-time life in an RV. I've been asked by passersby "How much did that rig cost you?" or had people I've just met ask me "How can you afford to do this? How much money do you make and what do you spend each month?"

I never had a stranger or new acquaintance ask me that about my house or condo. Not once.

For some reason though, people are so curious about living in an RV they don't even realize what they are asking. Perhaps it is the incongruity that inspires people who know me from circumstances other than campgrounds, but even total strangers, like the guy who fills up my propane at a Harbor Freight or the woman I park near when I stop for groceries, ask these questions.

Like most full-timers, I'm pretty forthcoming. It's nice to be able to encourage someone or to gently help them be a bit more realistic if they are contemplating a similar lifestyle for themselves.

Budgeting for life as a nomad isn't terribly different than any budgeting. Don't assume you will save money. It all varies depending on the lifestyle you choose. I've met people who travel on less than $1,000 per month and those who spend more than $6,000 per month.

The budgeting process is just what you should probably be using for any budget. Track your expenses for a few months. Write down everything you spend. Then categorize each item and decide if it is a need or a want. What spending would change on the road? You might, for instance, be able to cut your clothing budget down a lot, because you simply don't have room for lots of spare clothing, and may be dressing more often now for a more relaxed campground environment. Paradoxically, I spend a bit more on entertainment now, because I want to visit new places and many have admission fees.

Do you have a rainy-day fund? Money set aside in case you have an accident, lose a job, or become ill? Everyone should have one of those.

Do you have debt? A mortgage or car payments? Student loans? Can you get rid of some of that debt before embarking on a nomadic life? Pay off the highest-interest debt first and then continue to pay that amount against other debts. Many full-timers advise not to have any debt when you start out.

Because I sold my house in a very expensive area, I had considerable equity. I paid off my debts and owned my truck and trailer free and clear before I hit the road. That means that my "rent" is whatever I spend on places to camp. Campsite costs run the gamut depending on what you can afford and what preferences you have.

For me, that means being out in nature and rural areas. Whether there is a good mini-golf course, fancy pool, or restaurant on-site, much less a zip line or game room, pretty much doesn't matter to me. I'm not vacationing; I'm living. Not to say I don't vacation sometimes or occasionally treat myself and friends to amenities, but it just isn't the main criterion for me when selecting a place to camp. This saves a lot of money.

Short, free overnight stays interspersed with longer stays of two weeks to several months at state, county, or national parks also keep down my expenses. If I volunteer in exchange for a free spot or "boondock" (camp without connections to power, water, or sewer) or "moochdock" (stay at a friend's property) more often, I can save my "housing allowance" to splurge on expensive locations like Liberty Harbor, accessible to New York City, or resorts in the Florida Keys or Gulf Coast. My overall rent and utilities are still far less than they would be if I settled down in Florida, where I am a resident, or in Northern Virginia, where I spent most of my pre-nomad life.

My camping fees average $25 per day ($750 per month) when I take into account the number of "free" sites from volunteering, boondocking, or moochdocking, the money I spend on cancellation fees if planned reservations must be changed, and the fees for membership in discount organizations that allow me to stay at campgrounds for a vastly reduced amount. That $25 average also includes the overall cost of water, electricity, and sewer if provided at a campsite, but not propane or Wi-Fi or fees that I have to pay to dump somewhere I'm not staying.

I find I spend pretty much the same on food and supplies as when I lived in a house. Some of the supplies are quite different: instead of a snow shovel or vacuum bag refills, I spend money on black tank chemicals or silicon spray to lubricate window seals. I definitely use more paper towels, but I don't need a lawn mower.

Equipment requires space and carrying capacity. For example, it is easier to rent a kayak than pack one (at least it was until I bought an inflatable one with an air pump that I can use in calm waters). I prefer to rent a bicycle rather than carry it with me, because I don't often use one.

When you drive any vehicle, you spend money on fuel, parking, tolls, maintenance, and insurance. Those costs go up considerably when you're towing a trailer. The more frequently I move, the higher my gas expenses. On the other hand, my commuting miles are zero.

Just like a house, your RV needs home insurance, not simply automobile insurance. You want replacement value if you can get it, and personal liability insurance in case someone slips and falls when you invite them in for a cup of tea. You'll also want good health insurance that is portable to the areas you plan to travel. Again, there are many people who don't have that safety net. At least at first, part of the reason they opted for life as a nomad may have been that they could not afford those expenses. If something damages their rig—or themselves—they may need to rely on help from family, friends, or even strangers. But fortunately there is an ethic on the road where people help one another.

When all is said and done, most people I know spend from $2,000 to $3,000 per month in living expenses. Like any person making a budget, a nomad asks, "Am I creating needs for myself?" Depending on your resources, you may have more wants than needs, but when you pare things down to the basics, you'll find you can be happy with far less. This creates freedom.

I have the freedom to help others, and not to have to earn a living myself at this point in my life. Good insurance, careful spending, and saving over the course of my working life are now paying off. Still, storing up things or money does not guarantee security. I also have the freedom of knowing that whatever comes, God has my back. Like the rich man who built extra silos to store a bountiful harvest in Luke 12:16-21, we do not know when our time on this earth may end. Real treasure is in our relationships with others, and especially and beyond all in our relationship with God.

The financial benefits of smart budgeting are not a goal in themselves. How you choose to use them may take you closer or further away from your true home. Similarly, budgeting as a process viewed through the lens of faith becomes a less onerous chore for those not inherently fond of math and numbers. Offer your addition, subtraction, and estimation to God, asking Him to help you to turn fruits to blessings and challenges to something He bears with you. If you use your resources consistently with His will that we love Him and others, not as riches for their own sake, even the budgeting process will help you grow closer to Him.

Thus, we circle back to the context of the quote I used from Luke 14:28 to begin this chapter. Jesus's advice on prudent budgeting was in the context of warning that someone who chooses to follow Him and become His disciple needs to carry their own cross and renounce possessions and other attachments (Luke 14:25–27). Budgeting is a form of detachment in recognizing what may hold you back from freedom and making allowance for what is necessary.

That doesn't mean that one shouldn't also budget for gifts to others and yourself. Gifts to organized charities, churches, and people in need nourish your spiritual life and often come back to you in other ways. Personal rest and relaxation are as necessary for us as food, shelter, and water. We need to recharge our batteries, literally and spiritually. Like anything good taken to excess, living frugally can become a problem if overdone. Budgeting for rest and relaxation is like keeping your gas gauge in the safety zone. As we explore this thought in the next section, keep in mind that either overfilling fuel or running on empty creates a hazard. Budget for rest like anything else necessary for your journey.

For me, this is particularly important to help keep darkness at bay. My depression is like a wound that has healed but doesn't completely go away. It remains a hidden scar that can flare up again, particularly if I don't take care of myself physically, mentally, and spiritually.

## Battling the Darkness

A wise person once said that sadness is an ally of the Enemy. When you wallow in it, you feed it and let it consume you. The stickiness of it holds you down. You risk drowning and you find it hard to grab the lifelines surrounding you, because you can't see them in the murk.

As someone who suffers from chronic depression, I fight this battle often. I've been blessed not to have had a serious relapse in more than a decade. Is my mental illness an obstacle? No more than diabetes, or arthritis, or missing an arm or leg is an obstacle. You adjust for it. You take care of yourself and recognize the danger signs.

Sometimes I have a bad day and realize that I need to take extra good care of myself. For me, that self-care includes fleeing to the Real Presence in a church or walking in nature, consciously reflecting on the fact that I am a beloved daughter of the Creator.

My pride gets in the way in that I sometimes ignore pain until it demands too much. Being numb to pain can let you ignore it until it is massive. Following surgery, for example, the painkillers I took relieved not just the pain of the incisions but also a toothache. By the time I stopped the medication, I needed an emergency root canal. That can happen emotionally and spiritually as well.

Those closest to you play a role in letting you know you've reached your limits. My daughters and friends will tell me if I'm getting wound up and curt. When I catch myself continuing to grumble about things or engage in negative self-talk, I know those are danger signs. When I binge-watch Netflix in the wee hours of the morning rather than sleeping, it often is because there is something I need to work through, but I'm hiding behind artificial distraction.

Even with personal experience, it can be very difficult to help someone going through something similar. There usually isn't an easy fix for pain. It isn't like adding air to the tires on my trailer. When I try to share how much prayer and resting in the presence of God can help, I sometimes encounter hostility and have to just respond with gentleness and listening.

"I don't want to hear that this is all part of His plan. I don't want a God that lets the innocent suffer," more than one person has told me. They didn't want to hear me say that God allows but does not cause suffering.

There are no pat answers for the cry of the suffering, only partial ones. We don't have God's full perspective. Without freedom, there can be no love, only slavery, but at the same time suffering often comes from freedom, when God's children choose to misuse it. God respects our freedom to choose the good or the ill, even at the cost of suffering. He allowed His only beloved Son, the ultimate innocent, to suffer for our sins because we could not bear justice. He took it upon Himself, in our place, as a God of mercy voluntarily bound by the laws of justice and freedom that He created. Christ suffers with us and can turn our suffering—like His—into a greater good.

Theology is not always a great response to someone in pain, however. Pain often blinds us to reason whether we want it to or not. Perhaps one closes one's eyes and ears and refuses to see, which may be why Jesus so often instructs His followers to listen. His words "whoever has ears to hear let them hear" follow many parables (for example, Luke 14:35, Matthew 11:15, Mark 4:9). I know I cover my ears and close my eyes when I let myself get too busy and miss praying, or when, as I used to do a lot, I try to pretend that everything is all right and to distract myself from my own feelings through keeping busy. "That I may see" is the prayer of the blind man in the Gospel of Mark (Mark 10:46-52), but also of all of us.

The reality is that we don't necessarily get to see. Sometimes, we may receive glimpses of what lies beneath and beyond, but perfect knowledge awaits us only in union with God in Heaven.

Here on earth, most often in retrospect, we may see how the most difficult times led us to happiness. But when you are in those times, being told that your suffering is not in vain and will result in good is not always helpful.

Sometimes, like God does when we cry out to Him, you just need to be present and listen to someone in pain. You can pray silently and ask the Holy Spirit to help you say or do the right thing, but it is God that brings others to Him through his gentle and persistent invitation. You may assist, but you can't make it happen. There's no metric. Just trust and hold on to your peace so that you can share it, even if it is not received in the moment.

Helping others and reaching out to those in need assists in keeping you from stewing in your own problems. The healing power of beauty in Creation—especially when shared with others—chases away my own dark moments. For this reason, my small apostolate often helps me as much as it serves others.

## Letting Go of My Plans

Often our plans are not the plans God has for us. Letting go of our own seeming control over our schedules is a grace. The spiritual and practical rewards of looking for God's will in all things were brought home to me at the outset of my journey.

I'd hoped to never spend another stifling summer in the crowded metro DC area. To my surprise, however, I ended up camp hosting in Northern Virginia during one of the hottest summers ever. Camp hosting involves living for free on a park site in exchange for labor needed to maintain the park and provide a great experience for guests. It varies tremendously from place to place, ranging from cleaning to public relations, arts and crafts, registration, or office work, as well as being a roving ambassador of sorts for the park to assist campers by answering questions.

In May, I was camping near Fredericksburg, Virginia, a lovely town with many historical sites and great restaurants. I thought the RV park there would be a convenient place to stay while helping my daughter move from the Washington suburbs to central Virginia. However, the drive to my daughter's place in Fairfax was at least an hour with no traffic and potentially two hours with traffic. Faced with that daunting commute, I found a spot closer to her at a Northern Virginia Regional Park. I could only reserve two days, as it was right before Memorial Day weekend.

The park was a lovely surprise. It was very shady, with large campsites, and secluded from the surrounding major roads by the sheer length of the drive past day use areas of the park. I introduced myself to two friendly people who were cleaning the fire pit at a neighboring site. They were camp hosts and had just started their summer shift. I mentioned that I would be camp hosting in Florida next spring. They asked whether I might be able to do it now. One of the incoming hosts had broken her arm. The park needed a replacement quickly—no later than the end of June. They suggested that I stop by the camp store and apply.

Since the location was so attractive, and the camp hosts so welcoming, I picked up the application. I talked with one of the two supervisors who needed to interview me. Unfortunately, I was tied up with moving for the next two days and could not find a time to schedule an interview slot. I was leaving for Ohio right after that and was not available until the week they needed someone to start. The two supervisors had several interviews lined up and were going to make a decision before I'd be back.

Just then, the sky opened up with an afternoon thundershower. The other person who needed to interview me dashed into the camp store to get out of the pouring rain. It turned out he had fifteen minutes available to interview me on the spot, right then and there. It went well, and they told me they would make a decision very soon. If they did offer me the job, they wanted a several-month commitment.

I prayed about it and asked God what He wanted me to do. I had planned to depart for Colorado and Utah in late June. This position would require me to stay until mid-September. I prayed that if God wanted me to stay, then let me receive the job offer and I'd take it, and if He wanted me to go, then let me not receive it. If there were people He wanted me to get to know or things He needed me to do in Northern Virginia before embarking on my adventure out west, I'd accept another steamy summer here even if I was disappointed not to escape the heat. The next day I received a call offering me the position. As is often the case, what God placed before me turned out to be more fulfilling than I'd initially thought.

The campground provided a site with full utilities (or "full hookups" in camper parlance) plus a pool pass. In return, I was expected to be available for the equivalent of twenty hours of physical labor per week—cleaning bathhouses, cabins, and campsites, assisting with arts and crafts activities and special events offered by the campground, and being on call to help campers if needed. The physical labor substituted quite nicely for joining a gym.

I was able to be close to my friends and my daughter, and I made new friends with other camp hosts, volunteers, and park staff. My camp host experience has helped me secure other spots as I travel. Best of all, I now have a place I'm glad to return to periodically near my roots in Northern Virginia. There's an open invitation to camp host again, making it possible to stay for more than a few days in this expensive area of the country.

ROAD EAST FROM WHITE SULPHUR SPRINGS, MT

CHAPTER THIRTEEN

# SIGNPOSTS ON THE JOURNEY PART TWO

*"Heaven and earth seem to merge, my children, on the horizon. But where they really meet is in your hearts, when you sanctify your everyday lives."*

—Saint Josemaría Escrivá

As I moved from discernment to getting on the road, my signposts began to extend further into the distance. I began my journey by renewing my relationship with God, through more frequent prayer and listening. I let go of my doubts, trusted Him, and embraced what He'd asked me to do. Then, I moved to learning new skills and striving to understand how to follow His will in the admittedly unusual path of moving into an Airstream to live on the road with full-time nomads. There's no contradiction between trusting God and seeking to understand how to do what He asks.

I learned to perform tasks I'd never imagined myself doing, such as backing a trailer, dumping gray and black water, and weighing my vehicles. The daily work of living in my Airstream and pulling it with my truck became prayer. What seemed strange at first became my ordinary daily tasks offered to God. They were new steps in the path to spiritual growth.

For reflection and guidance, here are the signposts that emerged from the mist in this period:

 Offer your daily tasks, whatever they may be, to God at the beginning of each day. Even walking the dog or cleaning dishes can be a prayer.

 Looking back over your life, are there times when God sent you encouragement in the form of words or actions of another? How did unexpected events, like a storm or an illness, have an impact much greater than it appeared they would at first?

 How can you better connect to God? Where do you find Him or, more specifically, where does He find you?

 Make time each day to reconnect with Him. Throughout the day, simply glance His way and think of Him when you begin another task, drive more miles, or set out your clothes for the next day. For example, every time I wash my hands (and that's pretty frequently between the pandemic and trailer maintenance) I say a prayer.

What are your sources of power emotionally and spiritually? Look for those sources of energy and make sure you can access and use them. Are you getting enough rest and nutrition, including spiritual rest where you place your worries in God's hands and rest as a small child in His loving, fatherly arms?

 Be prepared to abandon preconceptions and your own planning if the road takes an unexpected direction, but check the signposts. Is this something God wants for you? Can you do it with the intention of pleasing Him? Stay close to His steps in the trail before you, and don't be afraid when it takes you places you've never been before.

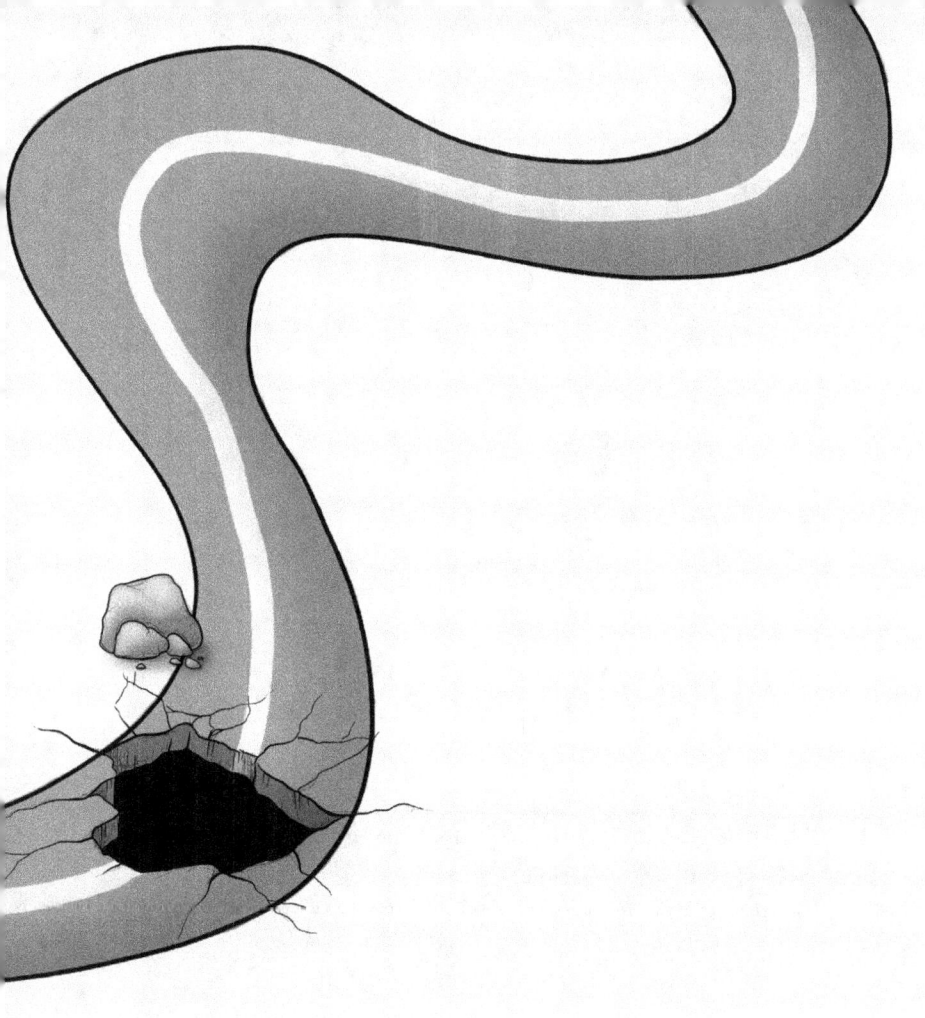

## Part Three

# LIVING ON THE ROAD

CHAPTER FOURTEEN

# DRIVING LESSONS

*"In order to journey steadily, we must apply ourselves to doing well the stretch of road immediately before us on the first day of the journey and not waste time wanting to do the last lap of the way while we still have to make it through the first."*

—Saint Francis de Sales

## No License to Tow

Before I picked up my Airstream, I asked the dealer, "What kind of license will I need to tow my trailer?"

"Just your driver's license," he explained. "There's no special endorsement or test you need to take, like if you were getting a commercial driver's license like professional truck drivers."

"Really?" I questioned, "But it isn't like driving a car . . ."

"No, there's some things you need to know, but it's easy to pick up. We'll show you so you can practice before you drive off our lot," he assured me. "You'll want to drive more slowly, leave more room for stopping, accelerating, and changing lanes, and take your turns wider than you normally would."

That basic advice still serves me well. I've also learned that if something feels off, pull over as soon as you safely can to figure it out. Trust your instincts. The time I left my trailer behind on the entrance ramp to I-10, for example, could have been much worse if I hadn't started to pull over as soon as I realized something didn't seem right.

I've also learned that making wide turns can mean making very wide turns. As I discovered driving just my pickup truck in Northern Virginia and DC, the truck alone did not have the tight turning radius of my little Mazda 3 sedan. On the other hand, my truck's big black twenty-inch tires didn't flinch if I ended up driving over a curb at a slow speed.

When I added the trailer, that changed. My Airstream had a lot less ground clearance than my truck. Once, I was pulling into a shopping center to stop for groceries before the store closed, on my way to a campground in rural Mississippi. I was tired from the long drive and eager to get to my destination.

As I made the turn from a small side road into the gravel lot, I accidentally drove over a small island between the road and the lot. The actual entrance was a bit farther down, but I'd looked at a cheery cartoon "turn here" sign and just turned immediately in front of the sign instead of past it.

My truck easily went over the curb, but didn't proceed farther after my trailer tires got to the same place. I felt some resistance, but figured the tires were just slipping on the gravel, so I put the truck into four-wheel drive to pull the trailer into the lot. My truck strained for a moment, then moved forward. I parked, looked back in the mirror, and realized I'd just left the rear bumper of the trailer on the curb.

Once again, impatience and being tired had been a bad combination. If I'd gotten out and looked when I felt resistance, or if I just had paid much closer attention to the turn, this wouldn't have happened. Or, if I'd made sure to carry the next day's food with me so I didn't need to shop on my way to the campground, I'd have avoided that curb altogether. I fumed to myself.

I sighed, walked over to the bumper, found the loose screws, and carried it all over to my parking spot. Fortunately, the storage compartment normally surrounded by the bumper was intact and its contents in place, so I didn't have to retrieve my stinky slinky from the lot. I already felt pretty embarrassed. I realized the bumper was too long to fit in the bed of my pickup. Nonchalantly, like I did this all the time, I pulled out an extra blanket, wrapped the bumper in it, and stowed it on the floor inside the Airstream. I stacked cushions around it so it wouldn't slide and damage the woodwork when I moved the trailer.

I ended up driving all the way to Florida with my bumper living inside the Airstream. I called the factory and asked about replacement parts, but the repair would be pretty expensive. Some friendly RVers in Louisiana looked the bumper over and told me they thought it could be straightened out and screwed back on, especially since I had all the hardware. I tried it myself with a neighbor holding everything steady, but the holes for the screws had stretched and the bumper wouldn't sit correctly. Later, I found a dealer willing to fit it back on using some washers, and I still use it that way. Like a few minor scratches elsewhere, the imperfections I know are there remind me to retain the lessons learned. Besides, they are like my wrinkles . . . well earned.

## Finding the Exit

Always know the exit route before you enter a new area. After I picked up my Airstream, my friend Amy went glamping with me at some beaches in Maryland. We both were desperate for coffee one morning as we drove a short distance to the next campsite. Normally, I make coffee in my rig, but I didn't have the system I use now and wanted something better than instant coffee. Eager for tasty espresso, we took the trailer in search of a Starbucks halfway between the two campgrounds.

By now I know that the coffee drive-through lane will not fit my truck and Airstream, but I was a towing newbie back then. I didn't see an overhead sign limiting the height clearance, so I figured I could just drive up to the window and order. Unfortunately, as we pulled into the driveway and headed to the window, I realized there was no way we were going to make the turn around the back of the coffee shop. A large metal trash bin blocked part of the area I'd have to swing into to clear the corner of the building.

I'd counted on being able to in effect make a U-turn by driving around the building. I didn't have room to turn around the whole rig on the one side of the building, which left me with no alternative other than to back up. The problem was that I'd have to back up onto the beach highway, and through the other cars waiting to get a quick coffee. Chastened, I backed up enough to pull into several empty parking spaces along the right edge of the entrance lane.

Having learned my lesson about driving decaffeinated, I went in with Amy to get our coffee. We pretended we had parked that way on purpose while chatting with the baristas, who were curious about the big silver torpedo outside the glass walls of their shop. Once we'd drained our coffee cups, we contemplated how to get out of the driveway.

My fearless friend Amy hopped out and stood at the corner of the entrance and the one-way highway looking for an opening in traffic. She had to wave off some vehicles that had their signal lights on to turn into the drive-through, her arms lifted and her hands waving like she was on a runway trying to direct a plane.

Finally, there was a break in the flow of traffic and she signaled me to go. I backed up with my hazards flashing, blocking two lanes of traffic. As soon as the truck cleared the curb, Amy quickly hopped in the passenger side and we drove off. People inside the coffee shop were clapping, and Amy waved at them cheerfully.

So now I make sure I'm stocked up on coffee. I don't drive when I haven't had my morning cup of java. The level of awareness of my surroundings, depth perception, and foresight needed is too high for a non-caffeinated me early in the morning. Towing and anything else that requires concentration when I'm not fully awake is a bad idea. In fact, life in general is better when I'm fully present and aware.

## Backing Up

My first experience backing up a trailer was two days after picking up my Airstream. A state park offered an experience of "the real Florida."

TOWING TIPS ON THE ROAD WITH BRUCE AND VERONICA

# TWELVE TOWING TIPS

1. You don't need a special license to tow, so educate yourself ahead of time
2. Never arrive at a campsite in the dark
3. Make w i d e turns
4. Realize it takes longer to stop, start, or change lanes
5. Coffee addicts: don't tow before coffee (or when tired—you have a bed in your RV!)
6. Best way to stop at a drive-through window while towing: DON'T
7. Slow down, get used to being passed, and don't hang out in passing lanes
8. Enjoy the journey and limit the number of hours or distance you travel in any one day
9. It always take longer to arrive at your destination than your GPS estimates: add fifteen minutes per hour as a rule of thumb, more if the speed limit is 85 and your safe travel speed is 60
10. After every rest stop or fuel stop, walk around your Airstream and inspect it. Is the awning still secure? Are the window latches still latched? Inspect your tires and hitch for damage. Check your tire pressure manually if you aren't using a TPMS.
11. Use a TPMS on your trailer tires
12. Know before you go: DO know the height of your rig and check for overhead clearance in tunnels, overpasses, and driveways with low-hanging tree branches; DO be aware of ground clearance on bumpy roads; DON'T drive into a parking lot, gas station, or narrow road without knowing your exit plan (which may mean backing up)

GO TO WEBSITE

It got real very quickly. After circling twice around the loop to my palm-shaded site, and eyeing the driveway skeptically, I retreated to the marina parking lot. There, I spent several very productive hours aiming for a pile of boxes and bright tape that I'd set up in at the edge of the lot, until I felt more of a sense of how far and how quickly the trailer would turn when backing into a spot.

I left the park feeling ready for a longer trip with the confidence that I could navigate a back-in site. My next stay in a back-in spot offered more parking lessons.

For example, don't hesitate to start over. Sometimes I don't have the right angle and must circle the campground loop and begin again. As you gain more experience, this all gets easier. You learn how far you need to pull ahead of the driveway you are targeting so that once your trailer pivots it will swing right into that spot instead of the foliage along the edges.

Never park in the dark if at all possible. Backing up in the dark as a solo traveler is hair-raising or, at least, hair graying. The glare from the backup lights effectively distorts the backup camera, so it is of little use.

On one of my first trips in my brand-new Airstream, I arrived at dusk at a campground. The lot I was assigned by the front office was at a ninety-degree angle from the road. Except for the entrance from the road, the site was higher than the surrounding land, with terraced retaining walls that made the back of the site about four feet higher from the ground than the front. Ditches for water drainage on either side of the entrance posed another steering challenge.

As I made several attempts and started over again and again, three different gentlemen appeared to give me advice on backing up. Unfortunately, all their advice differed. At that point, if I'd had the benefit of the experience I have now, I would have gone back to the office and asked for a different site, or if I could simply have stayed in one of the parking lots for the office or activity buildings overnight, I could have attempted backing into my assigned site in the morning with the benefit of daylight.

Like the Three Kings who altered their path on their journey home, it is important to take account of the circumstances and not stubbornly stick to a plan in the face of new concerns (Matthew 2:1–12). Recall that the Kings traveled first to visit Herod, the King of the Jews, as they searched for the new King whose birth had been heralded by a star. The murderous Herod wanted them to report back to him once they found the child, ostensibly so that Herod too could honor him. But the Kings were warned in a dream, and they had the grace to listen to the warning and depart from Bethlehem by a different way.

By contrast, my insistence on backing in that evening despite the negative conditions yielded a dent and some scratches. The dent was from turning too sharply so that my truck rear contacted the trailer, and the scratches were from when I took out a bush that I couldn't clearly see. Even though I traveled by Airstream and not camel, the Three Kings provided an example of flexibility that I would have done well to follow.

Help is nice, but never rely on what someone tells you unless you understand why they are telling you to turn the wheel and you have checked out the terrain yourself. For one thing, "turn left" or "turn right" can be quite confusing when you and the other person are facing different directions. Many experienced trailer towers who travel in pairs use walkie-talkies and agreed-upon terminology like "driver side" or "passenger side" when backing in. Also, always make sure you can see your helpful advisor in your mirror. If you can't see them, you risk running them over if they don't move quickly.

One very helpful tip I learned that evening was to place my hands at the bottom of my steering wheel and move the wheel in the direction I wanted the back of the trailer to go. However, you must do this slowly, as a little goes a long way. When you reach the pivot point where your trailer starts moving, it moves a lot faster than you think it will.

Later, I learned to use my mirrors and to stop, get out, and look a lot when backing up solo. You just have to resolve that you will keep doing this until you successfully park. Embarrassment has no place in backing up, even when several old guys around a fire turn their chairs around so they can watch you. Sometimes they'll applaud when you succeed.

GORDONSVILLE, VA

# SEVEN STEPS TO BACKING IN

1. When pulling up to a back-in site, drive your tow vehicle past the site; keep in mind that your travel trailer tires (rear set if you have more than one axle) are your trailer's pivot point
2. Starting over is your new normal
3. Place your hands at the bottom of the steering wheel; turn them and the wheel in the direction you'd like the rear of the trailer to go
4. Use "driver side" and "passenger side" for turning directions when working with a partner
5. Use your backup camera and mirrors; if you can't see where you are going, get out and look; repeat until parked
6. Make small turns; once the trailer starts to pivot, it pivots quickly
7. You can pull forward to straighten the trailer before backing in

GO TO WEBSITE

## Hitching Up and Checklists

When hitching up a trailer, you have to back your truck so the receiver is over the ball of the hitch and then use the hitch jack to raise the ball into the receiver. Inside the round receiver there is a lip. Once the ball is in place and the receiver locked, the lip and lock keep the ball from popping out of the receiver. Once, when I was new to hitching up, I caught the ball on top of the lip but didn't know what was wrong. It just didn't look right. Fortunately, as I was looking at it a neighboring camper came over to explain the problem. "You can't tow that way or the first bump may end up with the trailer going the opposite direction of the truck," he warned. I simply started over and worked until I had it right.

Another helpful rule for life with a trailer is never, ever hurry and don't talk to others when you are in the middle of your arrival or departure routine. Veteran RVers know that the time to strike up a conversation is not when someone has just arrived or is preparing to depart. Distractions can lead to skipping steps. In fact, if you are only staying one night, you may want to avoid unhitching altogether.

When rain is forecast for the morning of my departure, I'll sometimes hitch up in the late afternoon the previous day. Every time I've hitched up in a downpour, I've made a mistake, ranging from leaving my hitch jack down (very quickly discovered) to leaving behind a hose or wheel chock or leveling block (took longer to notice and retrieve/replace). Once I drove from my campsite to check out at the campground's office only to find I'd left my phone perched on my truck's back bumper! Fortunately, I noticed it when I walked around my rig for one last pre-trip inspection before leaving the campground.

Preparing for departure or setting up upon arrival is a process that benefits from a checklist. I still use one, like I'm a pilot preparing for launch, to be sure I don't forget anything critical, such as, for example, raising all the stabilizers before jacking up the trailer to hitch it to the truck. Turning off the water pump inside is also key, as jostling of taps on the road could lead to a flood inside and an empty water tank upon arrival.

Over time, I added a step to my departure process. After towing a short distance, I pull over, get out, and double-check everything, including the tires and the hitch pin. I do this as well before getting back in my truck to tow again after I stop for gas or a meal. I learned the routine through tough experiences, so I'm sharing it to hopefully save you from my bumpy learning curve.

## Weather

Living full-time in an RV heightens my appreciation of the many things beyond my control. In particular, I've acquired a healthy appreciation for the power of weather.

A year ago, I stayed a couple of months at a state park in Alabama with some fellow RVer friends. When strong thunderstorms with a chance of tornadoes threatened, we needed to have a plan in case the tornado watch turned into a tornado warning. We could stay in our trailers and RVs and, if necessary, move to a concrete bath house, or we could head up to the lodge before the storm hit a couple of miles away within the park.

I did not want to have to run across a wet field in the rain to a bath house, so I decided to drive up the mountain to the lodge once a tornado watch was announced. There, I could set up my laptop in the lobby with several others. We didn't head to the lodge's underground concrete corridors until there was a tornado warning.

In fact, it turned into quite a festive atmosphere. I brought some crackers and cheese, others had wine, and someone else had chips from the vending machines to share. Campers are used to bringing their own setups with them (a cup, a fork or spoon, and a plate) for potlucks or impromptu happy hours. We were still in the midst of a pandemic then, but we sat appropriately distanced around tables in the bar area and watched through panoramic windows as storm clouds rolled in over the lake below. Several campers had brought their dogs with them. Penny was with my daughter in Florida, but I've sheltered in place in concrete bathrooms with my canine companion on other occasions.

When everyone's phones and portable radios started going crazy with tornado warnings, the hotel staff opened the doors

GORDONSVILLE, VA

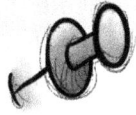

## ARRIVAL AND DEPARTURE TIPS

- Use checklists for arrival and departure so you don't forget anything and you perform tasks in the correct order—for example, chock your wheels before unhitching your trailer!
- Arrival and departure are bad times to socialize
- Never leave your awning open when you are away from your RV
- Things break when you travel. This is normal. Be prepared to fix things or to pay someone to fix them
- Keep a set of keys somewhere outside your Airstream
- Hang a lanyard with your keys on the door handle and wear it every time you go outside of your Airstream

GO TO WEBSITE

behind the bar. We all filed into the maze of corridors beneath the hotel that led to the kitchens. We chatted with one another as best we could while maintaining some distance and wearing pandemic masks. In an hour or so we were able to return to the lobby. After monitoring the storm's progress and weather predictions on the television, phones, and weather radios, we gradually departed to return to our rooms or campsite.

Always know the names of the counties you are traveling through or camping within. Often announcements about bad weather threatening are by county. While I have a useful app on my phone for weather and radar (AccuWeather), I also carry a hand-cranked radio that will pick up the National Oceanic and Atmospheric Administration (NOAA)'s emergency weather broadcasts in the event that my phone or regular radio do not work.

It is not a good idea to try to outrun tornadoes; however, having a home on wheels is great for running away from predicted bad weather. I've departed early on several occasions from a campsite where hail or powerful thunderstorms were expected, keeping track of the weather on my radio or using my phone to check the weather predictions when I stopped. For example, I once scored a great waterside spot at a coastal campground in Florida, but unfortunately the next day the weather prediction became dire in anticipation of Hurricane Zeta's shifting path. I canceled my plans for the rest of the week and drove away from the storm's track to avoid high winds, flooding, and severe thunderstorms with potential for hail and tornadoes.

Hail and Airstreams definitely don't mix well. Golf ball–sized and softball-sized hail is the worst, but even smaller diameter balls of ice can create dimples on aluminum. Larger hail can make dents that stress seams and cause leaks.

High winds need to be considered as well. If you are stationary, you can prepare by filling up your fresh-water tank and hitching up to your tow vehicle for stability. If possible, face your trailer into the direction the wind is coming, as it is built to withstand the air pressure of being towed at highway speeds. Putting the stabilizers down can help also. I've slept in my trailer in Montana through nights when fifty-mile-an-hour winds rocked it back and forth, like a giant silver cradle.

However, wind deserves even more respect when you're driving. I've learned to take high wind warnings seriously even if I don't currently feel the wind. If winds above twenty mph are predicted, I change my route or reservations to wait for better travel conditions. I learned this the hard way, on a highway in New Mexico.

## WEATHER TIPS

- Know the weather prediction along your route
- Know the names of counties along your route, particularly in Tornado Alley or when trying to run away from bad weather
- Respect the wind; reroute or delay a trip if winds are over 20 mph
- If camping in high winds, put down your stabilizers, fill your fresh water tank, and face into the wind if possible
- Locate the weather shelter near your campsite and plan how to get there
- Keep a "go" bag with water, snacks (for your pet too!), medicine, extra phone charger, and copies of important documents you don't normally carry in your wallet or purse
- Take your phone, wallet or purse, and pet with you if you evacuate

GO TO WEBSITE

CHAPTER FIFTEEN

# DISASTER STRIKES

*"God allows failure, but He does not want us to become discouraged. God doesn't require us to succeed, He only requires that you try."*
—Saint Teresa of Calcutta

### The Accident

I was traveling north on I-25 in New Mexico on a bright sunny morning. I'd stopped for breakfast a short while ago and was still enjoying the rest of my fragrant coffee. The red dusty hills on either side of the road stretched for miles until they disappeared into the desert. As the highway wound over bridges and past sharp crags of rock, I spotted the occasional limp windsock at the side of the road with a sign warning that this was a high wind area. There was little traffic. Occasionally, 18-wheelers and semi-trucks flew past me as I cruised along in the right-hand lane at about 60 mph.

Suddenly my trailer pulled sharply to the right then swayed left, right, and left again. My first instinct was to brake while I held the steering wheel firmly, hoping that would stop the sway.

Bad move.

Just as my foot touched the brake pedal, I remembered I should squeeze the manual trailer brake control on the dashboard instead. I reached for the sliding control but never made it. I was already enveloped in white and off the road. I could sense motion like being in some bizarre carnival ride but could see nothing except white.

As soon as my world stopped moving, I saw that my dog Penny was alive and looking up at me quizzically from under an inflated white air bag. I realized we had been in an accident and the airbags had gone off. A surge of adrenaline kicked in. My door had opened from the impact. I unbuckled and slid out from under my airbag without even turning off the ignition. I ran around the front of the truck to the trailer with the first thought in my head being "This is bad. Did I turn off the propane?"

Still attached to the truck, my Airstream lay on its side like a wounded whale beached on an alien shore. The propane tanks were intact inside their aluminum box. I quickly checked that the propane was off, then turned back to the truck, opened the passenger door, and picked up my bewildered Chihuahua.

By then, a man had reached the wreck and said firmly, "Ma'am, you've been in a major accident and you need to sit down." Obediently, I walked twenty feet away and plopped down on the ground, dog in my lap. He turned off the ignition on the truck. He and his wife and another kind gentleman retrieved my phone, my purse, and my briefcase. I sat there unmoving in the dusty red dirt, watching with odd detachment as other people stopped to see if they could help.

I could see my truck was badly damaged. Its wheels had sunk halfway into the ground. I was trying not to look at the Airstream. By then my thoughts had turned to thanking the Lord that my dog and I had walked away from the wreck.

I was very fortunate my seatbelt had held me firmly. The people who stopped to help said the truck had rolled up and down an embankment. It landed facing south instead of north. The trailer had yanked the truck around like a toy. Although the roof was badly dented above the back seats, it remained intact above the front seats.

I asked one tall man who'd joined the group of good Samaritans to take photographs of the wreck on my cell phone. Another man who stopped was an emergency medical technician. He asked me my name and the date and where I was going and whether I was in pain. I was not in any pain. I was too shocked.

The accident occurred in a rural desert area with many canyons and little traffic. No one else was involved, thankfully. The embankment prevented my rig from crossing over to the southbound lanes. The group of people who'd stopped to help decided three would stay with me until the police and ambulance arrived. The others wrote their names and telephone numbers down for me and wished me well before continuing on their journeys.

An ambulance arrived after about thirty minutes to take me to the hospital in Socorro, New Mexico. The paramedics unsuccessfully tried to take Penny off my lap, but she bared her two teeth and growled, menacing them with her gums. It was clear she'd decided she wasn't leaving me. I was able to walk to the gurney holding her and lie down with her on my lap. My blood pressure was dangerously high, and my heart was racing, but I did not have any abrasions or feel hurt then. By the time we arrived at the hospital, my neck, hip, and shoulder were aching from the impact of the seatbelt.

The nurses were awesome. They let Penny stay in my lap and I stroked her fur, grateful that she seemed completely fine. I figured out later that the airbag must have passed right over my pup as she slept in the passenger footwell. When the truck rolled, Penny fell into the deployed airbag rather than being hit by it as it burst into action. Either that or my guardian angel had grabbed me with one arm and her with the other. Perhaps both.

As the technicians wheeled me through the sterile white corridors, trailing my IV bag, the beeping sound of the monitors and people passing us in the halls did not distract Penny. She remained curled between my legs watching me intently with her big brown eyes and alert perky ears. Penny stayed with me during multiple X-rays and CT scans for injuries to my neck or skull. I had no major injuries, but skyrocketing blood pressure kept me at the hospital for several hours until it stabilized. One of the doctors became Penny's hero because he shared his beef jerky snack with her.

Upon my release, the sheriff very kindly drove me and Penny to one of the few hotels in town. He and his colleagues managed to find most of the things thrown clear of the truck and trailer and pile them all in the back of the truck before the truck and the Airstream were towed to a salvage yard.

The tow yard was closed until Monday, which was just as well. I needed some moral and physical support before visiting the remnants of my beloved tiny home on wheels and pretty lime-green truck.

## Doubts

That evening, I sat in the hotel room with my intrepid Chihuahua. My entire body was sore and I felt exhausted. I didn't think I'd hit my head, but bruises started blooming there and in many other places. I had a colorful welt matching the bottom of the steering wheel on my left leg, and I found that my coffee cup had apparently upended itself on the back of my yellow "Happy Camper" shirt.

While I was very grateful to be alive and that Penny was OK, that night I began to doubt whether I really had what it took to travel and tow solo. Despite the positive experience of over fourteen months on the road to this point, I was so discouraged. "Why did you let this happen, God?" I wondered. "I did what you asked and leaped out in faith to travel full-time. What did I do wrong?" After a long moment, I thanked Him again for sparing me and Penny in the accident. I asked him to help me conform my self-doubts to His will for me. The more I looked at the accident photos from my phone, the more shaken I felt.

As I reflected on every minute of the morning that led up to the accident, I recognized there were things I could have done differently, but nothing I did that directly caused the accident. Still, was God trying to tell me that my time on the road was over?

Penny looked at me, sensing my distress. She'd had a rough day too. After we were dropped off at the hotel, I'd carried her across the road to Walmart. No one objected to me bringing my small dog into the store. She was unusually subdued and did not do her characteristic challenge bark at other people near us. I purchased some toiletries and a change of clothes, plus pet dishes, dog food, and a mat for Penny.

After a restless night, I attended Mass the next morning just a couple of blocks away, at San Miguel Mission Church. The processional hymn was an old favorite of mine with a reassuring refrain, "Do not be afraid, I am with you." Later another song that proclaimed "you shall cross the barren desert but you shall not die of thirst" and "you will wander far in safety though you do not know the way" seemed to speak directly to me. After Communion, the cantor sang a cappella a verse from a song that I had never heard in church before, but had discovered while traveling. For me, this hymn—"The Summons"—captured what I felt God had called me to do. I had even shared a YouTube clip of it on my Facebook page many months ago. Hearing it at San Miguel that day comforted me as a very generous outpouring of grace.

I realized that God had everything in hand. I do know this and trust this, but sometimes I forget it. His gentle reminders were the reassurance I needed. It occurred to me as well that the Mass I'd attended just before the accident was at Our Lady of Good Help (aka Our Lady of Socorro) and where I ended up resting afterward was in the town of Socorro.

I was very grateful, I realized, for the kindness of the strangers who'd stopped to help me on the highway and the sheriff and nurses at the hospital. Also, I had very good health and vehicle insurance. Yet, here I was, miles away from my worried friends and family.

So I asked for help. I put out a message on Airstream Addicts asking if anyone in the area might be able to help me visit the junkyard and retrieve what I could of my belongings. More people than needed responded generously. Although a dear friend from the East offered to fly out and, if necessary, rent a car to drive me back to her home to recover, it turned out not to be required.

In addition to the offers of material help, many people lifted me up in prayer from near and far. In the first few days after the accident, the proximity of San Miguel Mission Church to my hotel continued to help me spiritually. After daily Mass one morning, I met a kind woman named Adriana. She treated me to a meal and showed me where she had painted Our Lady of Socorro in a mural down the street. I took that encounter as another sign that all would be well.

Stacey, a kind solo Airstreamer who lived nearby, showed up first to assist at the tow yard. She helped me get some bins from Walmart and make an initial trip to my damaged rig. Stacey's kind yet practical attitude was calming. When I first saw my mangled beauty, with her nose crushed in and windows broken, I cried. Where shards of plastic and metal dangled over the missing front bumper of my truck Bruce, it looked like it had been in a fight and broken all its teeth. The truck's dented ceiling and twisted frame reminded me of how things can change in an instant, and that they could have been far worse for me and Penny.

Stacey and I were unable to open the crushed door on the Airstream. Instead, we reached through the broken windows and rummaged around the truck bed to pull out some clothing and other items. I was glad to see that my prized Amish quilt was intact, although its lavender and purple squares were covered in red dust and sparkling pebbles of tinted safety glass. The quilt embodied fond memories of a trip with my children to Lancaster, Pennsylvania, several years before.

Others responded with different offers of help, including a woman who offered to loan me her Airstream if I could come get it in Minnesota. The message spread to other RVers as well. Marie, a "wrangler" for the local Sisters on the Fly, a national group of women who enjoy outdoor activities such as camping and fishing, contacted me and offered to coordinate help from women she knew. She organized several people, including Christine, a fellow Airstreamer, to retrieve my belongings from the wreck of Bruce and Veronica. Marie's friend Paula volunteered to drive two hours to pick up my items when ready and take them to her storage unit in Albuquerque.

On Wednesday John and Ellen, a couple of experienced Airstream full-timers camping nearby, met Christine and me to help extract more belongings from the rig. John was an engineer with an extensive knowledge of the mechanics of towing and Airstreaming. He brought a crowbar with him and managed to pry open the front door from where the door frame had bent it.

The first glimpse of the inside was pretty upsetting. Cushions and pillows were upended everywhere, with dishes, DVDs, boxes of pasta, and tea bags spilling out amid twisted pieces of wiring, white plastic pipe, insulation, and torn edges of aluminum. The cabinets had pretty much all exploded, with bits of pale birch and white scattered about. A light hung askew from the ceiling. The refrigerator was propped against the oven door. Ironically, an unopened and unused Tire Pressure Monitoring System was in the sink.

Ellen was an acrobat. She managed to squeeze into spots in between the stove, where a sole sneaker perched, and the refrigerator, which was leaning over the stove. Meanwhile, John methodically went through my scattered tools and appliances evaluating what might be salvaged. At one point, as we went about the weary task of extracting items and deciding whether to keep and clean them, or photograph them for insurance and discard them, John emerged triumphantly from the back of the Airstream holding an intact can of vehicle polish. "Lynda, look . . . this will buff right out!"

Christine had brought a pack of her dogs with her. Bridget, a small feisty black one, followed Alvin, a magnificent gray wolfhound with yellow eyes who towered over her. Alvin liked to lean up against people's legs to get acquainted and receive scratches behind his soft ears. Olive, the tiniest dog, curled up on a pillow that had fallen to the ground out of the Airstream's window. She seemed to be the supervisor of the whole pack, including the humans. The dogs' presence cheered me up considerably as I searched through the debris of my tiny home. Meanwhile, Penny stayed safely in her crate in the hotel room as the crash had not mellowed her fierceness toward other dogs.

Fearlessly, Christine crawled through broken windows, using blankets to shield her from the sharp edges. She wriggled over the mattress to find jewelry and medicine scattered all over the interior of my Airstream. She picked up tiny earrings that had fallen on the floor and found a gold cross dangling over the edge of a broken cabinet.

It physically hurt to see my home in this condition. My thoughts went to the people in Panama City that I'd helped, whose homes had been destroyed by tornadoes.

I was so grateful to have Ellen, John, and Christine there for moral and physical support. After taking a few loads of extractions back to my hotel room, Ellen helped me to clean dust off books and other items, while John carefully packed the storage bins I'd purchased. I set aside the items I'd need for my stay in Albuquerque.

The next day Marie's friend Paula arrived to pick up my full storage boxes and other bulky items like a ladder and camp chairs. She gave me a key to her storage unit so I could keep my RV-related belongings there until I was able to pick them up again. She and her daughters even organized my items in her storage unit for convenient access later.

Marie opened her Albuquerque home to me and Penny, giving us a very comfortable and safe landing spot for a couple of weeks. Her warm hospitality let me stay in the area to meet personally with the insurance adjusters and also recover my equilibrium enough to shop for a replacement truck. I drove the new truck back East with Penny in her usual copilot spot, stayed with longtime friends, and caught up with my daughters over a heartfelt Thanksgiving holiday. As soon as insurance proceeds came through, I paid off the truck and purchased a replacement trailer. I was back on the road in just over a month from the date of the accident.

During the aftermath of my wreck, other Airstreamers had my back in different ways. I never saw a single victim-blaming comment posted in the responses to my pictures of the accident. I suspect that Elizabeth Suzanne, one of the moderators for the Airstream Addicts Facebook group, had something to do with that. From Georgia to California, many Airstreamers offered places to stay while I recovered.

I was overwhelmed by the kindness of former strangers, now friends. At first, my pride was hurt that I had to accept so much help. "Lord," I prayed, "what am I supposed to take away from this?" "You can't do everything yourself," He reminded me. "Accept help from others because you are blessing them by accepting my help through them."

"But I thought I was supposed to be the one helping others," I said, puzzled.

"I never told you that I expected you to do everything yourself," He gently chided. "Remember you can do nothing apart from Me, but with Me all things are possible."

My doubts were really a lack of trust in Him. I doubted that I could do what He'd asked, even though He told me I could, in Him and with Him. And, He reminded me, "It might not look anything like you imagine. I'm asking for you to trust Me. Questioning how is fine, but not whether it can happen. I may not tell you My plans for you, but if I don't, that is for your own growth."

Fortunately, God is very patient. We've had the same conversation many times since. He knows when I most need reassurance and generously provides it.

Doubt often pursues me in my travels. Do I boondock enough? Do I have anything of value to say to the people who read my blog or who purchase this book? What if I get sick again?

I imagine literally bundling up all these circling thoughts, wrapping them like a present, and leaving them at the altar, at the foot of the cross, even if I have to do it again and again. Jesus always bears our crosses with us and for us, and my willingness to embrace mine in some way comforts Him. God is outside of time. Every moment is the present, so even now Jesus is having sharp thorns thrust onto his head by mocking soldiers for whom he would—and did—die for love.

He gets me. He knows my worries, anxieties, and doubts. Better yet, when I forget to lean on Him and run around like a crazed squirrel burying nuts for the winter, He gently reminds me and forgives me for my lack of trust.

How, for example, can I purport to help others develop a relationship with Him when I haven't succeeded with members of my own family? And how can I tow again when I fear what might happen the next time an unexpected set of circumstances converge to knock me off the road?

Well, I do what I can and leave the rest to Him. I can accept my

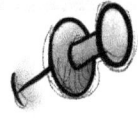 

# FAVORITE GIZMOS AND GADGETS TO PACK

Consider both weight and space in deciding what you need to carry. Some items are light and easily stored, yet really improve the quality of life traveling. I'm not including tools in this list, since several of the references listed in the Resources section at the end have good lists of tools. These are just items I've found particularly nice to have with me.

- Microfiber towels
- Rechargeable lantern
- Stacking bowls with lids
- Duct tape
- First aid kit
- Large bowl to do laundry in sink
- Plastic cups, wineglasses, and dishes
- Drip coffeemaker cup that uses a Keurig pod
- Long lighter for lighting propane gas oven
- Hand-operated weather radio
- Double-sided Velcro tape for hanging pictures and decorations
- Zippered, breathable bags for organizing clothing stored in overhead bins

GO TO WEBSITE

own shortcomings when my intentions are good, and let myself be a small child, who stumbles, falls, and cries, but whose very good Father always picks her up and helps her. This is an ongoing struggle. But I'm not alone and neither are you. Finding peace and joy in the midst of doubt is possible. It is not the results that the Lord is interested in, it is the effort. The little things we do count.

With this outlook, my anxieties lessened. I did take away some other lessons from the accident, in addition to greater trust and prayer and appreciation for being the recipient of help. I resolved to drive more slowly and be more aware of the weather. I purchased a smaller, lighter trailer to make it less likely it could pull the truck around and installed a TPMS (Tire Pressure Monitoring System) before leaving the dealer's lot. Now I visit CAT scales regularly to check my weight distribution. I've practiced more with the manual brake controller in my replacement truck.

Fundamentally, towing is serious business, not to be obscured by the joy of traveling. Even when nothing has gone wrong before, and even when you do everything as best as you can, disaster can suddenly strike. It turned out that a gust of wind and a blown tire were the culprits in my accident. Insurance handled the claims very promptly, professionally, and fairly. Most important, the generous outpouring of help from God and the people He brought into my life helped me recover relatively quickly.

Other challenges to full-timing are not quite as dramatic but still very real. As a nomad, you have to shift gears often and adapt to changing circumstances. Soon I resumed my journey as a Tin Can Pilgrim.

## The New Rig

Just over a month after the accident, I was back on the road with a smaller Airstream and a heavier truck. I realized I didn't need quite as much space as I'd had in the twenty-five-foot Veronica. My insurance came through with total loss payouts that let me replace the truck and Airstream. Downsizing by six feet in my tiny home and purchasing an older truck without all of Bruce's plush but unnecessary amenities let me keep something in reserve for future unexpected needs.

While insurance was evaluating my claims, I sought the intercession of Blessed Alvaro del Portillo, a kind man on the path to recognition as a saint. During his life on earth, he was particularly skilled with finances. In gratitude for the settlements, I named my new nineteen-foot Flying Cloud Airstream "Alvie" after Blessed Alvaro.

My new-to-me RAM 1500 truck was quite a bit older than Bruce but in excellent mechanical shape. I thought about calling it "Dimples" due to the marks a hailstorm had left on it, but decided instead to honor Saint Joseph, to whom I often pray. In recognition of my survival of the accident and purchase of the truck in New Mexico, I used the Spanish name "Jose." So, Alvie the Airstream now happily follows Jose the truck.

This second chance to downsize applied to the contents of the Airstream as well. Some items I had purchased back in 2018, recommended by other Airstreamers, I later sold at rallies to fellow travelers. A Magma cookware set for me wasn't worth the weight. Despite the rave reviews the heavy-duty pots and pans got from serious cooks, all I really needed for my cooking was a saucepot, a frying pan, and a casserole dish.

I also ended up donating a very large cooler that I'd intended to do double duty as an outdoor table and seat. I just didn't use it enough to make it worth the space.

Despite all my planning, after a year of travel, I found there were things I hadn't used. In round two of downsizing, I managed to part with nearly all my books and DVDs.

I had accumulated other items, like a generator that weighed about forty-five pounds and traveled in the back of my truck. When I lost that generator in the accident, I didn't replace it. I'm still contemplating if I really need one now that I have better batteries working well with my solar setup on the replacement Airstream.

This constant reassessment and winnowing of the items I carry is a feature of full-time life on the road. Obtaining a reliable storage unit is also key. I store items of sentimental value that I might want to have if I settle down in a house one day—or that my daughters might one day want. Some seasonal items are stored, but others I simply carry in a covered plastic bin in my truck bed.

My traveling mantra became "buy something, lose something" because I didn't have the carrying capacity to add things willy-nilly to my belongings. Everything had to have a purpose—including of course aesthetics—and ideally more than one purpose. Hanging on to a shirt that I liked but that shrank in the Laundromat dryer could not be justified by the thought that eventually I'd lose more weight and be able to go down a size. My clothes, like me, needed to live in the present moment.

Finding peace amid disasters, mishaps, or just the small challenges of each day became more of a way of life for me as I continued my journeys as an Airstream nomad. The saga of my accident and its aftermath made the rounds at many campfires. It ended up being a way to witness to my trust in God and my gratitude for His answers to prayer even when they were not what I'd expected. Witnessing to His divine love in all things occurs in many contexts in my life as an Airstream nomad, as you'll see in the next chapter.

CHAPTER SIXTEEN

# WITNESS

*"Go into the whole world and proclaim the gospel to every creature."*
—Mark 16:15

## Preaching Without Words

Sometimes it is hard to explain exactly what I do or say to preach the Gospel as a Tin Can Pilgrim. Often, it is simply bearing witness through words or action. It isn't about me. It's about God and developing a close relationship with Him so I can love the people He loves whether they are family, friends, or strangers on the road. What He has done in my life and in healing me, so I can be there for others, glorifies Him, not me. Living with God and sharing in His life is something accessible to anyone if they choose to follow Him. Like Him, I yearn for souls who do not know Him to welcome Him and share in His joy.

For instance, once in North Carolina, I was hiking with new friends and spontaneously commented, "What a beautiful fern and look at this tiny caterpillar! I love how God gives us these little wonders." That led to a conversation with someone I'll call Jim along the lines of "Do you think God made this just so we'd see it? That's a little weird and maybe even creepy to think some deity is watching us." "Not really," I answered. "He loves us and wants us to be happy. He is outside of time and knew that we would be on this glorious trail today. I have no doubt that we were meant to be here and see these things." "Well, whatever makes you happy," Jim responded. "If you want to believe that stuff, that's fine, but I don't think that way."

"How do you think?" I asked. Before he could respond, his friend Katie interjected, "Well, I think there may be a God, but He's not that involved." "How's that?" I asked and a conversation ensued about how much in love with us God is.

I've had conversations that started that way many times. This sounds very vague, but really all I'm doing is trying to live my faith and not hide it. I don't get to see results. That requires a lot of trust, especially from my former achievement-oriented self. "But what exactly do you do in your mission?" is not a question that has a definitive answer. I try to be open to the inspirations of the Holy Spirit and to witness through my actions and words what being Christian is. I'm just doing that in locations and with people that I would never have encountered if I'd remained where I'd lived and worked most of my life.

For instance, a camp host in New Mexico noticed the "Tin Can Pilgrim" sign on my truck door and asked me about it. When I explained what I do, he said, "I believe in the Creator, but not your God. Too many people use God as an excuse to do what they want and impose it on others." "I agree that saying you are acting on God's behalf or even just that you believe in Him doesn't mean you are actually following Him," I commented softly. "Whether we call Him the Creator or Jesus Christ, God reaches people in different ways. What do you believe about Him?" We talked and discovered commonalities in our beliefs, and then we prayed together.

Sometimes such conversations progress to talking about how even seemingly good people can act badly. I might suggest that my new friend read the Gospels to see how the apostles Jesus chose messed up again and again even when they had the benefit of being with Him. It isn't the people in the Church that bring us to

God; it's the Holy Spirit that may work through them or may have to work around them when they spectacularly fail.

## Extending an Invitation

Once in a while, there's a particularly clear example of how the Spirit is using my life as a nomad. One of my friends from a prayer group texted me to introduce Mary, a friend of his from his hometown who was living in an RV. It turned out that she and her husband were camping not too far from me at the time so we arranged to meet.

Mary invited me to lunch at their campsite. She bustled about setting up food and talking a mile a minute. She and her husband Tom had been full-timing for a couple of years. She offered me a drink of bourbon with lunch, which I declined, as I'm not much of a drinker and planned to drive to a shrine afterward. While we chatted, she poured herself a couple of refills and explained she was cutting back. She had been in rehab but fell off the wagon. I asked if she'd like to pray for help with that and she eagerly grabbed my hands. I prayed with her, asking the Holy Spirit to bring her peace and healing, to help her find a way to give up drinking again, and to bless her and her husband. I thanked God for bringing us together so we could encourage each other to follow Him more closely. Meanwhile, her husband finished tinkering with something he was repairing on his truck.

When Tom joined us, I mentioned to Mary that I planned to visit a nearby church and go to confession, as it was available that afternoon. Mary said, "I really need to go—actually, we both really need to go since we haven't been in so long. Can we follow you there?"

"Sure," I said. "It's a lovely church and you'll enjoy seeing it too."

She asked Tom, "Will you come with me and drive?"

He looked at her red-rimmed eyes and said "Yes." They followed me in their truck and we parked and went in together. I lingered in the Adoration chapel praying until they were done. Afterward, they told me they had made an appointment to return and talk with the priest as a couple. I needed to drive back to my own site, but they stayed longer to pray together in the chapel.

## Material Assistance

Occasionally the Holy Spirit inspires me to assist someone in a material way, like buying groceries for an elderly woman in line before me at the grocery store. She didn't have enough money with her and was fumbling through her purse to try to find change. As the clerk placed her bags in the cart, the woman's daughter came in from the parking lot to see what was taking so long. She thanked me, explaining that her mother had just gotten out of the hospital and did not have the right checkbook with her. I told her "God bless you both and I'll pray that she recovers quickly." The weary-looking daughter said, "Thank you, you really made this day a whole lot better." As she rang up my order, the cashier also thanked me for being patient and said she had done the same for someone else last week. "That's great," I remarked, "Just think how many people we might help when others pass it on when they can."

Material assistance may mean loaning a tent and cooking gear to a woman camper who needed to move out of an RV. She was sharing living space with a man seeking a relationship that she didn't want. When she returned my gear and left the camp in a camper van with another male friend, I gave her a book called *His Princess: Love Letters from Your King* by Sheri Rose Shepherd to encourage her to see her own value more, as God does.

Do these acts make any difference? I trust God that they will fit into His plan if He inspires me to act or speak for love of Him and to care for others He loves. Most often, I simply pray for the people I encounter and try to keep the commandments with cheerfulness and peace, to witness to God's love in small and gentle ways.

## A Canoeing Mishap

One of the most beautiful and peaceful experiences I've had so far was canoeing in the dark in the Everglades. Collier-Seminole State Park has a guided canoe trip at night once a month. Gliding through the mangrove-lined swamp with a full moon reflecting off the ripples in the water lets your imagination run wild. You imagine yourself as an explorer, alone in the wilderness, even though the glow sticks attached to the sterns of the other canoes twinkle in the distance.

I enjoyed this two-hour canoe trip so much that I signed up for the daytime one the next morning. This also was an amazing experience, although not entirely in the way I'd anticipated. I was able to take many close-up photos of birds. The still, dark water reflected the brilliant blue sky, the tangled brown mangrove branches, and other lush green foliage as we paddled through narrow winding waterways that occasionally opened into larger pools. Along the way, roots or "knees" and the occasional larger branch gave us lots of practice navigating.

The morning canoe group was much larger. The guides gave the same safety presentation as they had at night, focusing on the key rule of "do not lean" out of the canoe, along with its "do not stand up" corollary. As a precaution, the guests all donned bright orange life vests. One of the guides was my partner in the two-person canoe. He took the back steering spot, designated for the person with more experience.

Equipped with our paddles, we embarked from the shore, while a sleepy alligator watched from the opposite side. We followed a creek through mangroves, most of us heeding the advice to not lean but push off on the mangroves if we drifted into shore. The rangers pointed out a variety of ibis and heron. Little crabs skittered along the branches, but I didn't see any snakes or more alligators.

This turned out to be a very good thing.

Only ten minutes into our adventure, several canoes became enmeshed in the mangroves. My canoe partner called out instructions. He mentioned as an aside to me that he'd only had three people ever fall out of a canoe in more than seventy trips. No sooner did he speak than a middle-aged couple—who'd been visibly nervous about the whole canoe trip from the outset—made the mistake of leaning over to grab at branches so they wouldn't drift into the clump of canoes. Over they went!

Sputtering, the woman did the classic rescue float supported by her life vest, while her husband splashed about frantically trying to retrieve his hat. My canoe partner immediately leapt into the water to help her, dumping our canoe in the process. So there I was in the solid, murky black water of the Everglades. It was only three and a half feet deep as soon as I got my feet under me and stood, but I couldn't see more than an inch into it. I grabbed my sunglasses quickly before they disappeared beneath the murk.

My erstwhile canoe partner was very apologetic. He sheepishly explained that he'd just acted on instinct, not realizing he could have told the floating woman who didn't swim to simply stand up. Meanwhile, remembering that alligators don't really want to eat people, but might not be happy if you stepped on them, I shuffled over to the swamped couple without lifting my feet. God looks after the smallest detail in our lives, I reflected, and the group certainly had made enough noise that no respectable alligator or snake would hang around. Although the water was smelly, it actually felt cool and refreshing in the hot sun. I helped the guide drain and right their upside-down canoe. Another guide hopped out of his kayak and we righted my canoe.

I stepped back in gingerly while he held the canoe. My original partner got back in, and we continued the three-hour trip, rather pungently since the black water had a unique earthy aroma due to all the decaying foliage and other things I'd rather not think about. Later, it took three cycles through the washing machine to de-swampify my clothes and sneakers. I became something of a minor celebrity among the rangers because I didn't get angry and yell at the poor guide as they apparently had expected. It is a fruit of regular prayer to find joy in all situations, even an unexpected dunk in the Everglades. Besides, the guide was thoroughly ribbed by his colleagues.

I wish I could have given my joy to the drenched couple, who were loudly squabbling over which one had caused their canoe to tip. They found no humor in the situation and opted to return to the landing with one of the guides. They left my guide with the legacy of doubling the number of clients who'd gone into the water on one of his trips. They left me with an unusual experience of swimming in the Everglades and an opportunity to trust that God would keep me safe.

The incident also gave me a chance to respond to a question about how I remained so calm and enjoyed the trip. One of the most powerful ways to help people connect with their Creator is when they notice your peace and ask about it. When the rangers thanked me for keeping my cool and for not being upset, one asked me, "What's your secret?"

"I wouldn't be here if I didn't trust God," I explained. "It's really easy to see God in all the beauty of the Everglades, and I just knew that nothing would happen that He didn't have power over."

"Oh, well, that makes sense," he said, looking uncomfortable.

I realize he may have turned this into a fun story told at the next campfire, but my answer may have stayed in his mind. I don't know, and it is perfectly OK that I don't. When we stay close to Him, God may inspire what we do and say, but He leaves observers free to see it and respond to it or not. Sometimes that response can take a long time, as I well know from my own lengthy wandering back to Him.

## Singing while Scrubbing

Camp hosting also provides opportunities to witness in some odd ways. Cleaning campground bathrooms is one of the more onerous tasks of hosting. I found the scene in *Nomadland* very realistic when Fern is interrupted while cleaning by a gentleman who proceeds to use the urinal in front of her. People surprisingly often ignore "Closed for Cleaning" signs on bathhouse doors.

While this is a mere inconvenience for me in the women's bathhouse, it is more annoying in the men's bathhouse. Like Fern in the movie, I'd have to stop work and wait for the men to leave.

My friend Maggie tried to forestall awkward interruptions by locking the bathhouse door. I didn't feel comfortable doing that because of the fumes from the cleaning solutions. If I happened to slip and hit my head, it might be a while before someone went to get another camp host or manager with a key.

So I opted to turn my work into praise in a way that ended up being quite effective at discouraging men from ignoring the "Closed" signs. I sang hymns and worship songs at the top of my lungs as I cleaned. Perhaps they just thought there was a crazy person in there, but I never had any intrusions while belting out "Adoro te Devote" or "Glory and Praise to Our God." Routinely, I broke into song when I spotted someone approaching through the window. Whether it was my off-key pitch or something else, they always waited or left.

## A Biting Experience

Another opportunity for witness occurred at my second job site during hurricane relief in Panama City, Florida. There, with a team of twenty other volunteers, I was moving the remnants of downed trees and imploded sheds to a huge pile in the street for disposal. I'd just dragged some branches out to the street and stopped for a break to drink some orange Gatorade.

Suddenly, I felt a sharp sting behind my right knee. Thinking it was a fire ant that had crawled up my pant leg, I swatted at it through my jeans. It felt much larger than an ant and didn't squish. Somehow, a wasp must have gotten in there, I realized.

I felt another sharp sting higher up on my thigh, then another before I located the elderly owner of the home we were working in front of, to ask permission to use her bathroom. "Something's biting me under my pants and I can't get at it," I explained. She pointed me in the direction of the mobile home she'd been living in since the hurricane. As I ran toward it, dodging piles of debris, I felt another sting.

I quickly wiggled into the bathroom and pulled down my jeans. A two-and-a-half-inch scorpion with a curled tail was traveling along the right inseam.

I quickly grabbed the ugly critter with the fabric of my jeans and dropped the culprit on the floor. It immediately tried to scurry away under the door into the owner's home. Not having anything handy to grab it with and not get stung again, I stomped on it with my work boot. I called out to the homeowner and warned her there was a dead scorpion on her floor.

The stings already were swelling up into puffy welts so I washed them with cold water and soap while she rolled a can of hydrocortisone spray under the door. It was quite effective and stopped the pain. A few hours later, when I returned to the volunteer site to shower, only a few small red marks remained.

Meanwhile, back on the job site, my new friends on the volunteer team were very concerned. "How are you so calm?" one asked as she nervously examined her own boots and pants.

"I have a great guardian angel," I responded.

"Are you sure you feel OK?" she queried. "No shortness of breath?"

"No, I'm fine," I shrugged.

It had happened so quickly that it never occurred to me to be upset or frightened. The volunteer orientation video had warned us to stomp on the ground and hit piles of debris before touching them so we'd scare away any snakes. Fire ants were covered thoroughly. I carefully watched my steps to avoid hills occupied by these fierce biting ants. But no mention had been made of scorpions.

Snakes were of more concern to me. A little earlier that morning, before being stung, I'd let out an audible cry of surprise when a skink lizard with a snake-like head peered out of a crushed pipe that I was about to grab. Overreacting to a harmless lizard was embarrassing, so I didn't make a fuss later about what I thought was just a bug bite.

"Do you feel OK? You're not allergic to stings?" my team leader asked.

I shrugged again. "It's fine. I am going to roll my socks up over my pants legs now though, because I don't want to collect another scorpion."

I joked about it, but there was a deeper meaning. Sometimes you just know you are in the right place doing what you are supposed to be doing, and you trust that God's will is done in all things. If I hadn't been stung by a scorpion, I might not have pulled my socks up over my pant cuffs for the rest of the time I worked and I might have gotten bitten or stung by something worse. Sometimes God accepts my morning offering of the day's prayers, works, joys, and sufferings by allowing joy, and sometimes by allowing suffering. Occasionally, they come together. This was a very small suffering, but it came with great peace and an opportunity to realize how much I trusted Him. That was a beautiful fruit of the work that day.

Later, I realized the tale of the scorpion had become useful to others too. Several other women began tucking their pant legs into their boots or pulling socks up over them. And when I walked past the video orientation session for new volunteers the next afternoon, I heard the trainer say, "There she is, that's the lady who had a scorpion crawl inside her pant leg! This is why you may want to roll your socks up over your pants if they are not snug at the bottom, or even tape them." I waved, acknowledging my new status as an anecdote and pointed to my socks, which that day and every other for the rest of the week remained securely pulled over my pant legs.

## Hello Saint Joseph

On a quieter note, I also found the chance to help a fellow camp host by introducing her to Saint Joseph. Ellen and her husband Rich had been trying to sell their house in a rural area of Maryland for more than a year. The contracted sales had fallen through several times and they were excited that their closing with this latest buyer was finally set.

Unfortunately, this buyer backed out too, because of difficulties selling his own home. Ellen and Rich were scheduled to start their RV travels in a few months. She was so upset that I asked if she had tried praying to Saint Joseph, Jesus's foster father and the patron saint of home sales. She said, "I'll try anything at this point! Tell me about what Saint Joseph can do for us."

I thought Saint Joseph would be a great intercessor for Ellen and Rich. The devotion of praying to Saint Joseph for help selling a home is an old one. Some people will bury a statue of Saint Joseph upside down in their yard, then dig it up and display it in their new home when they're successful with the sale. Others simply ask for Saint Joseph's assistance as the provider and protector of the Holy Family.

Ellen agreed that "It sure couldn't hurt to try!" Accordingly, I gave her a statue of Saint Joseph and a prayer card. I also printed out an explanation of the tradition of seeking Saint Joseph's intervention for home sales. She thanked me and said they were headed back to the house for a few days to get it set for showing again.

Three days later she returned with great news. She hadn't felt comfortable burying the statue, but she had been diligently praying for help from Saint Joseph. The first day her house was relisted it sold for $10,000 more than the original deal, and the new buyer wanted a rapid closing. She and Rich would be able to go on their planned trip after all!

We've stayed in touch and may caravan to Alaska one summer. To this day, Ellen continues to check in with Saint Joseph and talks often about the experience. Witnessing to the power of prayer spread well beyond that one house sale.

Some of the most prosaic things offer the opportunity to see and witness to a deeper meaning within them. This is true of the ordinary activities of everyday life, including something as simple as the use of water.

Saints are people who were just like us but are now in Heaven. After lengthy investigation, the Catholic Church officially declares someone a saint based on evidence of holiness and of prayers answered after their death. Dying for one's faith as a martyr, like Joan of Arc in France or Charles Lwanga in Uganda, also is a basis for the Church to recognize a person as a saint.

Moreover, all those in Heaven are saints. There are many unknown to us or known only to their families and friends who remember them. I pray to intercede for the souls of the departed, even when I believe they must be in Heaven with God. In God's grace, no prayers are ever wasted. They can go to benefit those who have no one to pray for them. A holy priest I knew once told me never to assume someone does not need your prayers to get to Heaven. Only God knows us fully.

We can ask the saints to pray for our intentions. Because the saints are with God in Heaven, their prayers are more effective. While many saints, like us, were sinners in their life on earth, they overcame their sins by accepting God's grace to help them work toward holiness. They now look upon the face of God directly.

That is what we hope for, for ourselves and our loved ones. We believe in the communion of saints, that saints in Heaven are alive and in relationship with us. They can pray for us and even advise us in prayer as we seek to grow in virtues they mastered over the course of their lives. In addition, saints serve as models for us based on a saint's particular interest or characteristic.

CHAPTER SEVENTEEN

# THE IMPORTANCE OF WATER

*"When the well's dry, we know the worth of water."*
—Benjamin Franklin

## Water Supplies

Since I've been living in an Airstream travel trailer full-time, I've acquired a deeper appreciation of water. My current nineteen-foot-long Airstream trailer carries up to twenty-three gallons of fresh water in one tank, up to twenty-one gallons of gray water drained from the shower or sinks in another tank, and another eighteen gallons that passes through the toilet into the black water tank. When I camp in areas lacking water hookups or dump sites, I conserve water carefully so I don't have to leave just to replenish my water supplies or dump gray and black water.

Water weighs about eight pounds per gallon, so you need to consider this when towing. I try to travel with almost empty black and gray tanks and a full fresh-water tank. In fact, my trailer, like most Airstreams, uses fresh water as ballast. The tank's location and low center of gravity help keep the trailer stable when it's being towed.

If I camp at a site with a fresh-water outlet and a sewer hookup, water management is easy. The supply and disposal are unlimited, much like when I lived in a traditional house. Yet now that I'm temporarily stationary in an apartment for health reasons, I maintain many of my water conservation habits. Again, water is precious, and this is recognized more in drier parts of the country. We are stewards of our environment. Limiting wastewater helps lessen the burden of pollution on local ecosystems.

When I don't have an on-site sewer connection, my black and gray water tank capacities limit how long I can stay in one place without moving to find a dump site. I've seen some folks resolve this with a portable honey tank on wheels, but I have no inclination to store and transport such a thing. The "stinky slinky" hose used to dump black and gray water is plenty of contaminated plastic for me! It fits nicely in my outside back bumper storage, which doesn't lock, but I don't think anyone would be tempted to walk off with it.

Without a fresh-water source at your campsite, you have to remember to fill up your water tank with a hose when you have access to potable water. I dump dirty water before I travel and fill up with clean water at the first source after traveling. Whether parked at a campsite or somewhere else without easy access to fresh water, you can add more water without moving your rig by carrying water to your trailer's water inlet and using a funnel with a long hose, available at home repair and hardware stores. I carry several gallons of water in jugs in the back of my truck both for extra drinking water and if I need to supplement the supply in the water tank.

In a sense, water is life for the Airstream, just like we need water to live. Too much water in the wrong place at the wrong time, however, can destroy the Airstream just like we can drown or be swept away by a flood. The power of water is spiritual as well.

## Water as Life

Water is a symbol of life with religious significance in many faiths. For Christians, water is made sacred by Jesus through the sacrament of baptism. We thirst for Jesus, and He offers Himself to

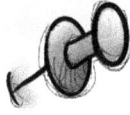

MEMORIAL FALLS, MT

## WATER TIPS

- Never let water run without using it and, if possible, collecting it for other uses
- Try Navy showers to conserve water: get wet, turn off the shower, lather, turn it back on, and rinse
- Consider alternatives for cleaning: baby wipes for people and paper towels to wipe off items before washing
- Humidity in a trailer is your enemy; avoid mold
- Create air circulation under your mattress (try a HyperVent underlay for an inexpensive solution or Froli sleep systems for added comfort)
- Create an exit for water vapor by cracking a window or vent
- Use a desiccant dehumidifier in cold, damp weather

GO TO WEBSITE

us as living water. Springs often have healing properties, such as the water that bubbles up from the ground in Lourdes, or nourishing properties, such as rivers of water streaming forth from a temple in the Old Testament. Water as a fountain of mercy from Jesus's heart also heals and sustains our hearts. In the supernatural, water is precious and life-giving.

Modern conveniences and easy access to plentiful clean water make us forget how the natural characteristics of water are almost supernatural. Water is for cleansing, for drinking, cooking, cooling off, warming up when heated, or soothing a scratchy throat or irritated sinuses. Humans can survive for weeks without eating but only a few days without water.

## Conserving Your Water

The importance of having enough water puts a premium on conservation measures. As we'll explore next, creatively conserving your water lets you stay longer in a place with no easy access to water and helps you value this resource that we often take for granted.

First, never let water run without using it. Don't use running water to get rid of the first layer of debris. Instead, wipe items clean before washing. I wipe all food particles or sticky residues off dishes (or me) with a damp paper towel or a wipe that goes in the trash. Then I wash.

Admittedly, this uses paper, but paper can be burned in your campfire or thrown out at a trash dump. Never leave trash in the wild or at your site: just carry it out with you if there's no way to dispose of it where you are camping.

Next, create a sudsy water supply rather than soap up with running water. Use some warm water in a bowl or cup mixed with dish soap to wash and scrub each dish or piece of cutlery first before rinsing with a thin stream of water. Scrubbing, not water pressure, gets rid of dirt. For yourself, apply the same principle with gentler soap or bath gel if you are washing your hands or face or having a sponge bath.

Never dispose of water without taking an opportunity to reuse it if possible. When you run a thin stream of clean water from a tap to rinse off soap, capture the rinse water in a large bowl. Dump or funnel the captured water into an empty water jug for use in the toilet. Be sure to mark or label jugs like this and store them in the bathroom, so they are not mistaken for drinking water!

Keep showers short and simple. I love my sparkling clean Airstream shower, but I don't linger in it unless I have a sewer hookup and water hookup. One quick uninterrupted shower easily uses one fifth of my tank. Instead, I capture the initial flow of cold water in a bowl or plastic bin for reuse, before it gets warm enough to start my shower. When the water is nice and toasty, I take a Navy shower: rinse, then turn off the water, lather up with soap and shampoo, then turn the water back on and rinse again. Repeat if needed, but avoid standing under running water if you're not actively rinsing. Some veteran boondockers also will stand inside a sturdy plastic bin in their shower and recycle that water for black tank uses.

Next, treat toothbrushing like a shower. Pretend the toothbrush is you. Rinse, turn off the water, use the toothpaste and brush, then spit and turn on the water to rinse again. Repeat as needed, finishing with a swish and spit of water or mouthwash.

Cleaning up also can be done with little water. After using them, wipe the sinks and shower with a paper towel or disinfectant wipe. It keeps them cleaner, avoids water spots, and removes the temptation to waste water by excessively spraying and rinsing.

Finally, consider alternatives. As we've all discovered in the time of pandemic, hand sanitizer can be used instead of soap and water. Disposable unscented baby wipes can take the place of a sponge bath or a shower. Dry shampoo can extend the time before you must wash your hair.

Some of these may seem extreme (or a little graphic . . . my apologies!). My point is that living full-time in a trailer helps me look upon water as a gift. In the most prosaic ways, it reminds me of the transcendental, of water as life and of grace through Christ as living water. When something must be conserved and used carefully, we appreciate it more and also enjoy it more when we do have the chance to be more liberal in its use.

## Laundry

This principle applies as well to laundry, one of the most water-intensive jobs anywhere. From uncontrolled soap bubbles to water hoses flailing about my Airstream's bathroom, laundry day in my rig can feel like I'm starring in a sitcom. What, you may wonder, makes doing laundry while camping so different from this chore in a house?

First of all, I don't have a built-in washer/dryer. While some RVs have this amenity, I have a more streamlined assortment of appliances in my Airstream.

For quick hand-wash items, I use a large bowl that fits in my sink. The disadvantage of hand-washing is that the items stay very wet, even after wringing. By the time I wrap them in a towel to absorb extra moisture, I've got extra items to dry.

My favorite laundry device is a semi-manual washer spinner. It has two tubs: one for washing and one for spinning. A small load—for example, one set of top and bottom sheets with pillowcases—takes about an hour counting all the time involved. Electricity powers the washer tub and spinner tub, which means I have to be careful not to run the air-conditioning or microwave at the same time I'm using the washer spinner.

The washer spinner poses other entertaining challenges. Once, I dropped the hose when filling the device, squirting water all over the Airstream. Another time the unbalanced load of wet clothing made the washer spinner take off like a thousand horses climbing stairs. Several times I've forgotten to close the drain hole before starting to refill the washer spinner with water. Still, despite the occasional mishap, it works well when I don't get distracted.

After washing, spinning, draining, refilling with water for the final rinse and spin and draining again, the washer spinner produces a small load of clean and damp laundry. My clothing, sheets, and towels will dry when hung on hangers inside my Airstream (either on the built-in retractable clothesline in the shower for items you may not want anyone who enters the trailer to view, or hanging from the bottom edge of the upper storage bins for everything else). If I use a dehumidifier or the air-conditioning, they dry in a reasonable amount of time (one day). Sometimes, I'll be at a campsite where I can hang wet clothes outside on a clothesline to dry. Laundry that dries in fresh air always smells wonderful.

The alternative is to do laundry when I visit someone with a washer-dryer or to use a commercial Laundromat. Although I've even had strangers offer to let me do laundry at their homes, there are limits to my sense of adventure. Unless I know the person and their laundering habits well, I may prefer a commercial venue.

Laundromats vary widely in their cleanliness, clientele, and environment. Almost always they are stifling hot and stuffy inside. The advantage is that at the same time I can do two or three loads of laundry that require different temperatures. Usually, all the clothing that requires the dryer will fit in one dryer.

However, once I add in the travel time, the fact that I still have some wet clothes I need to hang up at home, and the cost ($10–$15 for the amount of laundry I generate in a week), Laundromats rarely come out ahead. I use them when I have no sewer hookup at a campsite to dispose of the copious quantities of gray water generated by using my washer spinner. I also use them if I have a large quantity of bulky towels or a blanket to wash.

With water and sewer hookups, washing clothes in my Airstream is preferable. It costs less and, despite the many steps required, can be combined with other tasks like cleaning or cooking or answering emails while the washer is washing or the spinner spinning. Also, lifting bowls of water from sink to machine and lifting the machine to drain the water are nice weight-bearing exercises in lieu of lifting weights at a gym—tighten your core before lifting and use your leg muscles to lift, not your back.

Using the semi-manual washer spinner—even without resorting to the more labor-intensive tub, washboard, and wringer like my great-grandmother used—makes you realize what an onerous chore laundry used to be before modern conveniences. If I do laundry once a week, it is truly a laundry "day" (meaning a full morning or afternoon to get it all done). And that's for one person and a small dog!

At a minimum, doing laundry this way allows for some good contemplative prayer time in the midst of the cleaning steps. For a family, laundry in a travel trailer would provide even more of an opportunity for sanctification by offering up each bit of the mountain of sorting, washing, spinning, rinsing, draining, and hanging work. Who knew that laundry could be so much more than cleaning?! Perhaps we've lost something for the sake of convenience.

Still, don't get lost in accomplishing the task itself and forget why you are doing it. Like Martha when Jesus visited her and her sister Mary at Bethany, we need reminders not to be so distracted and anxious with daily household duties—or any other task—that we close ourselves off to listening to Jesus by focusing on the task itself. Martha busied herself preparing and serving food for her guests while Mary sat at the feet of the Lord listening to Him teach. In frustration, Martha asked Jesus to tell her sister to help her. Instead, He gently rebuked her by saying, "Martha, Martha, you are anxious and troubled about many things, but one thing is necessary. Mary has chosen the good portion, which will not be taken away from her" (Luke 10:38–42). I always thought He was being kind of harsh with Martha until I realized that by focusing on her resentment of Mary's failure to help her, Martha missed the purpose of her service.

When I replaced my first Airstream with a smaller one, I found that I had less room or weight allowance for my own washer spinner. Now I typically use a Laundromat or take up friends on offers to visit while I do my laundry at their homes. I've had some interesting conversations with folks in Laundromats and gotten tips on places to visit nearby. So I'm content that the social aspects of laundry compensate for the loss of the convenience of doing laundry in my trailer. Better yet, I also use that Laundromat time to read and pray, focusing again like Mary on listening to Jesus in the middle of the laundering task I'm offering to Him. I can easily lose that contemplative spirit though if the machine eats my coins! As in backing up the trailer, starting over can be a form of penance.

## Humidity

For all its benefits and necessity, water in another sense is an enemy of trailers. Humidity can wreak havoc, as can leaks that let in rain, and pools of water that appear outside your trailer.

Thanks to the advice of other Airstreamers, I knew to purchase some items to prevent humidity and mold. Under my mattress, on top of the plywood board it rests upon, I installed HyperVent matting. For people who live in boats and RVs, this material creates airflow under a mattress. It comes in rolls that can be cut to size. I struggled to cut it with scissors but was pleased with the result. No mold in my sleeping quarters thus far! There are other products that do the same thing, but this solution cost less.

We can also be our own worst enemy when it comes to water. We breathe out water vapor. When it is colder outside than inside, that vapor condenses on windows and even sometimes on the metal surfaces inside my trailer. Showers, cooking, and hanging clothes to dry also put water into the air.

So when you are creating humidity, create a way for it to exit. Run your kitchen fan when cooking and, if weather permits, have the screen door open. That helps if you're not the most apt cook (speaking from experience). Having the fire alarm go off while you're cooking is much more distressing in a small trailer than in a traditional home!

When you're showering, run the bathroom fan during and for half an hour after your shower. Wiping down the shower walls and floor with paper towels after your shower also removes moisture if you dispose of the wet paper right away.

For moisture created by breathing and heating, I leave a vent or window cracked to promote air exchange if I'm not using my air-conditioner. The air-conditioner dehumidifies the trailer quite effectively, but is of little use when it's cold out.

Finally, again upon the advice of experienced trailer dwellers, I purchased a desiccant dehumidifier for use in colder, wetter weather. Not only does this take significant amounts of water out of the air, it warms the trailer somewhat while it does this. If I'm boondocking, I save this water for toileting or rinsing bugs or dirt off camp chairs or my outdoor steps. Unlike gray water, it is clean. Nevertheless, I'm not inclined to drink it or use it on dishes. You also have to have electricity to run a dehumidifier. It pulls a significant number of amps, so it is not that useful when boondocking. In that case, you can place some containers of DampRid or a similar chemical desiccant in areas inaccessible to pets and children.

This sounds like a lot, right? Once you get used to thinking about water and humidity, though, you end up with a routine. It helps me remember how privileged most of us are not having to think about water. It creates greater empathy for those who live in areas where water is always scarce, even if they are not in a trailer or motor home. These measures also present occasions to thank God for the blessings He gives us, in that we have water. Being grateful changes your mindset, reduces stress, and produces peace.

## Lakes and Leaks

Water on the ground can also pose a challenge. Remember that you are camping, not just parking. Avoid low-lying places. You can sink into the mud, playing havoc with leveling and necessitating drier weather or the use of four-wheel drive to pull your trailer out of the mud. At Alumapalooza in 2019 there was so much water on the fields that tractors had to pull trailers out. While moochdocking in a friend's yard I've had to stay longer because of water that pooled around my Airstream. When "Lake Lynda" evaporated and the mud dried, I could leave without tearing up her yard.

Despite the prospect of finding myself in a mini lake, I love the sound of rain on the roof. The patter of drops and even the roar of a deluge lulls me to sleep in my Airstream. Unless, of course, the rain starts to fall inside. My bathroom fan had a faulty gasket, so the vent leaked whenever it rained. I used a bucket and let it be until I could get into an Airstream dealership to have it fixed under warranty.

A leak on the roof, though, is far worse because water travels. It may leak into the trailer nowhere near where it entered. For this reason, it's important to occasionally inspect the caulking on the outside of all your windows, vents, and on the roof itself. It is much better to repair a roof when it is sunny than to discover it leaks in a storm.

Since I am still leery of walking on the roof of my Airstream, I have the roof checked every time I need to take it in for any kind of warranty work. That way someone who can look at it from above may catch problems I can't see on my own with my ladder.

## Introduction to Religious Terms

Glossaries and in-depth explanations can be found in the Catechism and other sources in the Resources section at the end of this book. These are just simple explanations of terms people often ask me to explain, as I use them throughout the text.

**Communion:** used in two ways: a sharing, unity, or participation; the Sacrament of Holy Communion celebrated at each Mass

**Eucharist:** the actual body and blood, soul and divinity of Jesus Christ received in Holy Communion fully present within the outer appearances of bread and wine

**Mass:** Catholic liturgy of the Word (readings from the Old and New Testaments of the Bible) and liturgy of the Eucharist which literally transcends time and unites the participants with Jesus at the Last Supper and His Crucifixion. During Mass, bread and wine are transformed into the Eucharist. Participants are present and part of Jesus's Sacrifice on the cross at Calvary.

**Real Presence:** Jesus in the Holy Eucharist

**Trinity:** God is one God and three persons perfectly united in complete communion with one another: God the Father, God the Son (Jesus Christ), and God the Holy Spirit. Each person is distinct and is God, but there are not three Gods, only one.

**Holy Spirit:** The love between God the Father and God the Son; the third person of the Trinity.

**Parish:** a community of the faithful that go to a church in a particular area under the pastoral care of a parish priest and the authority of the bishop of the diocese

Not to carry the analogy too far, but this is not dissimilar to our spiritual lives. Sometimes we can tell what the cause is when something is going wrong; at other times, we can't see it clearly. Like any form of maintenance, daily prayer helps avert crises. Taking the time to listen to God and reflect on how the day went, what went well and what might have been handled better, clears my mind before I sleep. I turn my small faults over to Him to heal before they become larger and do more damage. Like the Airstream technician, He takes a wider view, from above. If ignored, small mistakes and failures can fester and hide unseen, coming out in more damaging ways. Keeping things running smoothly requires maintenance and placing things in His hands. This also helps recovery if an unexpected challenge overtakes me. So be sure to inspect your caulk for cracks and get expert help if needed.

CHAPTER EIGHTEEN

# THE RESTORATIVE POWER OF MEALS

*"We become what we receive."*
—Saint Augustine

## Cooking

The screech of the fire alarm went right through my bones. It seemed to bounce off the shiny walls inside my Airstream. I opened the door and put on all the fans to clear my tiny home from the smoke that had sparked the alarm.

I've never been a great cook. I was trying to sauté some tofu and veggies on my propane-gas stovetop and forgot that sesame oil burns at a much lower temperature than olive or vegetable oil. The smoke smell lingered for a couple of days, reminding me to not make that mistake again. Mistakes often are the best way to learn though, so I'm sharing my cooking misadventures and successes for those who wonder how you feed yourself when traveling full-time. And, like me, those not culinarily gifted will find that everything tastes better outdoors or at least in front of a window looking at gorgeous scenery.

My Airstream, like many RVs and some self-constructed kitchens in renovated vans, relies on propane gas for stovetop and oven cooking. Since I knew I'd be camping often without electricity, I did not choose the convection microwave option offered in lieu of the propane gas oven. My Airstream's space constraints also mean that I carefully choose what appliances and cooking devices make sense. This has led to discovering how to make toast in a frying pan—another good way to trigger the fire alarm if you set the heat too high and don't keep an eye on how brown the toast is getting!

Although many people swear by Instant Pots and Thermomixes, the cost and weight are not worth it for me. My main cooking investment is a small outdoor gas grill. I could have picked one that hooked into my stored propane tanks, but I didn't want the constraint of having the grill close to my Airstream and said tanks, so I carry the grill and a small bottle of propane gas with me in the back of my truck.

The first time I used my grill, at a campground in Montana, I tried setting it up on the picnic table, but gusts of wind made it impossible to light. I ended up using the Airstream as a windbreak. I set up the grill on the ground out of the wind and turned a camp chair on its side to shelter it further from stray breezes. Cleaning it was difficult, so now I pre-spray the grill and then use a grill stone to scrub it.

My best bet when cooking is to keep it simple. Many Airstreamers and other nomads I've met can make the most amazing gourmet meals in their propane gas ovens (using a pizza stone so heat distributes more evenly) and even over a campfire. My contributions at impromptu potluck meals tend to be on the appetizer side or fresh fruit and vegetables. To date, my most creative effort might have been peach jam with some chili powder dabbed on top of bits of soft cheese on crackers. I also happily contribute marinated raw meat to those who grill for a crowd.

Still, I can boil pasta with the best of them. Now that pasta itself comes in protein-packed and veggie-infused forms I find I can easily make a complete meal using it as a base. It is inexpensive, light to carry, easy to store, and I can add in another protein or fresh vegetables easily.

## Food Storage

I keep a small stock of canned soups, tuna, chicken, and beans under my sink, close to the floor. Small items go in the compact pantry on the side of my refrigerator. Larger foodstuffs, like pasta, flour, rice, coffee, and cereal, find a home in an overhead bin above the dinette table.

My spice rack is a slim one, taking up a section of one of the shelves in my pantry. I always have a multiple-purpose lemon pepper, Italian seasoning, and everything bagel. Pepper, salt, turmeric, cinnamon, ginger, curry, chili powder, rosemary, and basil give me a broad range of seasoning options when I don't have access to or carrying capacity for fresh spices. Small bottles of flavored oils, vinegars, and marinades start out in the pantry, but may move to the refrigerator once opened.

Keeping food cold presents its own challenges. Refrigerators in travel trailers are notoriously finicky. They must survive bouncing around on the road while towing. If ammonia-based, they need to be level to work correctly and maintain their life span. Also, they take a long time to cool when you first start them, and warm up quickly when you open the door or add more food.

Forty degrees is the magic number. Above that, you run the risk of food poisoning. Since I've experienced that a couple of times in my life when not living on the road, I'm highly motivated to avoid a repeat in my Airstream.

I threw out quite a bit of food until I learned some tricks to keep it at the right temperature. Keeping a thermometer inside the fridge and using a fan to circulate air on the outside compartment is essential. Leave airspace around your items and try to position your Airstream on your site in a way that minimizes direct sun against the portion adjacent to the refrigerator. Parking in direct sun without an awning that shades the exterior outside the refrigerator can stress the appliance's cooling capacities in warm weather.

Lower temperatures can be an issue as well. At thirty-two degrees, salad freezes and becomes inedible unless you can cook it or make a smoothie out of it. I drink oat or almond milk, which rarely seems to freeze. I'm going to add a 12-volt rechargeable fan to the interior of my fridge to help air circulate. Otherwise, the temperature can vary considerably from the cooling fins to the bins in the bottom.

Finally, a good cooler is very helpful. I initially purchased a very large Arctic cooler that could keep ice unmelted for five days, but I found that the size and weight did not justify the limited use I made of it. Now, I have a small, well-insulated one to keep in the truck when traveling. I purchase ice and use an insulated bag when I need to empty the fridge for defrosting.

Cooking isn't just a matter of access to food, storage, and a heat source. It also involves considering how you will wash ingredients and clean up afterward. Always keep in mind that the fewer pots you use for prepping or cooking, the longer your water will last without needing to refill or dump.

Finally, food is much more than just being fed physically.

## The Deeper Meaning

Meals are wonderful for connecting with people. A good meal shared with friends or strangers nourishes the spirit. It reminds me of a movie from the 1980s called *Babette's Feast*, based on a short story by Isak Dinesen. This leisurely paced film tells the story of a stranger to a town inhabited by a strict religious sect that views pleasure with suspicion. She uses an unexpected windfall to create a gourmet masterpiece for others, most of whom have not treated her well. The meal brings together people who were divided. Babette's extravagant and gratuitous love poured into the gastronomic delights she creates literally transforms the receivers.

I'm no Babette, but in any shared meal there is power to bring people together. Indeed, *Babette's Feast* is an analogy for receiving the body and blood of Christ in Communion. When I was finally able to receive Communion again during the COVID pandemic in spring 2020, I felt like parched dry land finally being watered. For seven weeks, due to lockdowns, I'd been unable to go to Mass in person and receive the Eucharistic body of my Lord and God. Finally, I found a church in Owensville, Missouri, that had just opened for in-person Mass with precautions.

I entered the church wearing my mask and read the instructions posted for safety. Every other pew was closed with tape. Tape marked spaces six feet apart on the aisle. Near each entrance a bottle of hand sanitizer invited use. Immaculate Conception Catholic Church is a lovely example of Midwestern Catholic churches. Wooden beams arch over decoratively painted walls, and a traditional sanctuary holds a tabernacle centered on the wall behind the altar, beneath the crucifix. Above the crucifix, a beautiful round, stained glass window depicts Mary with angels.

The morning sun filtered through the colorful window into the church. Pale blue and gold carved stations of the cross illustrated Gospel scenes of Jesus's Passion, from His prayers in the Garden through His death on the cross and burial. These delicate and detailed carvings were recessed into the side walls and separated by narrow, rectangular stained-glass windows. Statues of Mary and Joseph carrying the child Jesus welcomed parishioners to the left and right of the sanctuary. I felt at home.

I took a spot in the third pew to the left. Six other people prayed silently, scattered about the church in separate pews.

Father Wayne presided. During the homily, he described the safety measures that he asked us to follow as a matter of charity. The sign of peace and the distribution of the Precious Blood remained suspended. We could remove our face masks while seated, but every time we left the pew we needed to wear the mask.

To receive Communion, we were to go up in single file, six feet apart, wearing a mask, then pull down the mask before extending our hands to receive the Eucharist. That way we would not be fumbling with the mask while holding the consecrated host. After consuming this Divine Food, we were to put the mask back on before starting to walk back to our pew.

Father Wayne explained that the bishop asked that everyone receive in the hand for now, rather than on the tongue. Kindly, Father Wayne demonstrated how to hold our hands, as apparently many people in that parish normally received on the tongue. It was a good reminder for me to cradle one hand in the other and wait for the priest to place Jesus in my palm.

Through the entire Mass, I couldn't stop breaking into a smile, hidden under my mask. Tears gathered in my eyes at the time of consecration, knowing that I soon would receive my Lord whom I love and adore. While I have grown to appreciate spiritual Communion, Catholicism is a physical religion that unites us with Jesus. He humbly becomes our food so that we may become part of Him as He becomes part of us.

At each Mass, Christ is truly present—body and blood, soul and divinity—in the representation of His redemptive sacrifice on the cross. The Sacred Body and Precious Blood are not symbols hiding under the appearance of bread and wine. Rather, during Mass Jesus's sacrifice transcends time and space. He becomes present sacramentally on the altar. All time unites with the one unique and sufficient moment of Christ's sacrifice, as it was at the first Mass, the Last Supper. As we pray and receive Him, all the angels and saints rejoice there with us. Also, at each Mass, we become united with every person participating in any Mass anywhere and with all Masses ever. We receive the actual body and blood Jesus sacrificed for our salvation, so kindly hidden in the outer appearance of bread and wine. This incredible miracle happens at Mass, because God longs to be with us and for us to be with Him.

Being deprived of this sacrament for weeks was no small matter. It was like being deprived of air or water. Something essential was missing.

Yet, good came out of the pain of missing this meal. The intimacy of receiving the Eucharistic Lord is something I hope I never take for granted again. The availability of livestreamed Mass when one cannot reasonably find any way to travel to a live Mass hopefully will outlast the pandemic. Another thing I've found all over the country is that the need to keep space between communicants in line to receive means that Communion takes much longer. This unanticipated benefit places the focus on the most important part of Mass—our union with Him. It gives us more time to anticipate receiving Him, then to quietly rejoice and invite Him to stay with us. Like the leisurely pace of *Babette's Feast,* it allows us more fully to absorb what is happening as we unite with Him and others around us—there, faraway, and in eternity.

CHAPTER NINETEEN

# SEEDS

*"No act of kindness, no matter how small, is ever wasted."*
—Aesop

## Inspiration

I see much of what I do as helping God sow small seeds. To do this, I need to focus on Him and what He wants, not get sidetracked by being too fond of my own plans, distractions, or impatiently leaping ahead. This requires a daily check-in with prayer and being willing to listen to the inspiration of the Holy Spirit.

Mass is where I find my best inspirations. God speaks to me quietly through Scripture and in meditation before or after Mass.

I remember the Mass the day I started radiation treatment for cancer. Being temporarily grounded for health reasons instead of living in my tin can took some acceptance. One benefit was always being able to get to daily Mass, whether livestream or in person. As I was a bit apprehensive about the treatment, I arrived to Mass extra early that day to have time to pray.

There were multiple messages that morning. The Gospel was the familiar parable about the tiny seed that grows into a mustard tree, a beautiful lush large tree in which birds come to nest. When I was a girl, my grandmother gave me a little bracelet with a heart-shaped round glass bead holding a mustard seed. I don't know where that is now, but the seed stayed in my memory. The theme of seeds became integral to my mission as a Tin Can Pilgrim.

At that Mass, Father Thomas spoke about his personal experience of the fruit that comes from planting seeds. His great-grandparents lived in a small rural village in Vietnam many years ago. At that time, families were lucky to have two meals a day. Many only had one. Often, the only food was sweet potatoes gathered from the fields.

A small girl, perhaps seven years old, cared for children while parents worked. She frequently was hungry, so Father Thomas's great-grandparents shared their meager food with her. Many years later, those sweet potatoes blossomed into something wonderful.

At that time, Father Thomas was living in the United States, trying to figure out how he could afford to go to graduate school. He was visiting Texas in the last year of his seminary education and assisted at Mass in a church. Someone he knew there told him about a woman who wanted to meet him because she came from the same area of Vietnam.

When they were introduced, she asked if he knew this particular family that she remembered from her childhood. He said, "Yes, that is my family name. I'm the great-grandson of the couple you knew as a girl." Delighted, she invited him to stay with her and her husband for a few days.

Before he left his new friends, the woman told Father Thomas, "I know you are having financial troubles trying to continue your education. I will pay half your tuition for graduate school if you need help." Her gratitude for the kindness of his great-grandparents so many years ago was a beautiful fruit of the seeds sown in the past, now making it possible for their great-grandson to pursue his dreams after ordination. Although Father Thomas eventually obtained scholarships, he remains grateful to this day for this woman's assistance at the outset of his graduate education.

## Unconscious Impact

Occasionally, God lets me see how small seeds sown through my journeys bear fruit. While attending an Airstream rally in central Florida last spring, I met many enthusiastic Airstreamers who enjoyed kayaking. I signed up for two trips along the Hillsborough and Weeki Wachee Rivers. On one of these adventures, I got to know Nancy, a lovely woman who suffered from an illness that left her unable to walk, but very able to paddle a kayak. As I took photos from my own kayak, I captured several of her and her husband joyfully paddling in theirs and enjoying the beauty of the river. Later, I shared the photos with her and we became friends on Facebook.

Several months later, Nancy reached out and asked me for prayer. She was facing another health challenge requiring her to be immobile for months. She wrote that she knew I was a praying woman, and explained that her and her husband's trailer had been parked near mine in the field where we camped. After I hitched up my trailer, just before pulling out of the field, she saw me make the sign of the cross over my truck. That made an impact on her, and she felt comfortable asking me for prayer. I was very grateful to be able to support her in that way. But it also was a glimpse of how God uses what we do even when we are not aware that our actions are being observed. Prayer before towing is a habit, and I just never considered that anyone might notice!

## Prayer in the Bathroom

Making an explicit connection to God the Creator, as a higher power, and ultimately as a divine Trinity of persons in communion with one another, takes courage. Sometimes people get your choice without any comment. But even when they don't ask, never underestimate the impact of your actions on others.

For example, I attended an Airstream rally at Jackson Center in May 2019 called "Alumapalooza." Airstream owners of all generations gather for the annual event at the Airstream factory, cheerfully dubbed "the mothership." With a schedule full of informative how-to presentations on maintenance and renovation of Airstreams, and a social schedule featuring an ersatz "Gong Show" for charity plus music and barbecues, this is a time to celebrate all things Airstream. It also turned out to be a time of trust and gratitude.

Airstreamers celebrate corniness, including pink flamingos. One woman even dressed as a giant flamingo for the "Gong Show" competition, where groups of campers performed skits and songs.

Airstreamers also promote "glamping" or glamorous camping. Honestly, any camping not involving a tent and having the benefit of a bed is pretty glamorous to me. Yet Airstream glamping takes this to new heights. Gourmet cooking classes and drink mixing demonstrations immediately filled up at Alumapalooza.

Proximity as well as group activities ensure that you get to know other Airstream owners at the rally. Hundreds of Airstreams of all vintages and sizes park behind the factory and in a grassy field on the other side of the small town. In rally parking, you are quite close to all your neighbors, with nothing to separate you and just enough space to put up an awning. You get to know others very well, as everyone participates in the same camping experience.

This year that bonding was intensified for early arrivals. The evening before the rally began a line of severe thunderstorms and tornadoes passed through Ohio. Several powerful twisters touched down in Dayton and nearby Celina. Neighbors woke one another, and we spent some time together taking shelter in the concrete bathrooms inside one of the Airstream factory buildings. Intense rain, high winds, and lightning appeared intermittently for a period of a few hours, accompanied by tornado warning announcements on our cell phones.

One of the couples sheltering in the bathroom with me, Robert and Maria, began to pray the Rosary. I pulled out my Rosary from my pocket and prayed aloud with them, holding Penny in my lap. We invited others to pray with us and several joined in, as the words are easy to learn and in some prayers common to many Christian denominations.

After the weather radar apps on our phones showed the storms had passed, we all trudged across the wet ground back to our trailers on the other side of the field. The experience deepened our appreciation of the beauty of the stunningly colorful skies reflected in our Airstreams the next morning. Before the rally ended, the Airstreamers also took up an informal collection for one of the charities helping storm victims.

My neighbor in the field later told me she felt that our prayers helped save us from any damage. One never knows the mind of God, but all prayers are put to good use. The sense of calm that settled over our group in the bathroom blessed us all with the fruit of praying together. Praying in public also testified to others about the source of peace and joy accessible to all.

## Deliberate Sowing

Another time, the Holy Spirit inspired me to help sow a seed by answering a question without watering down the truth. I was accosted by a homeless man outside a café in downtown Washington, D.C. I can still see him, rather apologetically asking for a dollar to help him buy food. He was a young man with old eyes. I told him I would not give him cash, but I would be happy to buy him a meal. His face lit up and we entered the café. He asked if I could wait for the food with him so no one would throw him out. We chatted a little as we waited for the takeout sandwiches and coffee.

As we departed with the food, he asked me, "I want to know, why did you do that?"

I looked at him and answered truthfully. "Because when I look at you, I see Jesus."

Startled, he wondered aloud, "Last week someone said the same thing to me. Maybe this is a message."

I suggested he pray and ask Jesus what He wanted. I told him I believed he would find a way to get out of his current situation and pass the kindness on to someone else in the future.

I never saw him again, and I don't know what happened. I don't need to, because I know God will use this however He sees fit. My part is just to follow His promptings in helping to sow those seeds.

## Sown by Others

I've also experienced seeds being sown in my own life by others. As a teenager, I worked one summer at a small newspaper in a resort town. One of the employees, a woman in her early twenties, was a born-again Christian. I can't remember her name, but I can picture her thin, earnest face, long brown hair, and slightly bulging blue eyes. One day, she asked if I was saved. I told her I didn't really believe in God but had been raised Catholic. She responded that I should pray, because God exists.

Then she seriously recounted how she saw Jesus outside her bedroom window when she was thirteen. I nodded and thought to myself, "This woman is wacky, but she's nice." I dismissed her as some sort of hysteric or perhaps someone who'd experimented with mind-altering drugs.

Many years later, though, on the day my friend David died, I remembered her testimony to me. It made an impact that someone articulate and intelligent actually did believe this stuff enough to tell me and risk my laughter.

Another seed fell into my hands at Lake Guntersville, Alabama, at the start of COVID-19 shutdowns. I was at Lake Guntersville for what was supposed to be an annual conference of several hundred entrepreneurs working from their RVs. Although the conference was canceled, about forty attendees like myself had arrived early and planned to stay late to enjoy the lovely state park and see friends from previous conferences. So we gathered outside with others for socially distanced potluck meals, hiking, and campfires. A few conversations and time spent together grew into friendships. Others I met there remain acquaintances on Facebook.

One man I was introduced to near the end of my stay had been a solo RVer and gig worker for many years. I gave him one of the cards for my blog. Next time I saw him there in Alabama, he said he'd looked at it and read my articles about being called to serve God. "You should just tell people that. I'm an atheist but I like to argue about religion." While we didn't have much more opportunity to talk then, what he said got me thinking. His comment helped inspire me to write this book and to be less anonymous in the blog.

## The Fruit

It can be hard to quietly try to help others find God, or rather to help them realize He is searching for them! I try to be sensitive to others' sensibilities and approach them where they are, with respect for their freedom. I pray about it and ask the Holy Spirit to assist me in saying and doing what will be helpful for each person I encounter. He most often asks me to extend a small, gentle invitation to see God's love in Creation and the events of life.

At the same time, sometimes I'm called upon to give a reason for my joy and to explicitly address faith. That was the case when the ranger in the Everglades asked me how I stayed so calm after being dumped into swampy water. It can be hard to say Jesus is the reason or to speak the name of God. Often the world is hostile to religion and suspicious of "religious" people, in many cases because individuals have been hurt by the sins of people identifying themselves as religious. When you proclaim good, you must act consistently with what you proclaim or risk undermining the message. With great faith comes responsibility to respond to it generously and not segregate it within the four walls of a church, synagogue, or mosque. Rather, that faith must permeate all we do so that the light of God shines through us, revealing Him to others through our actions.

CHAPTER TWENTY

# BEING PRESENT

*"Today was a Difficult Day," said Pooh.*
*There was a pause.*
*"Do you want to talk about it?" asked Piglet.*
*"No," said Pooh after a bit. "No, I don't think I do."*
*"That's okay," said Piglet, and he came and sat beside his friend.*
*"What are you doing?" asked Pooh.*
*"Nothing, really," said Piglet. "Only I know what Difficult Days are like. I quite often don't feel like talking about it on my Difficult Days either.*
*"But goodness," continued Piglet, "Difficult Days are so much easier when you know you've got someone there for you. And I'll always be here for you, Pooh."*
—A. A. Milne

## Presence

The meaning of compassion is to suffer (Latin passio) with (com). When we share common or similar experiences, we can better walk with others who are in pain. For this reason, the losses and illnesses I've experienced in my life have been gifts. They let me be more sympathetic and understanding of others when they are going through difficulties.

When people are in the middle of a major disappointment or especially a genuine crisis, it is hard for them to see that it may end up being a gift. Often it takes time for us to recognize the impact what we're going through will have in the future.

Once in a campground in Alabama, I met a very friendly extended family who arrived in a large RV next to me a couple days before I left. Grandparents, children, and grandchildren clearly were enjoying their family time together, with lots of little ones drawing with chalk, riding their bicycles, and exploring the park.

One mom saw me walking Penny as her fearless toddler made a beeline for my small dog. We got to chatting about her work in the pro-life movement, while the kids watched me rub Penny's belly, as she does not like to be approached by strangers, even small ones.

The grandparents also introduced themselves and invited me over for a meal one night. I was talking with the grandma when she received a call from a daughter who lived a few hours away. Her daughter invited her to attend a screening of the movie Unplanned the following night. The daughter's parish had purchased a block of tickets to provide free to parishioners. Grandma couldn't go, but she remembered I'd commented that I was leaving the next day to camp at a park near where her daughter lived. "Would you like the free ticket, Lynda?" she asked. "Yes," I answered. "I've been looking forward to seeing that movie." She arranged with her daughter for me show up at the movie theater in Cullman and look for the group.

I almost didn't follow through, because I was tired from hitching, towing, and unhitching my rig. Yet I really wanted to see the movie, especially after Grandma and her daughter had gone out of their way for me to use the free ticket.

When I pulled into the theater parking lot, I looked for the church group. A woman wearing a white cross necklace was standing at the entrance holding a sheaf of papers. We made eye contact. She asked "Are you here for the premiere?"

I said, "Yes, I was at Lake Guntersville and met a couple who told me about the movie and had family at Corpus Christi parish."

She said, "Oh, you mean the Smiths."

"Yes, did someone call and put my name on a list?"

"Oh, no, but that's fine," she smiled. "I just happen to know they're at Lake Guntersville this week." She gave me the ticket and I went in.

I picked a seat at random, next to two women. During the ads and previews, the woman to my right introduced herself. We started talking and realized that we both had lived in Northern Virginia. I mentioned I'd worked at Tepeyac, a pro-life medical practice. She asked if that was the one headed by Dr. John Bruchalski, as he'd delivered several of her children. We were surprised to find we both had children delivered by Dr. Bruchalski decades ago, two in the same year! We chatted and found we had other things in common, including the traumatic loss of our marriages. She asked what had brought me to Alabama, and I explained to her how I was living full-time in an Airstream as a pilgrim.

After the movie she gave me her name and number to get in touch so we could talk more about life as a nomad. It turned out that she was considering purchasing an RV and working from it. She was about to embark on a new stage of life, just as I had done the previous year.

God surprises me all the time with an unlikely series of coincidences that lead me to just where I should be. When He brings people into my life, or invites me to be vulnerable with the people already there, He blesses me by giving me a chance to walk with them, to befriend them, just as He and others on His behalf have done for me in my life.

In essence, being present to others, not only to talk about faith but to show its impact through my actions, is at the heart of my mission as a Tin Can Pilgrim. It can be at the center of what you do as well, whatever your circumstances in life. We find ourselves when we reach out to others.

## Volunteering

When life is difficult, when you feel sad or lonely, one of the best ways to break out of the dreary box you find yourself in is to do something completely different where your focus is on others.

Even today, I find that the easiest way to get to know people in a new location and to get over any feelings of being a fish out of water is to volunteer. Opportunities abound for RVers to do this, from camp hosting, to disaster relief, to home building. Many of these come with a spot to park your RV and even hookups for utilities.

I discovered camp hosting in Florida in part because I was volunteering after Hurricane Michael. When I had traveled through the Florida Panhandle, I'd been struck with how miles and miles of highway cut through the carcasses of former forests. Splintered tree trunks, some neatly lopped off by tornadoes, others in heaps of lumber, were everywhere. This was five months after the hurricane. As I approached towns, I realized how many homes had debris and blue tarps on them.

A friend of mine was organizing a mission trip for hurricane relief through Samaritan's Purse in Panama City, Florida. Although the dates for that group mission didn't work for me, the organization was willing to accept individual volunteers, train them, and put them together in teams with groups of volunteers to get to work right then and there.

This was a great experience for many reasons. I'd never done anything like it. Although I was familiar with tools and fairly handy as a single mom, I didn't know what a "mud-out" was or how to anchor a tarp on a roof. Nor had I ventured beyond my comfort zone to see and hear firsthand from people who'd just lost all or most of their belongings, or even suffered the death or injury of a loved one.

I showed up bright and early for orientation. Along with a hundred other men and women, and some children there with their families, we prayed and asked for God's help to serve others. I was issued a bright orange shirt and work gloves. I'd used a chain saw before, so I was willing to do that if needed on my job assignment. The orientation covered safety and sensitivity toward the persons receiving volunteer help.

Each morning the teams of workers prayed with one another before setting out for the day. We also prayed with the homeowners, if they were amenable, when arriving at a job site and when finishing up work there. In addition to prayers at meals, a couple of evenings per week there were volunteer-led devotions available. I did not participate in those as it was the only time I had to get to Mass or pray my daily Rosary. I generally was so tired from the physical labor that I went to sleep around 8:30 p.m.

We shared excellent meals in the church that housed the many volunteers staying in single-sex, dormitory-style quarters. And in the evenings after dinner, while all were still gathered at the common tables, homeowners and volunteers spoke about how God had touched them during the day. The locals tearfully expressed their gratitude, some saying how difficult it was to be recipients of aid when they had always been the givers. Others talked about how much hope it gave them just to know that volunteers cared. One woman spoke of the joy that shone forth from the volunteers as they did the hard manual labor needed to clear her yard of fallen trees and debris. All echoed what the chaplains and crew leaders told us: that we were being the hands and feet of Christ.

Most of the work turned out to be clearing garbage, downed trees, twisted fences, and remnants of exploded buildings. Because I had my trailer and Penny to care for, at first I volunteered only a half day, commuting back and forth from my campground at a state park north of Panama City. Later, I added a week to my commitment and parked my trailer in a lot across the street from the church, with several other RV dwellers there to assist.

The work was physically challenging but very rewarding. Teams of orange-shirted volunteers would arrive at a site en masse. The team leaders then conferred with the homeowner to make sure all were on the same page regarding their needs and the work to be done. One or two volunteers would keep the homeowner company, as a friendly ear to listen if the person wanted to talk about the traumatic disaster that had led to the need for volunteer assistance. Volunteers also were open to sharing their faith in Jesus if the homeowner was receptive.

Meanwhile, like a busy swarm of bright orange ants, the rest of the workers completed the debris clearing, mud-out, roof tarping, or other projects needed. Blue-shirted chaplains from the Billy Graham Rapid Response Team visited the job sites and were available to minister both to volunteers and homeowners. Everyone was encouraged to do all aspects of their jobs well, even the smallest things, like picking up handfuls of insulation or raking clean a yard once massive tree trunks had been removed. Each part of the debris clearing was work done for God.

At my first job site, I met Clara, a woman about my own age who normally lived with her son and his family. Her smile was tentative. Although her whole family had survived Hurricane Michael by sheltering at a nearby relative's home, her son's home had collapsed into a heap of twisted siding, steel beams, clothing, and children's toys. For six months, Clara had been living in a small trailer next to a huge pile of rusty metal and rotting furniture. Today, a crowd of people in bright orange shirts gathered at the property to help. Her son arrived with some friends and joined us. By the end of the day, the yard was clear. Clara smiled as the volunteers handed her a souvenir Bible and we all prayed in thanksgiving for being able to help.

Back at the state park, the rangers at the entrance had noticed that I left early each day wearing my bright orange volunteer shirt. They all recognized Samaritan's Purse and knew about their hurricane relief efforts. One gentleman, literally named Ranger Rick, thanked me for using my time to help the community. He asked if I'd consider volunteering at the park as a camp host next year. We agreed on a several-month time frame for next spring.

Ironically, I never got to volunteer there, because Florida shut down its campgrounds when the pandemic struck in spring 2020. However, the fact that I'd lined up a camp-hosting gig in Florida actually helped me land one in Virginia.

## Overcoming Loneliness

Loneliness is a challenge on the road, but also in other settings. The alienation of modern society, particularly during the COVID-19 pandemic, isolates us even when we dwell in very populated areas.

There certainly are times on the road when I arrive at a new destination, or am traveling between locations without stopping long, and I wish there were someone to share the driving, the chores, and the adventure. Sometimes I do travel with friends, but most of the time I'm by myself except for my dog. Still, I'm never

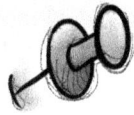

## MAKING FRIENDS ON THE ROAD

- Get a dog (or a goat)
- Carry the ingredients for S'mores and offer to make them for strangers you meet
- Build a nice campfire, put out several chairs and a cooler, wave and invite campers walking around the campground to have a seat and refreshments
- Join a caravan or attend a rally
- Walk around the park or camping resort and say hi to your neighbors
- Sign up for organized tours or events at your park or campground
- Visit a local church and read the bulletin of events
- Volunteer with fellow campers at an organization like Habitat for Humanity or Samaritan's Purse, or as a camp host
- Carry personal calling cards and exchange them with other campers— design your own or pick a design inexpensively from services like Vistaprint

GO TO WEBSITE

alone. I can pray and tell God about my day and listen to Him. I also have several stalwart friends whom I call on a regular basis.

Beyond seeing loneliness as a condition that needs to be cured, it can become an opportunity. The best remedy is reaching out to someone else who is marginalized or alone. Helping others dispels our own loneliness. When we reach out by a phone call or visit, we encourage them but we also satisfy our own inherent nature that desires to be in communion with others.

When you choose to love with Jesus's love, despite how you feel, you give hope to those who experience your love. Where you put love, you find love.

Why do we so often feel alone in our own skins? We lost the perfect harmony that we were created for and that Adam and Eve had with God and each other before the Fall. Our restless hearts ultimately are satisfied in our true homeland, in God's presence. While we may touch this place in moments here on earth, particularly in the beauty of nature, our longing for our true home won't be satisfied on this side of eternity.

By acknowledging that, we free ourselves, through trust in God's promises, from the present sorrow of loneliness, to embrace hope. Hope is the expectation of eternal happiness based on trust in God. The grace to access that hope makes my nomadic life a marvelous adventure indeed. I long to share that, to give you a reason for my hope. If what I write illuminates this vision for just one person reading this book, the occasional difficulties of my journey are well worth it.

CHAPTER TWENTY-ONE

# FINDING COMMUNITY

*"Faithful friends are a sturdy shelter; whoever finds one finds a treasure."*
—Sirach 6:14

## Nomads

The movie *Nomadland* beautifully illustrates how diverse people find community on the road. It tells the story of an initially reluctant van dweller who travels from gig jobs to the Rubber Tramp Rendezvous in Quartzsite, Arizona. Along the way, she meets other nomads, many portraying themselves in the movie. These characters include Bob Wells, the founder of the podcast *Cheap RV Living* and the Rubber Tramp Rendezvous. A few years ago, Bob and others formed the nonprofit Homes On Wheels Alliance, Inc. to assist and support nomads in need.

Through actual nomads and actors, *Nomadland* realistically captures the instant camaraderie among travelers. Sitting around the campfire talking and sharing a meal is how I've met many friends on the road.

However, *Nomadland* doesn't tell the whole story, only one slice of it. The film focuses on people who at least at the outset appear to have no good alternatives to being nomads due to economic stress. Actually, the people I've met on the road range greatly in age and economic security. Some are retired with resources and are volunteering or working because they like to work. Others are young with families. Some homeschool, or "roadschool," their kids. Some journey to work, like traveling nurses. Others work from their traveling home, as RV entrepreneurs in a host of online and technical jobs. Some, like the protagonist of *Nomadland*, may start out on the road for one reason but stay because they come to prefer their independence as well as being close to nature and seeing new sights. They become more fully alive.

Still others have roots in land somewhere. They may own a site, an RV park, or a house or condo that they rent rather than inhabit. Or, for economic reasons, they may technically be nomads, but not really be able to afford to travel much.

Finally, there are part-timers. They are mainly people who do this for fun and travel. None of these categories is exclusive, and people tend to move from one to another and back again. "Snowbirds," for example, don't move their RVs much but settle in two or three different areas each year based on pleasant conditions. When they travel, it is more to change their weather.

We are all made for community. Whether you are an introvert or an extrovert, you can find your community, your "tribe" living on the road. In many ways, it is easier to connect with your nomadic neighbors, even when they are temporary, than it is to connect with people in an apartment building in an urban area. Nomads are more aware of their surroundings and others within them. They live life at a slower pace, not as caught up in constant frenetic activity. In short, the lifestyle encourages being present in the moment. Living on the road makes one more receptive to connecting with others and through nature with the Creator.

## Animals

One of the best ways to connect with others while traveling is through the animals that accompany their owners on the road. I find that most people who camp not only are friendly and community-minded, they love their animals too. Having a dog creates many opportunities to get to know other people on the road.

My little dog Penny is a feisty seventeen-year-old Chihuahua. She transformed from an urban condo introvert to a camping and traveling dynamo, then, during the pandemic, back to a sleepy lapdog who likes to curl up by the fireplace.

Among other things, she is in charge of campsite security. She accomplishes this by sounding like a much larger dog if anyone comes right up to the door of the trailer. While I do have to pick her up so she won't bark if a friend visits, I'm glad she's so protective.

The best strategy for friendship with Penny is to ignore her and wait until she initiates. People who bend down and try to talk to her are immediately suspect in her little doggy brain.

Penny is great company for me as a solo traveler. She helps me keep to a schedule since she has internalized when I set my alarm and when it is time to go to sleep. When we tow the trailer, she is quite content to curl up in the footwell of the front passenger side of the truck and usually goes right to sleep.

One morning in a park in Florida, I'd just finished making myself a cup of tea on my propane stove when Penny started to scratch at the trailer's door and whine. "Time for a walk, girl?" If she could have nodded, she would have, but her wildly waving plume of a tail answered for her. I clipped her leash to her collar and she pranced happily down the folding stairs outside.

Penny eagerly sniffed along the edge of the campsites following the looped road we'd just driven in on. As we turned a corner, I saw a large Airedale and a tiny Scottie across the road, next to a large RV. The Airedale was tethered while the Scottie wandered free amid the several camp chairs. When the Scottie started barking, Penny the fierce Chihuahua answered back. Suddenly the Airedale stiffened and leapt, pulling its tether right out of the ground. The big dog charged directly toward us, pulling the tether line across the back of the knees of its owner, who tumbled to the ground.

Everything happened quickly. Penny shed all semblance of bravery and ran behind me. The Airedale pursued, teeth snapping. I yelled and tried to grab both dogs, but they were moving too fast circling around me. Suddenly, Penny screamed and let out a series of high wails. I kicked at the Airedale and grabbed my dog who continued to yipe. By then, the terrier's owner had gotten up and raced over to collect his dog. Other RVers poured out of their campers.

My hands were wet and I could tell Penny was bleeding. I wrapped her in my sweatshirt and ran to my camper. The Airedale had nipped her on the rump, but the rest of the moisture was dog saliva. Two RVers followed me and pulled up the local emergency vet number on their phones. The wife of the man who'd been toppled by his Airedale came over and gave me her number and her vet's number, assuring me that their dog had had all his shots and had only ever attacked another dog once before. Another man came over with the mug I'd dropped to return it to me.

Fortunately, I got Penny to the vet quickly and she was able to get stitches. The vet obtained a faxed copy of the Airedale's vaccination records. Upon our return to the campground, I mentioned what had happened to the ranger as I cradled Penny in my arms. She looked pathetic with her shaven rump and big brown eyes. The ranger told me that dogs are not supposed to be left tethered even when their owners are nearby. He was incredulous when I told him that the Airedale's owner mentioned that the dog had "only" bitten another dog once before. He offered to talk to the owners and make sure that they kept their dog in their trailer at all times except when they were walking it on a leash. That didn't make me feel particularly secure, so I planned to leave the next day.

Penny, however, had become a minor celebrity in the park. All sorts of fellow campers came around to see how she was doing. Several I hadn't met yet waved me over to their campfires while I cautiously walked Penny in the opposite direction of where the attack occurred. The Airedale's owner returned to my trailer, told me she was so glad Penny was all right, asked the amount of the vet bill, and wrote me a check on the spot. She looked genuinely distressed.

The next morning, I found that she and her husband had packed up and left. Apparently, other campers had expressed to them and the rangers that aggressive dogs should not be in the campground at all, even if being kept in the trailer and only taken for walks on a leash. Some of the RVers I met over the course of the next few days stayed in touch with me, always asking about Penny.

Full-time nomads have many different kinds of pets. My friend Mary traveled with her bunny, whom she took for walks on a leash and let roam about her Airstream. Shelly, a kind lady I met in Robertsdale, Alabama, has a brightly colored parrot named Woody who accompanies her. Britt and Josh, two young RV entrepreneurs, have an amazingly cute white cat with a squished face who perches on top of their furniture and surveys the area around their campsite. My friend Jeremy lives in his RV with a rambunctious black curly-haired dog named Remmy, who always finds a way to introduce Jeremy to his neighbors by bounding over to play. Miss Dixie, a playful German shepherd, travels in an Airstream with her human, Laural. We've had many adventures together, including persuading Miss Dixie not to pounce on migrating tarantulas in the New Mexico desert.

Just as in many other living situations, pet owners instantly have something in common with other pet owners. That commonality can grow through sharing stories about their pets, hanging out in the many dog parks found at campgrounds, and watching out for one another in the event of a power outage or delayed return from a hike. Again, this community develops more quickly and, thanks to social media (who doesn't love posting pictures of their pets?), sustains itself until we meet again.

## RV Entrepreneurs

As I traveled from campground to campground, many of the people I met asked if I had a blog. Some of them did not do Facebook and recommended I start my own page to write about my journeys and stay in touch. Several years earlier, my children had to teach me how to use my iPhone, so I was a little intimidated at the idea of having an online presence beyond the very user-friendly Facebook. I started searching for a class on how to create a blog and ran across the RV Entrepreneur Summit, a conference put together by Heath and Alyssa Padgett, a couple of digital nomads.

Digital nomads are those who work full-time online from their rigs. Many have YouTube channels, blogs and vlogs, or online shopping sites. Acronyms like SEO (search engine optimization) and terms like "click-through" and "conversion rate optimization" form their language. This was all foreign to me.

I decided to take a leap in faith and go to Lake Guntersville, Alabama, for the 2019 RV Entrepreneur Summit. Workshops on "Secrets of Successful Nomad Bloggers" and "Solo Travelers" looked interesting, but my real target was a workshop on "Zero to WordPress Hero." The speaker, IT guru Julia Taylor, literally would walk me through creating a blog.

Julia, a thin, fit twenty-something full of energy, had the patience of a saint. Her presentation was at warp speed, and my laptop kept spinning the blue circle of death instead of connecting. I raised my hand to ask multiple questions and took copious notes. Fortunately, everything was recorded and available later. Julia generously met with me (and others who needed extra help) on an individual basis to help us get through the steps of creating a WordPress blog. By the time I left Lake Guntersville, the *Tin Can Pilgrim* blog was a reality.

Even better than the classes were the people I met. From SEO marketers to pet sitters and virtual assistants, beer crafters and musicians, Etsy creators and real estate investors, members of this diverse group all had in common their love of travel and the freedom of working and living on the road. In addition to the variety of workshops and speakers at the conference, these mostly young, energetic entrepreneurs went hiking and mountain biking and enjoyed many meals together. I made some friends with whom I stay in touch even now. The following year, about forty of us camped together again at Lake Guntersville, even though the 2020 Summit was canceled at the last minute due to the pandemic.

This group ran the gamut from a retired teacher who looked exactly like Santa Claus and his wife who taught yoga classes online and in person. Another couple with grown children had left their day jobs and now traveled full-time visiting craft breweries and blogging about them. Others did mysterious things with social-media marketing and other online activities that I still don't fully understand, but which included creating and maintaining websites for corporate clients. There were solo travelers, married travelers, a family with seven children in a school bus, van dwellers, families who lived in huge upscale rigs with fireplaces and multiple rooms, and even a few hardy souls who tent camped, hoping to acquire a van or RV in the future.

Many of these travelers did gig jobs, such as camp hosting or inspecting gas lines. There were several life coaches, photographers, and artists, some of whom sold jewelry and coloring books via Etsy. One enterprising young couple had a business purchasing and refurbishing Airstreams. They hoped to set up a bed-and-breakfast park using the Airstreams. I met Mary, an author with a just-published book about living full-time in a sixteen-foot Airstream as a disabled person. Mary also ran a pharmaceuticals company and supervised several employees remotely from her rig. One of the conference presenters, Heather Ryan, aka "the Tax Queen," provides tax services for "location-independent" business owners from her rig, as an enrolled agent authorized to practice before the IRS in every state. She and her husband are both digital nomads, having lived full-time in their RV since 2016. Heather also offers online classes on finance and taxes for the full-time RV entrepreneur.

In fact, the how-to industry, whether by coaching or classes, is a perfect fit for digital nomads. Many have blogs and courses about how to transition to full-time RVing, how to repair RVs, how to find work camping opportunities, or how to do just about anything while traveling.

Thanks to the RV Entrepreneur Summit I've been able to reach many more people through my writing than in person. The *Tin Can Pilgrim* blog, and now this book and whatever else grows out of it, have become part of my ministry. Because I am not commercializing my blog, I deliberately chose not to seek ads and corporate sponsorships. Instead, I've created a *Tin Can Pilgrim* Patreon account for people who'd like to support what I'm doing and receive advance or behind-the-scenes access to projects in process. While not everyone can join me on the road, some want to do more than virtually follow me, so they now have an avenue to do that as Travelers, Wayfarers, Companions, Sojourners, or Pilgrims.

## Snowbirds and Long-Term Campers

Some of my happiest times traveling have been when I've stayed longer in one place. I'm thinking of the time I visited a small RV park in Robertsdale, Alabama, just off Route 10. The sense of community there was strong.

The owner, George, treated his long-term residents as an extended family. While I was there, he hosted a Mardi Gras celebration. This potluck event, with main dishes and king cake, courtesy of George, drew many campers into the recreation hall. There, to cheers and maneuvering and the delight of visiting grandchildren, George threw colorful beads, moon pies, stuffed animals, and small toys to the residents. People in wheelchairs smiled, shouting "Throw me somethin' mistah!"

They encouraged me to participate. I scored about a month's supply of moon pies and several necklaces that I wore later to a parade in Mobile. The toys and animals that landed in my lap were re-gifted to children at the RV park.

Quite a few folks told me with pride that Mardi Gras had originated in Mobile and suggested what parades I should attend. Of course, while in Mobile, I also visited the historic grand cathedral in a square in the center of town. And I visited the USS *Alabama*—again at the urging of the RV park residents, who when I returned wanted to know what I'd thought.

Opposite my campsite in Robertsdale, I met Smitty, a retired veteran who always seemed to have a glass of whiskey in his hand. I was puzzled when he asked if he could wash my truck for me. At that point I still had Bruce, my big green truck. Smitty said he didn't have anything to do and really liked my truck. At first, I was reluctant, as I felt concerned for his health and knew I could take care of the truck myself. But something made me say yes, because he looked so hopeful. Well, that man practically detailed the truck. He took several hours painstakingly removing all the road crud that marred its bright green surface and large, black-rimmed tires.

After he finished, Smitty shyly asked if I had a computer. His had broken a while ago, he explained. He had a diskette with a slideshow of pictures of his father, who'd passed away a number of years ago. The funeral home had created it from family photos Smitty provided for the viewing, but Smitty hadn't been able to view it in years. He and his wife, who was bedridden with lupus, had settled into the RV park. Like others, they were essentially living in their RV as a stationary home.

We sat at a picnic table outside his trailer and I popped the diskette into my laptop. Smitty's eyes glistened, and he explained that this was the first time since the funeral that he'd seen these photos. I knew I would have played his memories for him if he'd just asked, but I realized that washing the truck was his way of keeping his dignity. He did me a favor, so he could ask me for one.

We got to talking about his wife. She was always feeling poorly, he said, and didn't come out much. I asked if she would she like to pray with me. His face lit up, but after stepping inside he returned and said that she'd appreciate it if I just prayed for her by myself. So I did. I also prayed for Smitty, in thankfulness for his generosity in cleaning and polishing my truck and giving me the opportunity to do a kindness for him. I continue to pray for them and others I've met on my journeys.

I found this sense of community again in an RV park in Deming, New Mexico, at the end of eight miles of a dusty unpaved road through the desert. Some people had lived there for thirty years. Others were temporary visitors like myself. The residents immediately invited me to join their activities, card games, and potluck meals. They also told me where to look for the resident jackrabbits at the edge of the campground and warned me to be careful on trails where rattlesnakes liked to warm themselves in the sun.

On the other side of the country, I'll always remember New Year's Eve at Bee's RV Resort in Clermont, Florida. Road signs announced Bee's with cheery aphorisms and cartoon characters.

At Bee's I enjoyed walking around the rows of rigs with many sites decorated in Americana and inventive kitsch. This contrasted with the nature trail and ponds, where a pair of graceful gray long-legged cranes kept watch. The yard statues of fanciful critters and rows of colorful flags and wind chimes, however, served as handy directions back to my campsite (as in, "turn left at the flower pinwheels, then right at the fountain with three gnomes bathing, and pass the row of cartoon racoons").

Bee's is an older-style large RV park. The facilities were very clean, but the rigs were packed in very tightly. I got to know my immediate neighbors very well, because I'd see them every time I opened my door!

Friendly residents zipped around in golf carts. An older gentleman warned me to watch out for baby rattlesnakes in the puddles on the dirt road when I walked back to my trailer at night. I'm pretty sure he was kidding, but I carried a lantern with me so I wouldn't trip over anything. Everyone strongly recommended the huge meals at the Honey Pot, the on-site restaurant famous for its fried chicken and pot roast.

I volunteered to help decorate the "Beehive" activity center for the New Year's Eve Party, hanging stars and tinsel. A disco ball completed the atmosphere. It reminded me of transforming a school gym into a winter wonderland for a prom many years ago. Residents and transient campers showed up with glittery hats and danced to live music provided by a local country music band. People at my table shared bottles of beer, and a few kind elderly gentlemen, prompted by their wives, asked me to dance too. The folks at Bee's definitely enjoyed ringing in the New Year!

During my stay at Bee's, I learned how to play all varieties of bingo. Sarah, a perfectly coiffed elderly lady, was intent on her bingo game. Nonetheless, she kindly guided me and let me use one of her prized set of markers on my cards. The tension in the air was palpable as the numbers were pulled from a hand-rotated wire basket at the front of the room. People who continued chatting during a game were promptly shushed by others. Clearly, the regulars did not want to miss anything!

As we talked in between games, I realized that Sarah was one of the non-mobile full-timers. Her husband had passed away and she was trying to make ends meet on $750 of Social Security benefits per month. Yet she did not seem to feel sorry for herself or anxious. She had many friends and clearly had found her tribe.

### Sisters on the Road

Another tribe I've found on the road are women who tow trailers or drive RVs by themselves. Whether they are solo full-timers or are part of a couple where only one likes to camp, these women are a natural support for one another. I joined the Solo Streaming Sisters Facebook group led by Lindy Brown, as well as Sisters on the Fly, a national group for women who like to camp, hunt, fish, and engage in other outdoors activities, such as Marie, who helped me out so much when I had my accident.

Sisters on the Fly engage in quite a bit of organized volunteer work and, like the Solo Streaming Sisters, can be counted on in a pinch for impromptu help. Over time, the Solo Streaming Sisters group gave birth to the Airstreaming Women's Network. This network provides a platform independent of Facebook to support and educate women seeking fellowship with other women as they tow trailers or drive RVs.

## Airstreamers

There are also Airstream owner subgroups for owners of nineteen-foot Airstream travel trailers, Indie Airstreamers for anyone who travels solo, and a host of other specialized tribes. The built-in family of the Airstream community is enhanced by membership in the Airstream Club, formerly named the Wally Byam Caravan Club International. Through rallies and caravans, these groups build great camaraderie among owners of the silver bullet.

I've even met several good friends at maintenance visits to "the Mothership" in Jackson Center, Ohio. The Airstream factory has a "terraport" where Airstreamers can park while receiving factory service. There are definitely some bonding opportunities while waiting for your rig to be repaired! I first met my friend Laural and her dog Miss Dixie at the terraport. We've traveled together several times since.

At Collier-Seminole State Park in Florida, fellow Airstreamers invited me to an elegant happy hour at a picnic bench, complete with fancy canapés and wine tasting. When Airstream owners see one another on the road, they wave and flash their lights. I've caught up with some at a gas station on the way to a rally, including the driver of the fancifully named "Lilo," towed by another Solo Streaming Sister.

The Airstream Club recognizes its iconic founder in many ways. The magazine is called the Blue Beret after Wally's signature headgear. To this day, officers wear blue berets. The Airstream Club issues "Big Red Numbers" for each member. Wally Byam initiated this practice in 1951 with his own Airstream, #1. The numbers traditionally are placed on Airstreams to help identify them during rallies and caravans, since they do look alike. Red stars placed on either side of the number identify how many years the owner has been a member of the Airstream Club, one star for every five years.

Regional clubs and units offer their own smaller rallies and activities. The largest gathering of Airstreams is the International Rally, which in the past has had as many as 4,000 attend and in recent years approximately 650. Most rallies are much smaller, whether national, special event, regional, or local by unit. Some private groups also organize Airstream rallies, such as Alumapalooza held on the grounds of the Airstream factory.

At rallies, Airstream owners and prospective owners socialize and learn about their rigs, with seminars on everything from cooking a gourmet meal to replacing rivets to changing a tire. For instance, the Swiss Festival National Rally in Ohio is like an Amish food and sightseeing immersion experience combined with a celebration of all things Swiss cheese. It took a maintenance-oriented rally for me to figure out how to set up and take down my awning correctly! I've attended a wonderful "Farm Life Rally" literally on a farm, where activities included an impromptu ukulele band and kayaking on a nearby river.

Caravans, where as many as twenty Airstreams journey together, are another bonding experience within the community. These range from history-oriented expeditions like "Nuts for Ruts: Finding the Oregon Trail," to the California Architecture, Food and Wine Caravan, which explores fine food, fine wine, and architecture, stating up front that "if you are a beer and hot dog type of person, this caravan is probably not for you." Caravans are not inexpensive, but the kitty fee for a caravan normally covers all campsites, activities, and many meals. They may last from fifteen days to two months and explore areas like the U.S. or Canadian

Rockies, Georgia, Alaska, Mexico, and Cajun country.

Club members who have a home base may choose to offer courtesy parking to other club members. Many property owners also offer other perks, such as a hookup to electricity or local sightseeing advice. Guests usually reciprocate with a small gift or thank-you card.

The downside of all this clubbiness is that Airstreamers sometimes are perceived as snobs. The expense of acquiring an Airstream usually is a lot more than other RVs. I've had strangers ask me many times "what did that cost you?" or comment "you could buy three of my brand for that." Referring to all non-Airstreams as SOB or "Some Other Brand" plays into this image. However, in fairness, an Airstream retains a lot of value compared to other brands. When properly cared for, it will last much longer, even three times as long, as a non-Airstream.

I honestly considered whether the Airstream cachet might be an obstacle for me in trying to connect with all sorts of people. Yet, in the end, I need to have a safe, comfortable home that I like to be in when my home is a tiny one on wheels. The positive aspects of being part of the Airstream community far outweigh any negatives.

CHAPTER TWENTY-TWO

# CHURCH COMMUNITIES WHILE TRAVELING

*"Since we are travelers and pilgrims in this world, let us think upon the end of the road, that is of our life, for the end of our way is our home. . . . Many lose their true home because they have greater love for the road that led them there."*

—Saint Columban

## Welcoming the Stranger

As I visit churches, whether for worship or as a pilgrimage destination, I find another opportunity for community. My faith community refreshes and strengthens me on my journey. While some of these are onetime encounters as I travel from location to location, I've found temporary homes at many parishes in places I've stayed for weeks or months.

To find local churches, I'll often ask at a campsite. I also use the MassTimes app (hint: be sure to put the actual address of your destination in Google or other navigation apps, as sometimes direct links land me at a location several blocks from where I want to be).

Because I visit shrines and religious sites, I keep a running list of recommendations or places I've researched. Many times, I can combine a visit to a shrine with Mass. Since the Mass always has the same parts and usually the same Bible readings wherever you go, there's an automatic familiarity.

## Temporary Homes

One of my favorite church communities while traveling is Saint Rita Catholic Church in Santa Rosa Beach, Florida. Just a short drive from Topsail Hill Preserve State Park, Saint Rita serves year-round residents, snowbirds, and tourists. People tend to sit in the same pew when they attend daily Mass. After a few days at Saint Rita, I started to recognize others by face. On Sunday, the enthusiastic young priest, Father Mike, asked visitors to stand and introduce themselves before Mass. That was very helpful as a couple of people approached me and struck up conversations after Mass. In particular, I met a widow named Katherine with a down-to-earth sense of humor. She invited me to events at Saint Rita, including a concert and bingo, where I met other parishioners. Every time I go back there, I look for Katherine and greet Father Mike.

Last time I was at Saint Rita, in January 2020, I volunteered to help out with the Friday Fish Fry. This is a big community thing in Catholic churches in non-pandemic times, but like many church activities it was suspended during the height of the pandemic in 2020–2021. For helping set up the dessert table, full of tantalizing baked goods donated by parishioners, and serving at several long tables, I received a volunteer T-shirt to supplement my scaled back full-time Airstreamer wardrobe, plus I enjoyed conversations with many guests.

During late summer and early fall 2020, I spent time on the Chesapeake Bay moochdocking at a friend's home. We attended Saint Anthony of Padua Catholic Church in North Beach. One Sunday before Mass, Father Stack, the pastor, asked if there were any lectors present and someone got up to serve. Since I've often lectored at my home church, I introduced myself after Mass and asked if they needed an additional temporary lector. Father Stack kindly interviewed me and let me volunteer as a reader.

Thus I was able to get to know some of the other lectors and cantors. Participating in daily Mass led to invitations to pray afterward with other Mass-goers. They gathered outside at the statue of Mary to pray the Rosary on Wednesdays and Saturdays. Eventually, I joined the parish Bible study as well, using my time to gain a deeper knowledge of the word of God through the socially distanced guidance of the humble but gifted Father Stack. Discussions with the parishioners attending the Bible study added to my sense of having found another home in this small, faith-filled parish.

## Festivals and Celebrations

I've been welcomed at many parishes even when my visits to the area were shorter. In New Mexico, I attended Las Posadas at Saint Jude Thaddeus Catholic Church in Albuquerque. Posadas is a nine-day reenactment of Joseph and Mary's search for shelter in Bethlehem before Jesus's birth. As I exited Mass, people urged me to stay for the event and handed me a candle. I speak a fair amount of Spanish, which helped with the bilingual procession and songs. With lit candles, the small crowd processed around the parking lot to the doors of different buildings. It was quite chilly in December, but the stars and luminaria scattered along the pathways between the buildings provided plenty of light and an illusion of warmth.

Young parishioners dressed as Jesus and Mary led the procession, followed by guitar players, singers keeping time with silver bells and wooden sticks, and some shepherds and angels. At each stop, we sang a part of a traditional song, "Seeking Shelter" or "Pidiendo Posada." This melody uses a call-and-response dialogue in which Mary and Joseph ask for lodging and the people at the door turn them away.

At the final stop, the crowd split into two parts, one behind the doors to the parish hall and the other in front of them. This time, when Mary and Joseph asked for shelter, they were let into a warm, brightly decorated hall full of tantalizing smells of food.

Tables and a buffet area were decorated with purple and silver. A large rainbow-colored star piñata dangled from the ceiling and an Advent wreath with glass containers for three purple and one pink candle graced a table full of song booklets.

I asked if a spot at a long table was taken, and the family seated there welcomed me warmly. The parish priest blessed everyone and read from the Gospel of Luke, while the musicians and participants sang more songs in between the readings. My favorite was "Vamos Todos a Belen," or "We All Go to Bethlehem." After prayers, everyone enjoyed delicious homemade food such as tortillas, chorizo, green chili, and sopapillas.

The following month, I visited Blessed Sacrament Church in Tallahassee, Florida, for Sunday Mass. The church was on my route from Ochlocknee River State Park, which had zero cell coverage but was famous for its rare white squirrels. One white squirrel obligingly showed up at my campsite for photos just as I was backing in.

The day I visited Blessed Sacrament turned out to be the Feast of the Child Jesus, celebrated with a Blessing of Santo Niño (the Holy Child) and an exuberant musical celebration. A kind lady that I sat next to during Mass urged me to stay for the festivities, and I'm glad I did.

The festival of Santo Niño de Cebu marks the arrival of Christianity in the Philippines in the sixteenth century. It is celebrated in Filipino-American communities throughout the United States. At Blessed Sacrament, many people of all backgrounds participated.

Carrying statues of the Child Jesus, candles, and flowers, women and men in traditional costumes entered the school gymnasium. A wide aisle separated rows of decorated tables, leading to the stage at the front of the gym. All of the parish priests lined up near the stage to watch, and a live band enthusiastically played. As the men and women in brightly colored costumes raised and lowered their arms, gracefully stepping in synchronization, they lifted up the flowers or statues in their hands. Drums and whistles punctuated the dance. Bracelets and necklaces with bells or flat coins tinkled as the dancers swayed on their bare feet in a tightly coordinated pattern. The men's striped vests matched the women's red-and-white striped long dresses and flower garland headdresses.

Men carefully carried on top of a red cushion a crowned statue of Santo Niño wearing an elaborate dress. Women followed, twirling and dancing with smaller versions of the statue in their hands. Many of the women wore brilliantly colored silk gowns with large square puffy sleeves and discreet slits in the long skirts. Turquoise-, pink-, purple-, and blue-clad ladies of all ages proceeded up the center aisle and placed their Santo Niño statues with the larger statue on a table in front of the room.

Finally, what appeared to be a queen of the procession entered. She wore an elaborate red dress and danced with another small statue. White and silver butterflies rested on the dancer's gown. Like the rays of a star, stiff metallic filaments fanned outward both from her headdress and a flat woven white straw circle on her back, from which a fringed white shawl dangled. Alternating pairs of women in black shirts, red sashes, and orange skirts lifted bouquets of yellow mums up and down in unison, followed by men in high-necked, long-sleeved white tunics and black pants making the same motions with candy cane–striped candles. Horns blared a triumphant call as the dancers smoothly dipped and turned.

The joyful procession ended with the dancers placing all their statues on a table at the front of the room. Next, the pastor offered a prayer and the crowd headed for the overflowing tables of food. Sticky rice, barbecue, spring rolls, empanadas, and all sorts of delicacies filled the plates of the grateful diners. At my table, I met several people who were parishioners and some who had traveled from other local churches to enjoy the occasion.

## Community in the Time of COVID

Obviously, as it has so many other things, COVID has limited this form of community as well. For many weeks in spring 2020, most churches in the United States were closed. When I stayed at Lake Guntersville, Alabama, I went to Mass at Saint William Catholic Church in the small town of Guntersville. The people at this parish were very friendly in an outgoing Southern way. Father Mark, the pastor, shared his time between Saint William and the

Chapel of the Holy Cross in nearby Albertville. He was determined to care for his parishioners.

When the pandemic struck, and churches temporarily closed, Father Mark immediately put into place livestreaming of Mass. He creatively found a safe way for people to receive the Eucharist in the parking lot after Mass. We lined up in our cars and watched the livestreamed Mass on our phones. After Mass, Father Mark came outside and set up at the side entrance to the church a small table with the Blessed Sacrament. One by one we drove up next to the table. He visited each open car window to say prayers and provide the Eucharist through the window. It was clear that he was moved by being able to serve his flock as much as he was, because we were able to receive Communion.

More recently, before my cancer diagnosis, I spent a couple of weeks in Gordonsville, Virginia, and found the same friendliness at Saint Isidore the Farmer Catholic Church. Despite our wearing masks and staying six feet apart, a few women approached me as close as allowed after daily Mass and invited me to attend a Women of Grace Bible study that had just resumed. There were only six people when I got there, spread out in a large room wearing masks, but they made me feel right at home. This came at a critical time for me as I was anxiously awaiting my test results.

Because of my choice to live as a nomad, it is not always easy to find community in local churches, but it is a great source of joy and refreshment when I do. It is one of the reasons I've learned to stay longer in one place. While the Mass and certain other elements of church practice are found everywhere, just as in any circumstance it takes time to develop even a modest connection to a particular group. Slowing down and being present in a particular area— where I can find spiritual nourishment myself—allows me to be more present to those whom God places in my path.

## CHAPTER TWENTY-THREE

# TRAVEL PLANS AND ROAD MAPS

*"If a man wishes to be sure of the road he treads on, he must close his eyes and walk in the dark."*

—Saint John of the Cross

## Reservations

My alarm chirped at 5:45 a.m. Outside my trailer the sky was just beginning to brighten. Bleary-eyed in the predawn glow, I patted Penny. At first, she looked indignant at her rest being interrupted, but then she rolled over for a belly rub. She burrowed back under the blankets when I picked up my phone.

I pulled up the reservation site for Florida state parks. There were several sites coming available eleven months in advance at 8 a.m. that morning, Eastern Standard Time. I opened several windows, one for each site, and completed the CAPTCHA puzzle for each. "I am not a robot," I mumbled to Penny.

I prayed while I waited for the minutes to pass. Periodically I refreshed the screens. After 5:59 a.m. Mountain Time, I counted to thirty then started clicking through the various windows to "Book This Site," hoping I'd manage to snag an opening through the electronic universe when it opened exactly at 8 a.m. EST.

There's always a tension between planning and not planning. I like to stay for at least two weeks in a site if possible, and in the same general area for a month or so. That gives me a chance to get to know people, see the sights, and perhaps even volunteer.

Also, some areas are just outside of my budget unless I get a coveted state or county spot. While many places have some free camping without hookups, the weather may make that unattractive or it simply may be so limited as to not be an option.

For instance, the Florida Keys have essentially no free camping unless you work your way up on a volunteer list over the course of a few years, serving first in the hot summer. The state parks there are gorgeous and a fraction of the cost of private parks; however, it is very difficult to secure a spot at one of them.

Once, I grabbed a last-minute cancellation in the Keys while camping at a Gulf Coast park. I cut my planned stay short and headed through the Everglades and Miami to Bahia Honda State Park for four days. Although the spots were closer to other campers than in most Florida state parks, lush foliage surrounded my site. A rocky beach for snorkeling and a pier for boat rides were just a short walk through a tropical forest trail. At night, campers gathered around fires and at the shore. Every evening, weather permitting, one couple played taps on their trumpets as the sun stained the turquoise water shades of purple, orange, and red.

Inspired, I renewed efforts to make reservations for the following year. What I discovered in my short stay, however, was that there are many snowbirds and full-timers who've become friends over the years and manage to coordinate their reservations to stay in the Keys for most of the winter. Florida only allows stays of fourteen consecutive days in one park during high-demand periods. A camper then must depart for at least three nights, before returning. Also, there's a maximum stay of fifty-six nights total at any one park in the course of six months.

Through many early morning efforts from time zones away, like the one I describe above, I managed to secure a series of reservations in the Florida Keys from November 2020 to early January 2021. Since my budget is $25 a night on average, I offset relatively expensive stays with free stays by boondocking or camp hosting. However, as happened for many people, my plans in 2020 were completely upended by the pandemic. Personal circumstances also intervened.

So I've learned to include cancellation fees in my budget. If I really want to be in a certain place at a certain time, I recognize that may not happen, that I will have to bow out for one reason or another.

Planning benefits my budget more than cancellation fees harm it. Monthly fees at RV resorts work out far better than daily stays. Also, there are many membership organizations that for the cost of dues provide free or very low-cost stays at private RV campgrounds or resorts. The definition of "resort" is malleable. It can mean anything from a small swimming pool and activities building to a community with a golf course, maintained trails, beaches with lifeguards, organized activities, and fine dining.

Normally, I'm not that interested in all the amenities. I'm happiest in natural beauty. This preference saves me a lot of money.

Nonetheless, there are definite benefits to staying at RV resorts. When traveling long distance, I like to alternate stays with power, water, and a dump station to compensate for stays without hookups. Also, in very warm or very cold weather, power is quite helpful. If I'm going to be in an area for a while, it is nice to have a community to get to know and return to periodically. Your friends on the road can find you more easily if you are in one location for a while, so hanging around helps maintain friendships already made with other nomads.

For this type of travel, I have a membership in Coast to Coast, which gives me low-cost stays of a week to fourteen days at a variety of RV campgrounds and resorts. Many others I know use Thousand Trails, Sun RV Resorts, or other membership plans.

The only catch of my low-cost plan is that sites may be booked only sixty to ninety days in advance, and there are blackout days for holidays and events. Nonetheless, it is a valuable tool in my camping bag of tricks. Good Sam and Coast to Coast also provide discounts on monthly stays at some RV resorts, as do Passport America and Escapees RV Club.

My first experience with a monthly stay was at a beautiful and isolated campground in Montana. I fled to that camp with my stimulus check after I became too nervous about exposure to COVID in a camp-hosting gig in Alabama. It definitely saved gas and camping expenses to be in one location, plus I gained a base for short trips to pilgrimage destinations and national parks within the vicinity. Unfortunately, the pandemic limited contact and opportunities to make new friends there or in the small town within walking distance of the campground. I planned to stay for several months, but an unexpected need for repairs and family issues necessitated a return to the East Coast. I definitely would like to return, and the experience helped me see the value of longer stays.

Another way to stay inexpensively in one location for a long time is to "moochdock," or stay on a friend's property. Local homeowner associations or zoning regulations prohibit this in some areas, but I was lucky to stay in a friend's yard along the Chesapeake Bay for several months last summer.

To park in my friend Karen's yard, I had to maneuver through an alley then back into a grassy area between two trees. That placed my front windows where I could see the bay while seated at my dinette. Natural shade from the trees kept the outside of the trailer cool compared to the hot sun beating down on my truck.

Over time, however, I realized my trailer was slowly sinking into the soft ground. I'd parked it using leveling blocks that looked like square, flat yellow Legos. Rain covered them when we had a few days of wet weather. I ended up waiting for a spell of dry days before I could move the Airstream out to my next campsite.

Many people who love traveling in their RVs less than full-time have fixed homes with ample parking space. As an Airstream International Club member, I benefit from the generosity of fellow Airstreamers who offer free stays for a night or two in their driveways or yards. Similarly, Boondockers Welcome is a membership organization that for a small fee annually gives you access to a list of RV owners willing to help out others by letting them moochdock.

If you have friends who offer you the chance to stay overnight in their driveway, accept graciously but be sure to ask them to send you photos. Once I stayed at my friend Jen's home near Raleigh, North Carolina, after a long drive. Her driveway was sharply pitched, which presented a challenge for not hitting the surface with any portion of the underside of the Airstream as I entered. Backing the Airstream in on an angle helps with that. However, Jen also had lovely trees overhanging her driveway, and she ended up armed with a pole clipper furiously chopping at low branches in her pajamas. Because the driveway's angle from the road was very sharp, I needed to back up and pull forward, then correct my angle and back up again several times. Opposite the driveway was a soft muddy ditch. Just before I was going to use my four-wheel drive to pull forward near the top of it, Jen mentioned that people frequently got stuck there. At that point, we opted instead to have me stay on a dead-end gravel service road at the end of her street. It was only one night!

That's the thing with living in a tiny home on wheels: if something doesn't work out, keep repeating that it is only for one night. I've had surprisingly refreshing stays on I-80 in Ohio where some rest stops offer one night of full hook-up RV parking for a modest fee.

Unplanned stops lead to encountering people you wouldn't have otherwise met and discovering places to stay you wouldn't have otherwise considered. Sometimes, an unplanned stop leads to a longer stay with adventures you might have missed if you'd kept following your original plans.

## Spontaneous Stops

I'm still acquiring the level of trust necessary to make traveling without any reservations work for me. I know people who live and drive that way exclusively. I like to have a plan and a backup plan, particularly since I'm a solo traveler. Nonetheless, some of my best discoveries have been entirely unplanned.

Last year, I crossed into South Dakota hoping to stay near a shrine. However, the weather forecast was grim, and it seemed more prudent to keep going. Various phone apps for overnight parking come in very handy in such conditions. RV Parky works well, as do AllStays and Campendium. Once in a while, I'll find a spot on the apps that I like well enough to keep it in mind for a future, longer, planned stay.

Harvest Hosts is a network of wineries, breweries, museums, stores, and more that allow self-contained campers to park overnight. There's an annual membership fee, and you are expected to patronize the host's business in exchange for a night of parking. Normally, you call a few days in advance, but I've had good luck with a same-day call if circumstances dictate. Although one night is all that is expected, on occasion a host has invited me to stay an extra night. For a modest fee, some places also offer full hookups or extended stays.

Of course, Harvest Hosts can end up being very expensive if you purchase a lot. Most places offer enticing wares (including books in church bookstores). I don't golf, so I purchased a T-shirt at a Harvest Host golf course. I did some Christmas shopping at an Amish museum and an alpaca farm. Breweries are great for beer, but sometimes food as well. Entry fees for museums count as a purchase. At farms and country stores, I've replenished my supplies with fresh produce, cheese, and honey.

What I like most about Harvest Hosts is getting a glimpse into very different lives. At Heritage Farm Suri Alpacas in Indiana, for example, I held a baby alpaca born only a few hours before I arrived. Mama Alpaca was not really into the whole nursing thing, so the owners had to milk her and bottle feed the baby at first. By the next day, things were settling down. Alpacas are both beautiful and comical with large expressive eyes and ears. This was one of my favorite Harvest Hosts stays. They offered beautiful items woven from alpaca wool as well as the wool itself.

Another beautiful stop in a completely different environment is Our Desert Homestead in Rancho Rio, New Mexico. The property overlooks the lights of Albuquerque, surrounded by deserts and mountains. I made my way up into the hills on a dirt road to this scenic site, the home of a family of five devoted to low-impact living. I purchased fresh eggs from the chickens they kept and chatted with a young man who was tent camping on the farm. The stars at night blazed brilliantly, like you could reach up and touch them. I heard coyotes in the distance (kept out of the homestead by fencing and two friendly rescue dogs). In the morning, I spotted a few hot-air balloons drifting through the bright blue sky.

The Green Valley Golf Club in Ohio was a humbling stay. The spot for parking was right next to an intersection. I'm a light sleeper and had the windows open, plus I'd had a bit too much coffee while driving. I woke up grumpy. Then I saw the beautiful sunrise and noticed a memorial I hadn't taken time to look at when I arrived. The manager explained that he built it to honor local vets. He served on the board of the Zanesville Veterans Appreciation Foundation. Among other services to local veterans, the foundation raised money for the Honor Flight to Washington, DC, for senior veterans to visit at no cost the memorials honoring their sacrifice and that of others who served. I was grateful to purchase a shirt supporting the foundation.

Point Labadie Brewery in Missouri provided a warm refuge on a rainy travel day. It was peaceful and quiet in the field by the brewery. Inside, happy guests enjoyed the beer dinner hosted by the owners and a local restaurant. Each course used beer in the recipe and was paired with a flavorful craft beer. I had a delightful evening with two young couples who were there to celebrate birthdays.

These overnight hospitality sites are not just a convenience, but a way to connect with others. Some hosts and fellow travelers become friends and follow my blog. Others want to learn more about what inspires me to live on the road full-time. I see my stays here as part of my ministry, sometimes giving others an opportunity to be charitable to me, as in my very first Harvest Hosts stay, at Cartersville Country Winery in South Carolina.

It was near Christmas, and I helped the hosts decorate their barn for a charity fundraiser. They kindly gave me a bottle of wine after learning about Tin Can Pilgrim and would not let me purchase it as the quid pro quo for the stay. Allowing others to express generosity can witness Christ's love as much as being generous oneself.

Another option for unplanned stops are stores with large parking lots that allow overnight stays with the hope, but not the requirement, that you patronize them. If I stop at a Cracker Barrel, Walmart, Cabela's, or Bass Pro Shop, I make every effort to buy a meal or supplies there. It is best to check with a store manager to confirm you can stay overnight, and to park in a remote corner where you will not block other customers. Don't be "that camper" who fires up a grill and sets out yard furniture like they are settling in at a campground.

Also, leave your spot cleaner than you found it. Dispose of trash in a trash bin available to the public, or take it with you to your next stop. If too many people leave a mess or interfere with other customers' use or enjoyment of the facility, then free overnight parking will vanish. Recently, many Walmarts stopped allowing RVers to rest overnight, because too many treated it like extended-stay camping.

Frankly, store or restaurant parking lots are not my choice for overnight stays. I'm a light sleeper. Just like at a truck stop, too many large rigs come and go at all hours. Whether it is headlights or engine noise, I find I don't get enough rest to make it anything more than a last resort.

A better option for my unplanned stops is staying off-grid in National Forest and other public land locations. This may require obtaining a permit, often on the honor system, where you write a check or pay cash to cover your camping fee, put it in an envelope with your name and vehicle information, and drop it in a lockbox. It also can be very frustrating to keep pulling into places and finding they are full. Again, various apps and Facebook groups can help you find spots.

I'm working on my sense of adventure, to be more open to staying at places spontaneously. One of the best features of life as a nomad is that I have wheels. I can leave or stay, altering my plans in a moment. Spiritually, it is a matter of trust that can be rewarded with delightful experiences.

An unplanned stop in Potosi, Missouri, for example, led me to a lovely small church where I met a pastor and two friends of his who were visiting from a previous parish. With small-town friendliness, they invited me to join them for a meal at an appropriately named local restaurant called the Bearfoot Cafe. As we entered, a large bear rug hanging on the wall greeted us. Humorous bear sculptures decorated walls and various nooks and crannies of this quintessentially small-town American diner. Later, Father Fleming gave me and his other visitors a tour of Saint James Catholic Church. He blessed me and gave me some healing oil to carry with me in my Airstream.

Another chance encounter touched me deeply at a small town in Michigan. I went to an evening Mass at Immaculate Conception Church in Three Rivers while headed to Indiana Dunes State Park. After Mass, several women stood around chatting outside and introduced themselves to me since I was clearly a stranger in the small town. Intrigued by my mobile ministry, they invited me to join them for dinner, but first stopped to pick up a shawl to give me from their prayer shawl ministry. They pray as they create the shawls, and the pastor blesses the knitted and crocheted work before they give it away. In this way, they too could participate in what I was doing by being present in a sense when I prayed in far locations with other strangers.

That variegated turquoise-and-blue shawl still has a place of honor in my Airstream. It survived a rollover crash in New Mexico and in fact held some items in place like a web against the broken door. I fixed the small pulls in the yarn, still grateful for that gift. If I hadn't slowed down and spoken with Nancy, Marie, and the other prayer shawl ladies, I would have missed an opportunity for fellowship in my journey west.

Living in the present means asking for God's guidance in small ways throughout the day. Humility means not getting so caught up in my own itinerary that I fail to leave myself open to the unexpected and to God's laughter. Often, His inspirations—when I recognize them—lead me to much better places than my own planning.

## Adjusting My Expectations

I've had to adjust my expectations on the road, mainly so far as planning goes. When I'm open to improvising and changing plans,

I enjoy life so much more. For instance, I met up with Laural, my fellow solo female traveler who's Miss Dixie's human, in South Dakota. She had a friend who was friends with the family that owns and runs the Crazy Horse monument. When we visited, we ended up getting an invitation to travel up to the construction site, literally walking out onto the arm being carved from the mountain. We hung out chatting with her friend's friend, enjoying a meal of buffalo stew.

Another big adjustment is making sure to take care of my own refueling and self-care needs, which require a bit more planning on the road. Admittedly, this was complicated by the economic shutdowns of the pandemics. Still, other campers often directed me to places where I could get my hair cut or go "junking" for lightly used clothing. The easiest thing to delay through forgetfulness and inconvenience—and the most important to stay on top of—is the regular dental and health appointments that are easy to neglect when you are feeling well. It's like that old adage about not waiting until it is raining to fix the roof!

I've found that it helps to block out in my calendar both the time I'd like to schedule annual appointments and a time several months in advance for making those appointments. That way, I can take care of several in one visit to the location where my preferred medical providers live.

As I write this, I realize I am very lucky to have that flexibility. When you don't have good insurance and regular doctors that you've established care with, you have to rely on urgent care. You need to have your own copy of all your records wherever you wander. In fact, it is a good idea to keep copies of important documents accessible, whether in a little fire safe or lockbox, or online. This applies to medical records as well as birth certificates and passports.

Another area in which my expectations needed adjusting was the length of time it takes to get to a new location. Driving my Mazda3 got me to my destinations before or near the time GPS estimated. That's not the case when I'm towing. Then I travel at a speed that may be far less than the speed limit, to be sure I can stop quickly or maneuver safely if I have to. Towing also means stopping more often, because it is not safe to try to use one hand on the steering wheel and the other to eat your takeout food when you are pulling thousands of extra pounds subject to wind and mechanical forces that suddenly might wrest that wheel from your control.

Going more slowly is actually a good thing. You have more flexibility to follow unusual signs leading to interesting adventures or to see more of the area on a local road. Large superhighways usually attract huge trucks that create slipstreams of air. I literally can feel my trailer and truck being pushed by the blast of air from an 18-wheeler coming up behind me. When a truck passes me, I slow down because the air it displaces then exerts sideways force on my Airstream. Taking your time with a lower speed and a less crowded slower road can buy you precious moments to respond effectively if something goes wrong.

Slowing down in life has the same benefits. When I was caught up in the whirl of the fast-paced, high-intensity life of a young associate attorney, I literally had no thought of self-reflection, of taking stock of where I was in life and where I hoped to be. It was a merry-go-round. Breaking my finger and having hip surgery forced me off the merry-go-round and created room in my life for thoughtfulness. The seeds planted by the Holy Spirit through others had a chance to sprout and bloom.

Still the lure of being busy didn't go away. Even today, I have to watch myself. I've concluded I'm an adrenaline junkie of sorts. When I undertake a project—or a mission—I throw myself into it with such enthusiasm that I sometimes leave myself behind. I create pressure for myself where there doesn't need to be any.

God's voice is quiet, a gentle whisper that we overlook when we surround ourselves with a cacophony of things, and things to do that seem very important, and to which we tie importance. We forget that we are loved for who we are, not for what we have or do. We are children with a very good, the best, parent who loves us unconditionally and supports us in all things good for us, who respects our freedom to make mistakes but is always there for us when we come back crestfallen at our own failures.

If one person finds this book speaks to them, or if they remember a story with some application to their own peace and joy, or if it helps in any way to allow them to connect with God the Creator, that is enough. I'd love to help many people with this book, if that's what God wants. The temptation to desire success as a bestseller, with invitations to talk shows and podcasts, and to know I've inspired others is just that: a temptation. These things are good if they are what God wants. If they are desired for themselves or for the warm glow of achievement I may feel or for validation that what I'm doing has merit, then they are an obstacle to my holiness. I desire to be a tool in the sculptor's hand, to be a guide showing those who feel lost and unhappy the signpost that can lead them to happiness. I desire this not for its own sake, but only insofar as it is what my Lord, my Beloved, wants and only as much as He wants it for me.

As a holy man once prayed:

> *O Jesus, meek and humble of heart,*
> *Hear me.*
> *From the desire of being esteemed,*
> *Deliver me, O Jesus.*
> *From the desire of being loved,*
> *Deliver me, O Jesus.*
> *From the desire of being extolled,*
> *Deliver me, O Jesus.*
> *From the desire of being honored,*
> *Deliver me, O Jesus.*
> *From the desire of being praised,*
> *Deliver me, O Jesus.*
> *From the desire of being preferred to others,*
> *Deliver me, O Jesus.*
> *From the desire of being consulted,*
> *Deliver me, O Jesus.*
> *From the desire of being approved,*

*Deliver me, O Jesus.*
*From the fear of being humiliated,*
*Deliver me, O Jesus.*
*From the fear of being despised,*
*Deliver me, O Jesus.*
*From the fear of suffering rebukes,*
*Deliver me, O Jesus.*
*From the fear of being calumniated,*
*Deliver me, O Jesus.*
*From the fear of being forgotten,*
*Deliver me, O Jesus.*
*From the fear of being ridiculed,*
*Deliver me, O Jesus.*
*From the fear of being wronged,*
*Deliver me, O Jesus.*
*From the fear of being suspected,*
*Deliver me, O Jesus.*
*That others may be loved more than I,*
*Jesus, grant me the grace to desire it.*
*That others may be esteemed more than I,*
*Jesus, grant me the grace to desire it.*
*That, in the opinion of the world, others may increase and I may decrease,*
*Jesus, grant me the grace to desire it.*
*That others may be chosen and I set aside,*
*Jesus, grant me the grace to desire it.*
*That others may be praised and I go unnoticed,*
*Jesus, grant me the grace to desire it.*

*That others may be preferred to me in everything,*
*Jesus, grant me the grace to desire it.*
*That others may become holier than I, provided that I may become as holy as I should,*
*Jesus, grant me the grace to desire it.*
—Cardinal Merry del Val, Litany of Humility

CHAPTER TWENTY-FOUR

# TRAVELING DURING A PANDEMIC

*"That my life is a gift. Jesus, I trust in You."*
—Sisters of Life, *Litany of Trust*

## Pandemic

I left Penny in Florida to visit with my daughter while I went to an annual conference of RV Entrepreneurs in Lake Guntersville State Park, Alabama, in late February 2020. I knew I'd be attending seminars and activities most of the day once the conference started. Penny would be happier with my daughter, who dotes on her every Chihuahua whim.

Lake Guntersville has beautiful sunsets that stain the sky and water with startling shades of purple, pink, and orange. Trails wind around the lake and up the mountain to the lodge. Trillium, ferns, and wildflowers abound. Quite frequently, the visitor will glimpse one of the eagles that nest at the edge of the lake.

In 2019 the park was the site of the RV Entrepreneur Summit where I created my Tin Can Pilgrim blog. Several of the friends I'd met the previous year showed up early to visit and socialize before the conference started. However, my oldest daughter called me a day or two after I arrived. "You need to stock up on hand sanitizer and cleaning wipes," she said. "This pandemic thing is serious."

I hadn't really been following the news and thought she was overreacting. I picked up some extras at the drugstore in town, just in case, on my way to visit the U.S. Space and Rocket Center museum in Huntsville, also known as "Rocket City." Quite a few of us went together to tour the museum and enjoy the first weekly "Biergarten," an annual German food, wine, and beer festival that normally begins in March and lasts until November. The Biergarten recognizes the German heritage of many of the rocket scientists who moved to Huntsville in the 1930s and 1940s. That turned out to be the last Biergarten in 2020 or so far in 2021.

As news about the virus later named COVID-19 spread, the organizers of the RV Entrepreneur Summit decided to cancel the conference. Most of us who already had arrived made the best of things and renewed friendships albeit with social distancing.

Penny's visit with my daughter ended up being extended indefinitely. I had planned to pick up Penny when I returned to Florida for a camp-hosting gig. However, Florida closed all its campsites in response to the pandemic. If I had already arrived at the state park where I was supposed to camp host, I might have been able to stay there and work on other maintenance projects even while the park was closed. Since I hadn't, I was out of luck.

Many full-time RVers were caught at loose ends as state after state closed their campgrounds or restricted them to state residents. Alabama didn't seem that concerned. In fact, when I went to extend my reservation, I mentioned that my camp-hosting gig in Florida had fallen through. The office managers asked if I wanted to apply to camp host at Lake Guntersville. Delighted with the opportunity to stay longer at the lake, I accepted enthusiastically.

For about the next month, I camp hosted there. Quite a few of my RV Entrepreneur friends remained at the lake as well, since their other reservations had been canceled or lockdowns made travel problematic. My job involved meeting and greeting folks checking into the campground, so I purchased some cloth face masks to wear and faithfully used my supplies of hand sanitizer. My coworkers and I drew chalk lines to assist with social distancing. I even adapted a tool used for picking up items out of reach so it would hold a clipboard and we could pass paperwork through the windows of arriving RVs without coming too close ourselves. This greatly amused most of the RVers. Hardly any of them wore a mask, as they viewed the CDC recommendations at the time with great skepticism, as an attempt to exert government control over personal choice.

Unfortunately, because all neighboring states closed their campgrounds, Alabama became everyone's destination. It was Fourth of July every weekend. I went from checking in twenty or so campers per night to more than one hundred. That made me uneasy because most visitors still did not wear protective masks. The camp hosts on duty had to remind guests frequently to stay in their vehicles while we checked them in or abide by the chalk lines we'd drawn to encourage social distancing.

Finally, the overcrowded conditions changed my comfort level with camp hosting there. In any event, social distancing limited opportunities to meet people and to get to know them and be a friend. It became increasingly difficult to have a sense of community in person. My daughters urged me to head for a less populated area and hold off on camp hosting for a while. When I received my first stimulus check, I reserved a site at a remote Montana campground and headed west again.

## Quarantine in Montana

After a long week of driving with short stops, I arrived in Montana at what I intended to be my campsite for the next few months. Surrounded by distant mountains and nestled into a grassy valley, my Airstream looked small against the Big Sky. For two weeks, I self-quarantined in my rig in compliance with Montana's requirements at the time.

This was no hardship. From my windows, I looked at snow-frosted mountains surrounding the campground. Like the

Southwest desert, the northern grassy plains contain an amazing variety of colors. Pale gold sheaves, red and brown bursts of wiry grass, and the purple skeletons of last year's wildflowers dotted the landscape. Patches of shorn bright green grass spotted with yellow dandelions bordered the edges of the RV sites, blending into the wilder terrain past the mostly empty rows of gravel and picnic benches.

Because the campsite was mostly unoccupied this early in the summer, I could walk around it and the neighboring fields without encountering anyone else. I did meet an enchanting variety of birds. One bird, a killdeer, pretended to be injured. With a piercing cry, she hopped away from where she'd laid eggs on the rock-strewn path, acting as a decoy for a presumed predator.

By contrast, sleek and shiny starlings soared and turned in the air as they battled the breezes. These little sharp-winged birds with white bellies and iridescent heads darted about defending the small birdhouses they occupied around the campground perimeter.

On one walk, I spotted what might have been some kind of brown cranes calling hoarsely in the distance. Black-and-white magpies and tiny golden finches flew all over the campground. One morning, I even saw a magpie chase a small rabbit. The magpies have a distinctive cry and look beautiful in flight, with long tails and white splashes of feathers on their necks and wings. They fly individually, while the finches congregate in groups, rising into the air like a shifting mosaic with bright yellow pieces.

When I walked along the country roads surrounding the campground, I encountered few humans but plenty of furry deer. Montana winters are harsh, and the deer's coats reminded me of ponies in the early spring. Their large eyes and comically expressive ears made me smile, grateful to God for the unanticipated companions.

While this was not how I'd planned to spend my summer, I made good use of my Montana retreat. The magnificent sky and vistas recalled God's constant presence. Remaining in one place for a while made me appreciate anew the need to slow down and get to know the location and people in front of me rather than constantly planning the next move. Inadvertently, the pandemic and quarantine helped me refine how to travel even in non-pandemic times.

After my Montana quarantine ended, I started to explore the rest of the very small town and found a rustic welcoming church to attend just a few blocks from the campground. Saint Bartholomew Catholic Church was close to the ground, with a steeply pointed roof that allowed winter snow to slide off before becoming too heavy. Certainly, the still furry deer that lounged in the sunlit churchyard appeared to testify to a challenging winter.

For the first time on my journey, I found it hard to integrate into a local church community. The small parish shared its priest with several others, so there was only one Sunday Mass and one daily Mass. Also, the pandemic impacted social life and the availability of community events, even when I traveled to other cities and towns in the state. I thought back fondly to church homes I'd found in other locations in a time free from the COVID-19 virus.

Although the pandemic complicated my efforts to find community on the road, it allowed me fully to appreciate the need to build rest and refueling into all journeys.

# CHAPTER TWENTY-FIVE

# FUEL STOPS

*"Come away by yourselves to a deserted place and rest a while."*
—Mark 6:31

## Natural

The excitement of moving to full-time nomadic life and getting started on the road may lead you to ignore the warning lights on your dashboard. When your fuel is low, you need to stop and fill up. Don't wait for the red zone. If I'm in a populated area with frequent gas stops, I'll fuel up when my tank is down to a quarter full. But in the desert or very rural areas, I'll stop for fuel at the half-tank point.

This lesson doesn't just apply to gasoline or diesel. You'll need to pace yourself while downsizing and you'll need to allow time to rest while journeying. In fact, rest itself is part of the journey.

For instance, I spent three weeks preparing my townhouse for sale in 2018. This involved a lot of hard choices and putting some items in storage to "stage" the house for prospective purchasers. As I got rid of the accumulated years of clutter and pared down the amount of furniture, the resulting open space and inviting placement made me realize I could have been living like this all along. Clutter infringes on peace, sometimes so slowly that you don't realize it's happening. When you walk through your home with the eyes of a stranger, you see things differently.

After preparing the house for my Realtor to show, I left town on a long-planned vacation. I have to smile in retrospect because God even took care of this detail. I'd planned the trip for more than a year, and yet the timing was perfect to give me a break from the admittedly stressful process of opening my hands and letting go of things to which I'd been clinging.

I left the house in my Realtor's capable hands and lived fully in the moments with my daughters. I was eight hours away in time and thousands of miles in distance, enjoying my first trip ever to Spain, with my grown children. While there wasn't a lot of physical rest on this vacation, my mind and spirit reset.

My oldest daughter and I rented a car and traveled through small towns, the seashore, and the foothills of the Pyrenees in northern Spain. We visited beautiful cathedrals and pilgrimage sites, sampling the local cuisine and practicing our Spanish. Then my youngest joined us in Barcelona for a week full of art and culture. The home sale was out of my control and out of my mind. Feeling the sun on my face on a boat cruise, or climbing up a winding trail to a fort, I could simply be in that moment.

When I returned from Spain, the house had sold and we had a closing date about a month away. Now I could continue the process of giving away or selling what was left. With travel comes jet lag, so I'd built in a slower pace for the first few days.

Gradually, over the next few weeks, I ended up sleeping on a mattress on the floor and eating from a chair using boxes as a side table. Soon I drove down to Florida to pick up my Airstream and move in. The bed of the truck contained all the items I initially needed, and I purchased groceries and trailer-specific tools and furnishings in Florida.

The physical demands of towing and camping also put a premium on rest. After my orientation and picking up my Airstream, I spent a couple of days in a nearby campground simply getting used to the trailer's features. I quickly learned how most nomads live life at a slower pace. They take time to relax by their campfires or under the shade of their awnings with old friends and new. In pre-pandemic times, they often started conversations and invited me to pull up a seat.

## Supernatural

We also need rest in a spiritual sense. For me, everything is centered around that quiet time I spend in prayer daily. I go to Mass daily when available. I also set aside twenty minutes to talk with the Lord at a specific time each day so I don't get to the end of the day without having had that time when He is my exclusive focus.

Prayer is a conversation with God. I might have little conversations with Him during the day, especially while driving or hiking. I'll pray before I start a task or sometimes when I'm meeting or listening to someone I've just met. These mini rest breaks, like sips of cool water, refresh me.

Resting in the moment allows us to refresh and refuel our spirits also, not just our bodies. The past is the past, the future is beyond your control, so live in the present. That doesn't mean that you don't plan. But you rest. You don't get attached to your plans and worry about what will happen if it doesn't turn out exactly how you envision. Leave it in His capable hands and deal with the people and circumstances in front of you that day.

This form of rest—resting in God—can take place anywhere. In fact, part of the secret to peace and happiness is knowing that you can rest anywhere at any time. We all remember that person who could nap anywhere, even on a bus during a school trip or in a hard chair during a lecture. I never manage to nap during the day unless I'm ill, but rest is always possible.

## Building Rest into Travel Plans

When I travel, I build in rest. I don't like to drive more than a few hours without stopping to stretch my legs, walk around a bit, and breathe deeply to let out the natural tension involved in towing. Over the months and years, I've found that it works best to intersperse periods of travel, where I stay overnight or every couple of days en route to somewhere else, with longer stays of a couple of weeks or a month. It is hard to get to know people and explore places if you are always on the move. Also, it's not a good idea to plan activities the day one arrives or the day one leaves a site. It creates too much artificial pressure to arrive sooner or depart earlier.

I know I need rest when I get "hangry," or respond with an expletive to being startled. If I start to feel shaky or tense, my tone of voice with others becomes strained and harsh. These markers are like the notches on my gas gauge. If I ignore them, I may end up having to rest not in the best place or at the best time. Literally, I run out of gas when I try too hard to keep to a schedule or a plan without incorporating downtime. Traveling in an Airstream means rest and food are available anywhere I can pull over for a stop, but that availability only helps when you pay attention to your fuel needs.

Deeper rest requires me to spend time in a deserted place. I'm an extrovert, but I need my time alone with God to recharge. Every few days, I make sure I've allocated some time for a quiet reflection or a walk by myself in a lovely location. I thank God and tell Him everything He already knows about my day, my concerns, my hopes and plans. I place before Him the things I worry about and ask Him to take care of them. The sense of peace and refreshment is like a soothing soak in a warm tub in winter or drinking a cold, delicious beer on a hot day.

Every month or so I'll make a mini-retreat where I spend a good part of the day doing nothing but being conscious of His presence. Typically, this involves prayer and listening to recorded or in-person preaching followed by silence to digest what I've listened to. A number of times a year I'll devote several days in silence to Him. This may take the form of an organized retreat at a retreat house, or I might simply select some books and sketch pads, turn off my phone, take a break from media, and quietly walk or sit outdoors.

Exercise as part of rest plays another part in keeping mind, body, and soul healthy. Hiking, kayaking, and swimming are my favorites, but I also like to sweat in hard physical labor like clearing debris after storms or cleaning bathrooms and cottages at campgrounds where I camp host. There is something about manual labor that connects me to Jesus the carpenter, Mary His mother, and Joseph His foster father. All work is holy and even the most ordinary tasks can become prayer.

All these forms of rest and refueling are just as important, perhaps more important, than filling up my truck's gas tanks and my trailer's propane tanks. I related to the scene in Nomadland when Fern bathed naked in a spring, floating in the water, a perfect representation of how we strip away everything to relax in God's beauty. Absent the nudity, I may sit on a beach and stare at the ocean or lie in a hammock under green branches.

Being in an actual restful location is not even necessary. You can enter into spiritual rest just through meditation and prayer. For example, I may imagine myself at a campfire on a cool, still night, holding the Infant Jesus in my arms. Curled up with the Baby in the folds of a woolen cloak, I rest my head in Mary's lap. She sings a lullaby while Joseph watches over us, feeding the campfire occasionally with sticks he has gathered. The occasional snap of sparks that drift up like fireflies are reminders of love, glimpses of light that replenish again and again. The stars slowly move across the sky as the Baby smiles in His sleep. Peace fills my heart as I gaze at Him with love, admiring His chubby fists and full eyelashes. I look at God, knowing He loves me and I love Him.

CHAPTER TWENTY-SIX

# BREAKDOWNS AND REPAIRS

*"The time to fix the roof is when the sun is shining"*
—John F. Kennedy

## Beyond My Control

As I travel, no matter how I pray, prepare, or practice, ultimately there are things beyond my control. A dealer installed the hitch on my current Airstream, "Alvie," with only three bolts instead of six on the tongue plate for the anti-sway bar. This meant that when the sway bar was in use it wasn't anchored securely. Several hours after leaving the dealership, I arrived at my destination to find the bar dangling in midair. The tongue plate had snapped in half.

Fortunately, this was a simple repair at another nearby Airstream dealership that managed to fit me in right away. They repaired the hitch with a new, properly installed sway bar. Thank you to JD Sanders RV in Alachua, Florida!

From this experience, I learned that it is best to double-check everything, not trust that even a well-reputed dealership has done everything correctly. Just because someone has more experience does not mean they cannot make errors. Ultimately, I'm responsible for my equipment and traveling safely.

The following month, I faced another challenge involving the same hitch. I'd just left the Foley RV Center and Airstream dealership in Gulfport, Mississippi, after they fixed a minor issue with my rear bumper.

I was driving slowly up the entrance ramp to a highway when something just didn't feel right. I spotted an area to pull over about twenty feet ahead. Just as I glanced in my rearview mirror, I heard a horrendous screeching sound. My Airstream wasn't where it should be, but was dragging a few feet behind. I deployed the brakes on the truck and trailer and pulled over at the place on the entrance ramp where there was room for my rig and put on the hazard lights. Fortunately, no one was following me closely.

To my surprise, I saw that my hitch had detached from the receiver. My Airstream perched precariously on the shank of the hitch. That long shank now rested on the concrete and accounted for the screeching noise as well as a curved white gouge in the ramp. One of the chains still held the Airstream close enough that the automatic emergency brake cable was still attached and had not deployed. The other chain lay on the ground. The pin for the hitch and the weight distribution bars were gone.

Amazingly, Alvie was not damaged and no one had run into us on the ramp. From the side of the exit ramp, I called Foley RV in a panic. I simply could not believe my hitch had fallen out (and was both shaken and very relieved that it fell out before I merged onto the highway!). A very concerned mechanic immediately came to pick up my Airstream and tow it back to Foley RV with his truck. He thought that the hitch pin must have broken, but neither one of us could find it along the road. We did retrieve one of the two weight distribution bars which had fallen off a block or so before I pulled over. The other had vanished. At least the newly repaired anti-sway bar with its six bolts remained in place.

Trying to figure out what had happened and decide whether to repair or replace the hitch, I called the Airstream dealership in Florida that had installed it when I purchased Alvie. I had a key lock on the hitch pin purchased from the dealership and had never removed the heavy hitch from the receiver. The service managers in Florida and in Mississippi thought it very unlikely that the pin had simply failed. With forty years of combined experience between them, they'd never had a pin just break.

Without the pin, the original dealership couldn't do anything for me warranty-wise and suggested that what had happened was that somebody somewhere had attempted to remove the hitch pin and steal the hitch. The truck had been hitched up to the trailer all of the previous day and during my one-night stay at a nice RV park in Louisiana. I'd stopped twice for gas, once in Texas and once in Louisiana, and enjoyed a short rest break from driving the previous day, but nothing had looked wrong with the hitch when I glanced at it before resuming my trip.

The morning the hitch fell off I'd driven over an hour on the highway to get to the Mississippi dealership for my minor bumper repair. I'd inspected the hitch and my setup as part of my normal checklist that morning, but my checklist then did not include handling the hitch pin itself to be sure it was secure. The truck and trailer were never unhitched at Foley RV and were only left unattended near the entrance to the dealership for fifteen minutes.

Perhaps someone had tampered with the hitch pin at some point and weakened it, perhaps it broke, or perhaps someone had managed to remove it outside the dealership despite the obvious difficulty of stealing the hitch when it was attached to the trailer.

In any event, it was a blessing that the hitch departed from the receiver in a way that did not harm anyone or anything except the hitch itself. I appreciated Foley RV's very prompt assistance and expertise that let me get back on the road the same day.

I ended up purchasing a new hitch with a key-locked hitch pin. No problems so far, but I did get a lot of helpful advice from fellow Airstreamers. In particular, I added to my safety routine. After the pre-towing inspection I always do, I now re-inspect my rig as soon as I've towed a very short distance. I also test the hitch pin itself to be sure it remains locked and secure.

The most important part of my safety routine remains recognizing that I am not in control of everything. I bless my Airstream and ask my guardian angel and the Archangel Saint Michael for protection before every trip. More than once, divine intervention has rescued me from danger while traveling. More common than something dramatic, however, are the little inconveniences that come with living on the road.

## Mechanical

A reality of full-time life on the road is repairs. Towing a trailer subjects it to forces not unlike an earthquake. Even a well-made trailer treated gently will need work.

As I enjoyed my campsite in Montana last July, I noticed a drip under my Airstream. A leak in a travel trailer is bad news. It requires immediate action to avoid far more extensive damage.

Water was slowly collecting on the ground under the pipe leading from my black tank to my dump valves. Quickly, I grabbed gloves and a paper towel to see what was leaking. Thankfully, it was not black water. A trickle of fresh water was running along the outside of the black pipe where it exited the belly pan. As water will, it traveled to the lowest point and dripped onto the ground.

Thus began the search for the source.

I explored all the areas of my nineteen-foot Airstream, inside and out, where there were pipes or water connections. It wasn't wet under the front dinette seat where the fresh-water tank and water pump live. Nor did I see any water on the floor anywhere or see anything wet under the kitchen sink. There was no water around the shower or the toilet.

However, behind and under the lavatory sink, I discovered a scant trickle of water slowly running down the interior wall of the Airstream. Drops were forming along the screws that held the connection for the thin white pipe emerging from the top hole between the inner and outer shells of the Airstream. The water ran down the wall, along the pipe, and followed the pipe back into the bottom hole between the shells. From there, the sneaky water somehow found an exit point along the exterior of the black pipe from the toilet. I dried the moisture under the sink, and left a microfiber towel wrapped along the pipe to catch any new trickles.

It had been raining, so I thought it might be a leak on the roof. I looked and didn't see any obviously deteriorated caulk. So I unhooked my outside fresh-water hose from the Airstream.

The dripping stopped.

Rejoicing that I could just fill up my fresh-water tank and use the interior water pump, I relaxed with a shower. Unfortunately, the leak in my Airstream started again, soaking my trusty microfiber towel under the sink. After I dried the area and replaced the towel, I turned off the water pump. I filled up some pots and bowls with filtered water from my site's outside faucet. Then began a few days of experimentation.

I used the sinks but not the faucets. For washing up or cleaning dishes, I heated water from outside on my stove then rinsed with cold water in bowls. I let the used water run down the drains. The leak did not return. I decided to turn the water pump back on, but not use the faucets.

Thankfully, no new trickles appeared when I turned on the pump. Encouraged, I flushed my toilet several times and was delighted to see the leak did not return. However, as soon as I tried the lavatory faucet, drops of water appeared. The same thing happened when I tried the sink faucet. The connections I could reach seemed tight. It was time to call for help.

Due to the COVID-19 shutdowns, I couldn't find a dealer anywhere within a several-hour drive taking service appointments. I called the Airstream factory and explained the situation. Fortunately, they were able to fit me in fairly soon to take care of the leak under warranty. So Alvie the Airstream and I hit the road again back to Jackson Center, Ohio.

Meanwhile, I bathed, washed, and cleaned like a true pioneer woman (or, at least, a Girl Scout). I lugged my water from outside in pots and pans and heated it on the stove. This worked for washing me and washing dishes, but I remained eager to get the leak fixed. If I hadn't been social distancing, I'm sure my neighbors would have been eager for me to get a real shower too.

Plans often change on the road and in life. A leak in my Airstream is not what I had expected. But responding with cheerfulness and asking for the grace to do God's will in all things makes unanticipated events easier to accept.

After all, perhaps there was someone in Ohio I was meant to encounter. Or it might have just been a way to get me back East for some other plan of which I was unaware.

For unrelated reasons, my youngest daughter ended up traveling to Virginia with Penny in May. I decided to detour after my repair appointment in Ohio to see her and reclaim my dog. Otherwise, I wouldn't have been able to pick up my furry copilot until much later in the year.

It turned out to be a timely decision.

## Physical

Since I was coming back East for Airstream repairs, I decided to take care of all my personal maintenance tasks at the same time. I was about due for a routine mammogram, needed my annual physical, and had some dental work I'd put off. Like many nomads who return to their original home for such appointments, I scheduled all my checkups with the doctors I'd used for years where I used to live in Virginia. My daughter and Penny were in the area, so I could visit them as well.

I was surprised when my doctor called to tell me that my screening mammogram had a suspicious area. At her insistence, I followed up with a diagnostic mammogram that revealed many "microcalcifications." These innocuous-appearing swarms of white dots on the mammogram film could not be detected by a manual exam. I didn't feel any abnormalities, nor had my doctor during my annual checkup. Further investigation was needed to determine if any of these might indicate cancer.

Following my doctor's recommendation, I scheduled a core biopsy. I managed to fit in a quick trip to Alumalina, an annual Airstream rally in North Carolina, before the biopsy.

I was hopeful the biopsy would prove negative. The procedure itself was very challenging. I climbed onto a table facedown with holes through which the doctor worked. Despite a local anesthetic, I felt like a giant sucking insect had stabbed me when the doctor inserted the hollow needles used to extract tissue. Afterward, it was like getting the worst mammogram ever, because my punctured breast had to be squeezed to stop any bleeding. That seemed to last forever, but I remembered to make good use of the experience by offering my pain for others in need of healing. All prayer requests received from friends or on my blog got a lot of attention that day.

Once I received the biopsy results, I canceled my plans for the rest of the winter. I had very early breast cancer. It was DCIS, or ductal carcinoma in situ, which thankfully could be treated with a limited surgery called a lumpectomy, followed by radiation and medication. It was not advisable to delay this, so I reluctantly gave up my six weeks of hard-won reservations in the Florida Keys.

If I had to have cancer, this was a very treatable kind. Catching it so early was a blessing. At my first meeting with my surgeon, we prayed together. It had been years since I'd had general anesthesia for anything, so I updated my will and healthcare directives just in case. My pastor visited and gave me the sacrament of anointing of the sick. This brought me great peace.

Many friends supported me during this period, with prayers and frozen meals dropped off for me to have when I returned from the operation. My friend Coleen even got up at a crazy early hour to drive me to surgery. My daughter was very patient with me and took care of the apartment and our dog Penny.

As I waited in pre-op, I prayed for those around me. My doctor described the surgical game plan in detail. He prayed with me again and let me keep my Rosary in my hand as they wheeled my bed down the corridor to the operating room.

It turned out that the lab results after surgery indicated that the DCIS was a very aggressive grade that likely would have spread if left untreated. In fact, I had a small "microinvasion" that warranted another surgery to check my sentinel lymph nodes, the part of the lymph circulatory system where breast cancer would travel to invade other areas. I pictured small British guards with big hats marching up and down a rope bridge.

I was so sure that I would not need more surgery that I was angry and upset at first when I learned I had to have the second procedure. It took Confession and a second anointing of the sick for me to surrender my fears to God and trust that whatever the result, He would be there with me.

Thankfully, no further invasions were found in the lymph nodes. My prognosis is excellent.

Having cancer meant I needed to put my beloved Airstream Alvie in storage for the first time. I paid a wonderful RV mechanic to prepare Alvie for winter weather storage. He drained and disconnected the water pump, emptied the tanks and pipes, and added nontoxic bright pink RV antifreeze where needed. Through a connection with a camping friend, I found a storage site close to where I'd temporarily be living, so I could occasionally check on Alvie. The timing worked out perfectly. I contacted the mechanic just in time to get the winterizing done before he was scheduled to be out of town for a while. After the appointment, I towed my Airstream directly to my newly acquired storage spot well before my surgery.

Also, my daughter and I were able to rent an apartment together for the duration of my treatment. It felt so strange even temporarily to move into a home without wheels and surrounded by other buildings and constant traffic. I felt confined and at the same time there was so much space.

I chafed at being fatigued and needing to nap once in a while, as well as having to be extra-vigilant about limiting my exposure to anyone who might be ill. Yet this period turned out to be amazingly fruitful.

For one thing, I'd been trying unsuccessfully to make progress on the manuscript that eventually would become this book. A friend of mine whom I'd visited since being in the area mentioned that she thought I'd benefit from a Bestseller Mastermind writing class she was taking for aspiring first-time authors, so I signed up.

Being still also left me with time to study and read and to reset again on my spiritual life. I'd drifted back into the bad habits of getting annoyed when things didn't go the way I planned and taking on too much. It also gave me a chance to reconnect with old friends in person and to spend valuable time with my daughter.

Writing about my journeys as a Tin Can Pilgrim let me uncover and internalize some of the lessons from life on the road these past several years. I needed reminders myself of the importance of slowing down, spending time with people—by phone and Skype at least—and focusing on others' needs rather than complaining about my situation.

And the writing class I took literally taught me how to go from a concept to what you are reading now.

THE BADLANDS, SD

## CHAPTER TWENTY-SEVEN

# SIGNPOSTS ON THE JOURNEY PART THREE

*"God made the world round so we would never be able to see too far down the road."*
—Isak Dinesen

Life on the road has been a lesson in humility and the need for radical trust in the Lord. Many opportunities to start over have come into my life. I would again slowly fall into the temptation to plan everything to the smallest detail and become too attached to my scheduled plans, rather than checking in with God. When unexpected dangers or joys upended my carefully constructed tower, I had to adapt and learn new languages.

Disasters and inconveniences became points of light in that they brought me back to His embrace in a deeper way. Instead of being the good Samaritan, I learned that sometimes I am the traveler who lies wounded in the road, dependent upon the kindness of strangers.

Community became a theme and a light to me. This wasn't just about Lynda traveling solo (with a small fluffy companion sometimes) and spreading light in multiple short stops; it was about building connections to others in relationships over time.

For further reflection and guidance, here are the signposts glimpsed as we wound through mountainous roads and deserts together:

 Do you attach your value to what you do and accomplish? Do you worry about the approval of others? Remember that God approves of you and loves you. When you have Him, you have everything. All things are small things in the end, except for the love we share in Him, with Him, and through Him with others.

 What do you cling to that may be an obstacle to you being truly free?

 What is scarce in your life? Do you appreciate it more? What is scarce in the lives of others that you can share with them?

 Think of a time when someone planted a seed in your mind or heart. How has it borne fruit? What seeds have you planted? What seeds would you like to plant? Ask God for help in discerning this in terms of the goal and how to accomplish it with Him, for Him.

 Reflect about the most difficult times in your life, when you or someone you loved experienced breakdowns, loss, or accidents. How did you respond? What came out of it? Upon reflection, what can you take away from the experience and use positively? Have you encountered someone needing support in a situation like you faced?

What communities are you part of? How do you help others and how have they helped you? At times when you feel sad or lost, reaching out to others, putting love where there seems to be none, helps love grow in you.

 How do you know when you need rest? What is the red zone on your fuel gauge? How can you form the habit of fueling up at a quarter or half tank, before it becomes urgent?

 What nourishes you, physically, mentally, and spiritually? Sit awhile in the presence of God. He's always there, waiting for you, so feel free to invite Him specifically to visit with you for a bit. Ask Him what nourishment He wants to provide for you. How can you receive His gifts?

 Set your alarm for ten minutes (you can gradually increase the time) and be alone to rest in the presence of God. Meditate on an image of safety and security. That could be floating in warm water knowing you are in the palm of God's hand, or perhaps being a small child asleep with the utter abandonment of small children, resting in His arms. Try this for thirty days. Keep a journal of your thoughts and what you experience. At the end of thirty days, read it. I'll be praying for you that you will find the inspiration He provides in love, to continue this practice daily, to grow ever more in relationship with Him.

## SPIRITUAL CHILDHOOD
*by Lynda Rozell ©2021*

After that crazy, intense, falling in love time of life
When it is quiet and peaceful,
It is easy to take you for granted, to crowd you out with things that I must do,
with events that seem important
Let me see what is important through your eyes, not mine.
I drift away, careless child wandering down the shore building sand castles
only to cry when they collapse.
Running after the glitter of bright shells,
translucent pale yellow and orange catching the sun, or so it seems . . .
Yet I ignore the sun burning me or the waves that creep under my feet
sucking away the sand with an inhalation then spitting me out
Falling back into your arms, you scoop me up, dry my tears,
brush away the sand, heal the stings.

I rest wrapped in a towel, in your strong arms, my head on your
shoulder under the umbrella.
And, there's ice cream, cool and sweet,
turning my sticky tears into sticky hands that you cover with kisses.
I rest in you, lulled by the waves and breezes,
the cries of gulls and sounds of children playing,
as I gaze enraptured at the whorls of a shell you placed in my grubby hands.
There, within the endless concentric swirls of peach and cream hidden
under the rough knobbled surface, I stay silent
until my tired eyes close and I dream secure in your love

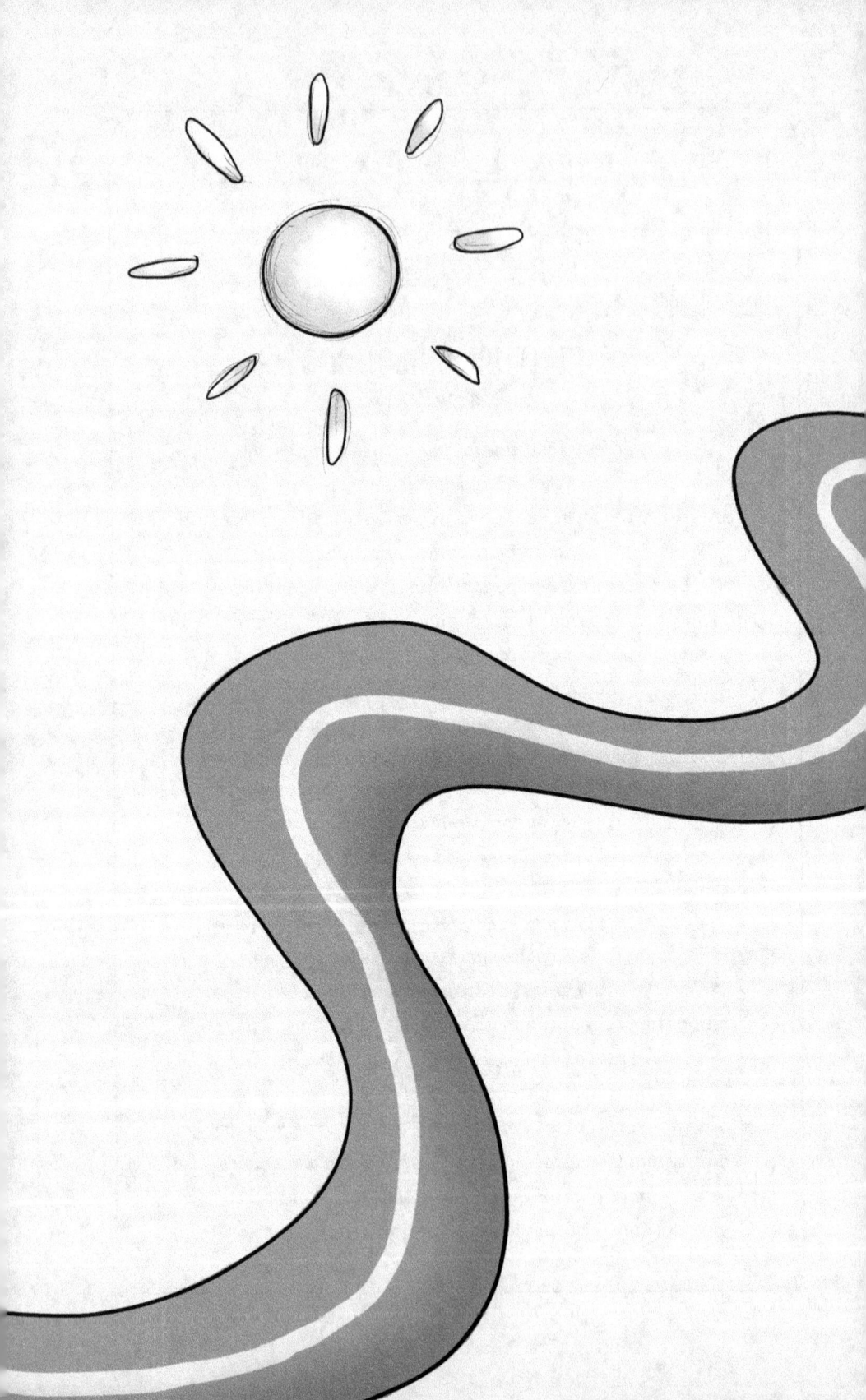

## Part Four

# RENEWAL ON THE ROAD

CHAPTER TWENTY-EIGHT

# CREATIVITY

*"For from the greatness and the beauty of created things
their original author, by analogy, is seen."*

—Wisdom 13:5

*"Ever since the creation of the world, his invisible attributes
of eternal power and divinity have been able to be understood
and perceived in what he has made."*

—Romans 1:20

## Creation Reveals the Creator

In Chimayo, New Mexico, there's a series of seven crosses outdoors along a bubbling creek. Rough blocks of reddish stone fit together in uneven pieces to compose each one. On either side of the cross, a stone arch leaps up from the earth, curves over the top, and flows back down to the ground, touching the ends of the arms. In the center of each cross a pale bas-relief sculpture on a round clay medallion depicts one of the days of Creation.

In the first medallion, light depicted by the pointed rays of a round sun on one side contrasts with the dark represented by textured dimples on the other side of the divide. One ray of light pierces over the barrier into the dark. Other medallions depict the division of the sky and the waters, as well as the creation of birds and animals. The sixth cross features an image of a Native American Adam and Eve gazing at each other and holding hands in the middle of leafy shrubs shielding them from the viewer. The final circular plaque contains only the words "And on the seventh day God ended His work and He rested."

This depiction of Creation within the beauty of the desert hills, expressed in rough stone and smooth clay, stayed with me as I drove away. I reflected on the creativity that seems to well up out of a life close to nature, and from my journey and those of other nomads.

As I travel, I discover again and again how the glorious beauty surrounding us in nature nourishes individual creativity in those who roam. In one of the most realistic scenes in the movie *Nomadland*, Fern offers a potholder she made to another camper at a swap meet. "Did you crochet that?" he asks.

"No, it's something else," she replies.

That insightful moment illustrates how those on the road, surrounded by God's creation, start to discover their own creativity. Being exposed to beauty triggers a desire to recreate it in a whole range of ways. This may include weaving potholders or penning poetry.

My friend Mary began drawing after she started living full-time in her sixteen-foot Airstream. She's now an accomplished watercolorist and sketches masterfully with pencils and pastels. She gifted me a lovely drawing based on a roseate spoonbill bird I photographed while kayaking in Florida. Mary chronicles her creative experimentation and growth on her social media feeds, encouraging others by her example.

I've also received gifts of art from Suzanne, whom I met in an Everglades campground. She paints on shells to make ornaments and wind chimes. Others decorate rocks and hide them at campgrounds. Nearly every rally has an arts-and-crafts and "garage sale" swap meet where artists both amateur and professional can be found.

The spurt of creativity that comes from being surrounded by natural beauty occurs even when not camping. My friend Karen, whose yard on the Chesapeake Bay faces out into an ever-changing panoply of water and sky, has been transformed by that beauty. Her prayer room faces out to the water, and the sense of peace there is palpable. Karen cans and bakes, and recently took up knitting. My birthday gift to her was a basket full of soft colorful yarn and knitting needles that she could use in her new hobby. Thus, the joy of created beauty can be shared by encouraging others to create.

Creative art and writing help connect us to other people and heal wounds. In fact, there's a whole therapeutic industry around helping people who are injured mentally, spiritually, or physically express themselves through music and art. Creativity provides a language and a lens that can focus and reflect on silent realizations. Art treats wounds by opening them up to sunlight. God softly drifts in through those openings, even to those resistant or fearful of discovering the joy of being loved.

Moreover, we are most human when we are most like our Creator. Creativity can't help but bring us closer to Him. We manipulate our environment to create something new from what already exists. Yet there is a big gap between us as images of God and the God who creates out of the void. The big bang theory postulates that everything came from a violent explosion of a super seed. It doesn't tell us where the seed came from.

All of Creation testifies to the glory of God. We can see Him in what He has made. Without exception, everyone I've met who lives full-time on the road perceives the beauty that surrounds them. It is one of the perks that lead people to choose this life and remain in it.

Unlike the animals, we are made to see beauty, to contemplate and enjoy it, and to participate in its creation. Through our intellect, we also can appreciate the inherent order and harmony of the physical laws of nature, expressing them through mathematical formulae. How would such order arise from a random, violent beginning?

Human consciousness also suggests we are not governed merely by an instinct for survival. The appreciation of beauty is written into the fabric of our beings, because we are created in the image of God who found what He created to be good or, in the case of humanity, very good. Similarly, a fundamental sense of right and wrong is intuitive, not merely taught.

Nonetheless, we don't always recognize God's hand in Creation or connect the beauty of a stirring sunrise or moonlight on waves to the greater beauty that lies within and above it. In this lifetime, at least, we cannot definitively see God in the way we see a snowflake or a mountain. Yet the breadth and majesty, the delicacy and intricacy of His Work can be seen everywhere. They speak to us of the Creator in the depths of our beings. It is up to us by the exercise of our free will to respond to the clues in our environment, by accepting the evidence of our senses as sufficient to convince us. God does not force us to believe in Him. He leaves us free to experience uncertainty. Otherwise, He would be forcing us to see Him and love Him. Love coerced is not love.

The beauty of Creation that calls to our hearts is the visible portion of God's outstretched arms inviting us to be embraced. God's fingerprints in our world are most striking in some of the places I've traveled.

## Through the Badlands

Pastel-striped buttes and fantastic shapes rise out of the plains in the Badlands. As I pass through South Dakota, I head for an overnight stop near Badlands National Park. Like nothing I've ever seen before, jumbled boulders with sharp edges make abstract art of a canyon. Rock formations evocative of those in underground caves rise like iced cakes.

As I drive, I praise God and thank Him for this unusual and terrible beauty. Winding bumpy roads lead me to drive very slowly, with a parade of others behind me. Tired, I head for my campsite to unhitch.

After making sure my rig is cool enough, I drink a lot of water and venture out in the ninety-seven-degree blazing sun. A stiff breeze pushes around the heat. It feels like being hit with a spray of hot air from a giant blow dryer.

I soak in the small details within the vast landscape. Round purple thistles in bursts of spiny thickets catch my eye. Swaths of rippling grass appear in the sunlight as if topped with shiny spun-glass filaments. Even a startled hare reminds me how life clings and blooms in all its varieties in what appears to be barren land.

When I stop to drink water, I listen to the silence marked by birdcalls and whispering grass. Other hikers that I spot seem to share the sense of hushed reverence and keep silent themselves. Waves of heat shimmer, like we walk within a mirage that could vanish at any moment. Instead, we stay in existence in the mind of God. It is places like the Badlands with their strange majesty that come close to revealing the Creator's fingerprints.

## What Lies Beneath

These fingerprints are found in many locations. In a place practically the opposite of the Badlands, I found them deep within the earth. There, in the absence of light, darkness has no color. I cannot see my hand in front of my face.

Water distantly drips, faintly echoing as I strain my ears to hear. The air is cold and my heart slowly beats. The soft breathing of me and my companions mingles with the sound of water. The air smells clean, with a sharp, bitter tang like salt.

I am not afraid, because I know God is present. For ten minutes we sit silently in the cool darkness. My eyes do not adjust because there is no light at all.

Then, our guide turns on her lantern. Twelve of us appear within a circle of dim light in the Lower Cave at Carlsbad Caverns National Park. Gradually we switch our headlamps on and smile at one another. For several moments, we remain sitting on the cool, slick rocks. We acclimate to light, like divers rising slowly through deep seas. Then we laugh and talk nervously, happy to be back in the world.

Far underground, we see "popcorn" made of stone contrasting with fantastic threads of frozen liquid that shimmer in the glow from our headlamps. Slowly, we pass through narrow crevices in stone walls and scramble over blocks of fallen rock to view the marvels surrounding us. A cavern filled with pools of water opens before us. Small bridges wind crookedly through the glistening still water. Occasional drops from the darkness above create ripples when they fall into the pools.

Little round pebbles or cave pearls lie scattered about as if dropped by a careless jeweler. Graceful molded spikes that hang down from the unseen ceiling and stretch up from the floor touch to form columns. Draperies of stone ripple like silk or the fronds of kelp forests in oceans. Translucent panels of amber-and-cream rock mimic curtains. Huge broken blocks of stone from a long-ago ceiling collapse bring home just how much rock separates our small selves from the surface.

The caves' intricate ornamentation and vast open areas remind me of stone carvings in obscure niches of great Gothic cathedrals. In these man-made cathedrals rising aboveground to the sky, artisans labored to create beauty in areas visible only from above. In the underground cathedral of Carlsbad Caverns, beauty emerged in the depths carved by unseen hands. Thousands of years ago, sulfuric acid hollowed out limestone to form a network of tunnels and caverns. Erosion and surface collapse opened entrances to the outside. Over eons, water sculpted minerals into art invisible to human eyes until recently.

Surprised by the glorious varieties of beauty below, I thanked God for His love that created delights not seen until we labored through darkness to find them. Like the beauty of a snowflake, or cell structure revealed by microscope, these remarkable formations unfolded long before anyone could appreciate them.

## Inspiring Our Creativity

Those who live full-time on the road frequently see and share such marvels. Gorgeous sunsets, striking waves, and winding roads amid snowcapped mountains punctuate their days. Nomads often post online pictures of the beauty they encounter. This beauty in turn seems to inspire creativity in those who live closest to it. Is it possible that by focusing on the essential, by downsizing, we regain something we forgot when we settled in cities, in towns, and in jobs that limit our creativity? Does living close to nature and the land nourish our right brains?

Certainly, my experience of life as a nomad sparked my interest in creative writing and photography. I've learned to slow down and look, to gaze at and absorb what I see, then to incorporate it consciously into my outlook. Nature and religious sites inspire me now to create pen-and-ink sketches and colored pencil drawings that I post in my e-newsletter and on Patreon and give to friends. A coloring book is in the works for next year.

As I travel, sometimes songs or poems suddenly bloom in my mind. Since becoming a Tin Can Pilgrim, art itself as a religious experience helps me see past the outlines of reality to its essence.

For example, once while driving north in Montana, I experienced a coalescing of the loveliness of the scenery with praise for its Creator. It was a conversation within my heart with Him, a dialogue of love with my God, overflowing onto paper when I pulled over along the side of the road. Encouraged by this love, I've learned to make myself vulnerable by sharing my creations with others. In that spirit, here is the poem:

### *A Gentle Conversation on the Road*

*As I drive the winding, climbing,*
*descending roads in Montana,*
*I see marvels unfold at every turn at every curve*
*Faraway plains and mountains*
*Trees sheltering rippling streams*
*A piercing bolt of purple flowers*
*swaying in the breeze*
*Vast golden fields of yellow blooms*
*Swaths of deep green fir trees like dark ribbons adorning*

the bronze-tipped grass hills
I love you, He says to me
Each delight I would have made just for you
As I died for you and would have done if you were
the only one I created

His love is so generous and expansive
Like a mother who loves each of her children
There is no limit on that love
The more children the more love

He sees us each
He is fascinated
with the smallest details of our days,
our humble sweet gifts clumsily made that we bring
to Him delight Him,
as the scribbles of a small child delight his parents who
hang art on the refrigerator door

Here, my Beloved God, is my poem,
my photo, my prose,
my feeble but heartfelt praise,
my return to You in small measure of what
You give in great abundance

Can I give you this, my friend, my sister, my daughter,
my fellow traveler?
Can I share this sense of His delight,
of utter abandonment in love?
Each bit of beauty is a caress, a kiss,
an embrace by the white clouds,
by the snow sleeping on the mountains,
even by the shadows

*as swiftly moving clouds play hide-and-seek
with the sun beams on the hills*

*He gives this to me—I praise Him and adore Him and bless
Him in thankfulness and amazement.
I wish to share it with you,
but I am the recipient not the Giver.*

*Can I help you open your heart to His ever-present, glorious,
all-encompassing Love?
Like another dimension, present but unseen, we see it
within our eyes, our hands reaching
our bodies breathing in deeply the scent of roses and pine
on the wind, listening to the silence.*

*Only He can give this to you and He does.
Receive it, dear ones, because you are dear to Him.
In knowing Him, loving Him, we know and love ourselves
and others and all He has created.*

## My Small Apostolate

The unnecessary beauty of creation calls to our hearts and invites us into its peace to listen. What is God, the Creator, the Universe saying to you? Ask Him. Look for answers in stillness and the silence of your heart. Like many others, I find that conversation or prayer in nature. It is there—and in front of the Blessed Sacrament in church—that God speaks most clearly to me. Or perhaps that is where I listen most attentively.

I try to make God known in the ways He invites people to a closer relationship, particularly as expressed in nature and through religious sites. I do this in a variety of ways, from volunteering, demonstration or witness, accompaniment or presence, all of which plant seeds. I may not recognize those seeds or see the fruit that comes from them. I trust that God will help me say or do what He intends for love of others and to invite them to His embrace. Whether you are a nomad now or just restless in your present life, He invites all wanderers to get to know Him.

We are all on a journey, a pilgrimage, with purpose, even if we don't perceive the whole. God has all of this—the pandemic, unemployment, suffering, and joy—in His plans. We just don't know those plans. He doesn't create suffering, but He turns it to good. The frustration of not understanding through reason is transcended by trust in faith. If you are not religious or spiritual, this may seem trite and circular. Yet what will satisfy your search for answers, your unspoken yearning for happiness?

Like physics to a caveman trying to comprehend the unseen, religion to the modern person may seem like magic, incomprehensible, contrary to science and logic. Science and religion, however, are not at odds—God created the rules of science, the laws of nature, the structure of the universe. Scientific inquiry itself requires hypotheses and leaps of faith.

Still, faith transcends what we can observe with our physical senses. Faith tells us that God loves us, that His plans for us are good, and that we are free to participate in them, to choose good. We are not slaves, nor is our fate predetermined. He seeks us out as friends, brothers and sisters, children and spouses, not as possessions but as gifts we choose to make of ourselves to Him, as He has given Himself to us.

That is why I think of my mission as an apostolate of friendship and relationship. Trust, common experiences, time spent together are what lead us to friendship. In turn, that relationship gives us more authority to speak about God. When a friend knows we care about them and love them, that friend is more likely to accept that we want what is good for them and that we want to share the good we know. Basically, I'm networking and introducing them to my best friend, God.

Part of friendship is getting to know the other person. That applies as well to my relationship with God. I spend time with Him, talking to Him through prayer, listening for His quiet voice. When you are in love, you want to know everything about the person you love. And when you are a friend, you want to know what your friend likes, understand your friend's life experiences, and be there in times of celebration as well as times of sadness. Well, God is just like that, as both friend and lover!

Reading through Scripture, and other spiritual reading, spending time in prayer, glancing at Him and thanking Him throughout the day—all of these deepen our friendship. Before I do work, I offer it to Him, whether I'm writing or scrubbing a bathroom. When I am delighted by marvelous vistas or small flowers, I share that joy with Him. Alpacas and frogs remind me He has a sense of humor, and so do the ways my plans are constantly upended. Part of my journey through life and especially as a Tin Can Pilgrim is learning to let go and trust Him, to truly believe that all things work for good, because He sees everything and He loves us wildly, passionately, and dearly, as if we were each the only person in the universe.

What I've learned in my life journey and on the road is a simple insight. God wants us to be who He created us to be, to find our true identity. My adventure is not unique to me. He invites us all to joy, by learning to trust Him, detaching from what separates us from happiness, and finding peace in that process. We find Him and enter into His joy in the present, in the small, ordinary moments of everyday life, whether that life is in a travel trailer or in any other setting.

CHAPTER TWENTY-NINE

# BECOMING YOUR TRUE SELF

*"We are God's children now; what we shall be has not yet been revealed. We know that when it is revealed we shall be like Him, for we shall see Him as He is."*

—1 John 3:2–3

## Trust

The fruits of my journey in life and as a Tin Can Pilgrim are trust, detachment, peace, and joy as I discover my true self. My fundamental identity is as a daughter of God. I am beloved. When I recognize that, I allow myself to receive love from God and through others. I also learn how to give love. The person God made me to be when He first thought of me is the one who follows Him, who wants to receive all His gifts, and use them for His glory and for His will.

That's a pretty big leap from my past self, who wasn't even sure there was a God. From childhood to life as a high-powered antitrust lawyer, to the loss of prestige and relationships, through my darkest days of depression, the challenges I faced in life led me to know Him. Taking the first step in recognizing His still small voice, to going deeper and trying to follow it until I found Him, was the first stage in my journey. Later difficulties further revealed Him as my source of strength and the one who truly loved me, whom I could trust fully. When you start to see His divine fingerprints, eventually you will want to grasp His hand, drawing you into a fully realized present. Trust is the key.

He kept calling me to trust Him, first by catching my eye with the silver Airstreams on the way to Richmond, then in exchanging my logical timetable for the one He wanted. I kept trying to put Him in boxes, to define my plans without Him, and again got caught up in a timetable I created. I drifted away from regular listening in prayer. Instead of putting what He wanted first, even if I didn't understand it, I created artificial deadlines with too much travel in too short a period of time. My self-created pressures led me into dangerous situations, like traveling without understanding the impact of sudden bursts of wind, or having to back out from a coffee shop I could not drive around. Still, at every moment, when I made a mistake, He helped me get up again.

You peel the layers away gradually when you are uncovering your real self. The most ordinary things become a conversation with God, a prayer, words of love whispered, exclamations of wonder and thanksgiving, a sacrifice offered in love.

It's like putting on eyeglasses for the first time in second grade when I didn't know before then that I needed them to see. The world became richer, amazing in detail previously unperceived. The leaves on trees, the veins on each leaf, leapt out of the cartoon trees I'd seen before. The strands of my mother's hair, the shades of color in her green-gray eyes, let me see her as a new person. A remarkable diversity of color and shapes emerged from what I'd thought with uncorrected vision was a smear of brown field.

Your inheritance as a son or daughter of God is to recognize what is beautiful, true, and good and to be free to choose it. You are made for Him as we all are, in all our marvelous diversity and differences. We will rejoice with Him in eternity, in joy we can only imagine on this side of the curtain. At your core, you are completely free and whole. The wounds of life, the scar tissue that constricts your free movement, do not define your true self. You can choose to love where there seems to be no love and to receive the love He gives you.

In my past life, I lived as a slave to fear. I sought others' approval and affection. My attachments to things and activities that offered a semblance of happiness were actually an obstacle to joy. I let a mere shadow of reality obscure what was true. But God never gives up on any of His children.

Life on the road has clarified what I was already coming to know: God approves of me and loves me. When I fall, He always picks me up. It is my job to turn to Him in the exercise of my freedom, even though my knowledge may be limited. I choose to follow my heart, trusting Him in a world where many other things are distracting and appealing, but ultimately not trustworthy.

Faith leaves the past behind and draws the future into the present moment. Worrying draws a false, negative future into the present, obscuring your view. When you worry, you think you have to do everything yourself. When you trust God, you bring Him into your present and live with Him there. You realize that His role is the primary one. You will more clearly see His hand in the past, find Him in the present, and have hope in His comfort and peace in the future.

God is a good person, the best. Trust Him. Don't let words and circumstances get in the way of trusting and believing in Him and humbly asking for His help. He always answers prayers, just not always in the way we plan.

Discerning His will for you in one sense is simple: He wills your happiness. In another sense, finding the road to that goal takes time and a willingness to surrender to His will in little steps along the way. Seeing the Airstreams glowing silver on the side of the road was a bit of a "Saint Paul on the road to Damascus" moment, but the real purpose God had for me took longer to discern. He asked me to trust Him without understanding it all fully, but encouraged me to seek to follow His path for me, as it gradually unfolded. He called me to follow Him, to be docile to His will, to search for it using my mind and the skills He gave me, while trusting that if I made a mistake, He would still turn it to good, so long as my intention was to do what He wanted.

    The beauty of nature revealed in my travels and the communities I found on the road also led me to a deeper knowledge of Him, in seeing His hand in all things, both marvelous and difficult. A wise man once noted that we, with our earthly vision, always see the reverse side of the tapestry, the one with the knots, not the beautiful creation woven by God on the other side. When we are mired in the tangles and crossed threads, we fail to realize that happiness comes later. In reality, we don't need to figure out what the other side of the tapestry looks like or how it is being woven, but just to trust that God who loves us is weaving something beautiful from all the knots. A poem popularized by Corrie ten Boom, author of *The Hiding Place,* put it best:

> *My Life is but a weaving*
> *between my Lord and me;*
> *I cannot choose the colors*
> *He worketh steadily.*
>
> *Oft times He weaveth sorrow*
> *And I, in foolish pride,*
> *Forget He sees the upper,*
> *And I the under side.*
>
> *Not til the loom is silent*
> *And the shuttles cease to fly,*
> *Shall God unroll the canvas*
> *And explain the reason why.*
>
> *The dark threads are as needful*
> *In the Weaver's skillful hand,*
> *As the threads of gold and silver*
> *In the pattern He has planned.*

*He knows, He loves, He cares,*
*Nothing this truth can dim.*
*He gives His very best to those*
*Who leave the choice with Him.*

## Detachment

Trust leads to detachment as we start to realize that our happiness is not something we must create for ourselves. From my initial downsizing and move into an Airstream, to losses experienced as I traveled, to being grounded for medical treatment, every step of my journey brought greater trust and more detachment.

To paraphrase Saint Augustine, we have a restless longing that wealth and power cannot satisfy. This is the longing for God that only He satisfies. Former lives, even memories or mourning for lost things and talents, can bog us down and get in the way of loving where we are now. In the Old Testament, the Israelites wandering in the desert after being led out of slavery in Egypt missed the cucumbers and onions they had enjoyed in their past lives. They clung to the memories of the past and security, not appreciating their new freedom or the God who provided it. Like the Israelites, we often struggle with leaving our onions behind. We get lost in the desert looking backwards, rather than discovering the incredible peace and joy to be found in the present moment.

Detachment from our faults is really what is at stake. I struggle with my own pride. Like the disciples James and John, who sought the places of honor at Jesus's right and left, I seek my own desires and self-aggrandizement at times. I make conversations about me, rather than ask enough questions about other people.

In this process of detachment, just like backing a travel trailer into a tight spot, you must start over and over again. Be at peace in this process, because God is infinitely patient and forgiving. He's not one of the old men watching at the campsite who might laugh at or applaud your efforts. His support and acceptance are unconditional, and you don't have to entertain Him. All He wants for us is that we accept the love He offers and give it back to Him and to others.

Detachment is not simply downsizing from possessions and letting go of a desire for approval. My journey as a Tin Can Pilgrim teaches me that I need to detach from what I do. In eagerly seeking to follow the promptings of the Holy Spirit, I can overdo things, running from activity to activity, from place to place, equating success with results. God wants all our efforts, even the small things we have to offer, like the five loaves and two fish. He blesses our small efforts and transforms them into something magnificent, a feast that feeds thousands and still leaves behind many baskets overflowing with His abundance.

At the outset of my journey, I realized that by letting go of things I was holding on to I could discover my real self. Thinking back to how I named my first Airstream Veronica, or "True Icon," I realize now that one secular meaning of "icon"—an idol or subject of great attention and devotion—proved oddly prescient. Although I didn't realize it at the time I purchased my trailer, I would end up taking great delight and pride in it, in acquiring skills to maintain it, and in the sheer joy and adventure of traveling. But ultimately, I needed to detach from the Airstream itself and more deeply embrace its religious meaning as an icon.

In the religious sense, icons serve as pictorial representations reminding us of eternal truths. They should point us to worship of God, not become objects of devotion in and of themselves. Veronica the Airstream, as the means of carrying out my mission, could not become its goal. It was only a symbol that pointed to an ultimate goal. The loss of Veronica and Bruce, with my miraculous uninjured survival (and that of Penny as well), became a time for reassessment and further detachment. It was a deliberate decision to purchase a smaller Airstream and older truck, to retain some resources for future needs, and to slow down, to spend more time in one community at a time rather than moving around so frequently.

Even so, I delight in the gift God made to me of my tiny home. That delight needs to be a thank-you acknowledging His goodness, for His glory. I like little Alvie the Airstream so much that I need to remind myself not to be overly attached to it. When I stayed in my friend Karen's yard on the Chesapeake Bay, each morning I'd get up and thank God for the beautiful sight of the ever-changing water and sky. I'd admire the Airstream sitting there reflecting the clouds in the sky. It took me a while to realize that I needed to be sure to restrain my fondness for the pretty, shiny thing and instead praise God not for the Airstream per se, but for how it helps me fulfill His will in my pilgrim journey.

When I detach from things I'm fond of, from my own wishes, even from evaluating the success of my efforts, that makes room for me to be filled by what God wants for me. Detachment leads to peace.

## Peace

Like many nomads, I find God's peace in landscapes. As I've mentioned before, the movie *Nomadland* demonstrated this effect in the scene where Fern literally soaks in a spring. Like a dry sponge, I soak in peace when I walk along the shore hearing waves, smelling the salt air, and seeing small shorebirds with delicate legs run toward the exposed wet sand, then back away from the waves again.

There's a stillness in nature when you hike by yourself. When you walk alone on trails, your senses are heightened, hearing the drowsy buzz of insects, feeling the coolness of deep green shade after crossing a sunlit meadow. Surprises, like the glimpse of a bright red cardinal or a small, curious golden finch, punctuate the walk.

Grass sighs in the breeze and small rivulets of running water sing as they turn into streams passing under my feet when I cross wooden planked bridges. The saltiness of sweat dripping down my face and the coolness of water from my flask are intensified by the quietude. My own heartbeat seems to be the loudest sound until I hear the trill of unseen frogs calling. I draw overwhelming comfort from this solitude, not as an experience of loneliness but rather as a form of communion with the Divine.

The same peace comes from sitting before Jesus physically present in the Eucharist in a tangible way to strengthen us. I can bring to the altar and to the foot of His cross all the worries, pain, and anger I have. I leave it there with Him. He's bigger than me and can handle it.

There's a story from a saint who asked a farmhand, "What do you do when you spend time in Adoration?" "I look at Him and He looks at me," the simple man answered. He sees us, He loves us, and He accepts who we are, while calling us to leave behind anything that interferes with being who He created us to be.

How does life as a nomad lead to this peace? You don't have to be a nomad to find it, but you do have to journey to it. Your journey may take place in your home, your work, wherever you meet God and accept His invitation to walk with Him. Sometimes that means He carries you on His shoulders because you are not able to walk.

Peace, however, is easy to lose. When I start grumbling to myself, or let fly with angry words when something doesn't go my way or someone makes a comment that irritates me, I know I'm not at peace. At that moment, I return to fixing my gaze on God. I remind myself that He is peace. He is present, and nothing happens without Him. In returning to trust, I rediscover peace.

## Joy

Joy comes from the absolute abandonment of everything into God's hands. The slightest movement of your thoughts and mind to Him, calling out in affection, thanksgiving, praise, repentance, or need, is a prayer. He allows us to draw closer to Him and receive supernatural joy. Yet when we pray, it is not like going to an ATM or vending machine, as my pastor recently reminded me. When we expect God to do exactly what we ask in prayer, we may lose faith if He does not. What we think we want often is not what we receive, but what we receive will be what brings us the greatest good.

Ultimately God offers us Himself, a person who is love incarnate and divine. We discover the joy of being loved. Fear, by contrast, destroys our love and trust. If we mistakenly view God as vengeful or uncaring, we turn away from Him and lose our joy. Friendship, marriage, and our own relationship with God fulfill the deepest longings of our hearts. We are not alone, even if we may feel lonely or misunderstood at times. Trust, detachment, and peace lead us to find joy in the ordinary things of everyday life, whether that life is in an Airstream travel trailer or an urban apartment.

CHAPTER THIRTY

# SIGNPOSTS ON THE JOURNEY PART FOUR

*"The Road goes ever on and on
Down from the door where it began.
Now far ahead the Road has gone,
And I must follow, if I can,
Pursuing it with eager feet,
Until it joins some larger way
Where many paths and errands meet.
And whither then? I cannot say"*
—J. R. R. Tolkien

As you approach the end of this journey with a Tin Can Pilgrim, realize that the road goes on. Your journey never ends until you reach your true home in eternity. Along the way, you will grow closer to God if you follow His signposts. He offers Himself to everyone, everywhere, at all times.

Some discover Him through creativity. Life on the road makes you more fully alive as you are closer to nature, able to see and absorb the beauty of His Creation. You realize that you have that same spirit within you that breathed life into this world.

Whatever the means that opens your eyes, as you see more clearly, you find Him. Trusting Him leads to detachment from things and activities that may be obstacles to a closer relationship. As you detach, you find peace and the promise of joy. As His children, we are all heirs to that joy.

Thank you for journeying with me in my adventures as a Tin Can Pilgrim. May these signposts continue to guide you to find the others the Lord has placed in your path to Him. Here are some questions and reflections to help you discern that path:

 Where do you see the hand of the Creator?

 Have you ever been inspired as an adult to learn a new form of art or craft? What inspires you to sing, to compose, to write, to draw, to build? Discover your own creativity by trying something new—a poem, a song, a drawing, a carving, a building, cooking, painting—whatever draws you. If nothing does, then pick something anyway and try it.

 How can you share that gift to inspire others?

 How do you experience joy?

 Is there a time when suffering in your life led you to peace and joy?

Do you know deeply, in the very essence of your being, that you are loved and that joy is your inheritance? Consider that and ask God to increase your faith.

 Who can you pray for? Offer the small tasks of each day for that person. No prayers are ever wasted, as God hears and uses them all.

 How can you live your life journeying with God?

 May you find happiness in the journey and the destination.

# CONCLUSION: AROUND THE NEXT CORNER, OVER THE NEXT HILL

*"Go someplace you've heard about, where you can fish or hunt or collect rocks or just look up at the sky. Find out what's at the end of some country road. Go see what's over the next hill, and the one after that, and the one after that."*

—Wally Byam

## Encouraging Others on Their Journeys

Hopefully, this book entertained you with tales of my journey and you learned something about living full-time in a travel trailer. More important, I hope it helps you to find your path and the courage and inspiration to follow that path. God has specific plans for each of us, to make us happy. If I've prompted you to start a conversation with Him, to listen and to pray, I'm grateful to have guided you to take the first step in your journey.

Life on the road is a process of becoming detached from things and activities that drain my time and energy and keep me from growing closer to my Creator. Traveling is a way for me to truly embrace whatever God wants for me and to be content in the present.

Before I hit the road, feelings of being trapped in my life and vaguely discontent without seeing a clear alternative had frustrated me for years. I never really came to terms with losing the abilities and privileges I'd had as a highly successful lawyer. I felt shame over the failure of my marriage and other mistakes I'd made. I tried to compensate by doggedly acquiring skills in a new field in which I believed I could easily succeed, by dating as if finding a new husband were the measure of success that would compensate for my failed marriage, and by maintaining the go-go-go parenting style typical of a highly competitive urban culture in which success is measured by the amount and type of extracurricular and academic activities in which your children engage. This was a setup for disappointment and dissatisfaction. Leaving it behind set me free to take a different path.

Not many people are called to life on the road. Most of us are simply asked to journey in place. My pilgrimage in its essence is a search for the manifestation of the Divine in the world. Where I end up on the physical journey isn't as important as the spiritual destination. I could have found joy and peace where I was, if I had understood that sooner, without ever living in an Airstream travel trailer.

Thus my message for you is one of hope. No matter how bleak and disheartening things may seem, or how counterintuitive the possible solutions, things will get better. Trust Him. He'll never let you down, because He loves you beyond all imagining. He wants only good for you, even if you have to walk with Him through many dark valleys to get there. Sometimes, that even means letting Him carry you.

In the end, He is God and we are not. Through humility and with His grace comes the possibility of a union with Him to which He invites each of us. I'm grateful to be a small part of that invitation, by sharing with you my transformation into a Tin Can Pilgrim.

Whether it means that you live life on the road as a nomad or not, that you make changes by accepting His invitation, that you look at your current life with new vision, depends on you.

May the traditional Irish blessing hold true for you on your journey:

> *May the road rise to meet you,*
> *may the wind be always at your back,*
> *may the sun shine warm upon your face*
> *and rains fall soft upon your fields.*
> *And, until we meet again,*
> *may God hold you in the palm of His hand.*

## Looking Down the Road

As I write this, I'm starting to plan for the coming year. I'll spend a couple of months camp hosting. Physical labor will build back my stamina for life on the road. All the lessons I've learned about maintenance and safety will inform my preparation of my Airstream Alvie for travel. I'm going to weigh everything I put back in my empty, winterized trailer, for example.

Most importantly, this time of reflection and renewal of old ties and relationships will regenerate my future travels. Writing this book has helped me with self-discipline. Living with my daughter in a small apartment—that seems spacious to me, but also reined in somehow—has renewed my appreciation for the freedom of nomadic life. Encouraging her as she looks for her first full-time job has also reminded me of the difficult challenges posed by the pandemic and the economy.

Yet, what I know is hope. I trust in God, who always wants what is good. Even cancer has had its silver linings—being treatable, helping me grow in empathy for those with physical ailments, and reinforcing the value of friendship, of being able to receive as well as to give.

So where do I go from here? Practically, I'm volunteering in New Mexico and perhaps Colorado. I'll spend time with people

I've met before, and make new friends who winter in Arizona and other warm, dry Southwest regions. In January, I've made plans to renew my acquaintances with friends in Florida. After that, who knows?

Making plans but letting go of them if the Spirit moves me in another direction is a valuable lesson I've learned in my marvelous adventure as a Tin Can Pilgrim. It is a mystery that you become who you truly are by not clinging desperately to who you think you are. You find happiness by letting go, by recognizing it right in front of you, in the present moment. When you find the One who loves you, who made you to be loved, you find yourself as well.

Although I may not know where I'll end up geographically, I hope my journey will lead me to be more flexible, more open and attentive to the workings of the Spirit, and more willing to follow wherever God leads me to serve Him and others. Spending time with people, listening to their concerns, and helping them find the source of real joy continues to be a marvelous adventure.

As Bob Wells would say, "See you down the road!"

# RV TRANSLATION AID FOR BEGINNERS (GLOSSARY)

**AC** – alternating current power; 120-volt AC power comes from a power pedestal in a campground, a generator, or an outlet in a residential "sticks and bricks" home

**Adapter** – in RV parlance usually a device that changes one type of power to another type

**AGM** – deep cycle marine batteries that do not require you to add water periodically

**Amp** – short term for ampere, the base unit of electric current or the flow of electricity

**Batteries** – really big batteries used to store power for your RV; see AGM, and Lithium and Wet Batteries below

**Black Water** – famous song by the Doobie Brothers; slang for swamp water; or, for RVers, any water and accompanying stuff that passes through the toilet and is stored—you guessed it—in the black tank

**Boondocking** – camping without connections to power, water, or sewer, usually in a remote place; a form of dry camping

**Camp Hosting** – work at a campground that is compensated in part or in full by provision of a campsite

**CAT Scale** – nothing to do with the kind that purr; a scale with flat plates on the ground that you drive over to weigh each axle of a trailer and tow vehicle

**Chocks** – device to prevent wheels from rolling, usually triangular graduated plastic blocks but may be wood blocks, stones, or metal braces that fit between two wheels in a double-axle trailer

**Class A** – largest drivable-style RV, built on a very strong heavy-duty frame

**Class B** – drivable RV built on a smaller frame than a Class A or C, typically a Mercedes chassis

**Class C** – drivable RV with sleeping area or storage loft above the driver cab

**Class D** – trick question: there is no Class D

**Converter** – the Holy Spirit . . . oops, wrong glossary! Device that changes AC power to DC power

**DC** – Location of the Capitol of the U.S. Yes, but also direct current power, the type of power that operates 12-volt devices such as lights and fans in an Airstream or other RV and is stored in batteries

**Dry Camping** – camping without precipitation? without booze? Perhaps, but more typically refers to camping without hookups, whether on public land, a park, a campground, or a parking lot; boondocking is a form of dry camping that occurs in a remote location

**EMS** – a surge protector on steroids, this electronic management system device detects low voltage, high voltage, reverse polarity, faulty grounds, overheating plugs, and other dangers for your RV electrical system (no, not UFOs . . .)

**EZ start** – device to reduce the amount of power an air conditioner initially draws when started or cycling back on

**Fifth Wheel** – a single person two couples go out with? No, this type of trailer attaches to the bed of a heavy-duty truck and has two levels with lots of space inside

**Flamingo** – tropical aquatic bird with long legs and pink feathers; iconic for Airstreamers for reasons lost to history, you'll find flocks of plastic flamingos and other flamingo-themed clothing and paraphernalia congregating at Airstream events

**GAWR** – Gross Axle Weight Rating, or the maximum weight that each axle of your tow vehicle is built to carry

**Glamping** – glamorous camping, as in an Airstream, often accompanied by fine wine and gourmet food

**Gray Water** – water and anything else that drains through the shower and sinks into the gray water holding tank

**GVW** – gross vehicle weight; includes all the fluids, cargo, and passengers, as well as any dealer-installed items

**GVWR** – gross vehicle weight rating; the maximum weight your vehicle frame is built to carry

**Hitch** – device to attach item being towed to vehicle doing the towing

**Hitch Ball** – the round ball on a hitch designed to fit inside the circular hitch receiver attached to a trailer

**Hitch Pin** – the solid piece of metal that goes through the hitch receiver on the truck to fasten the hitch in place; locking hitch pins are best

**Hitch Receiver** – either the empty rectangular metal inlet on your tow vehicle, for inserting the hitch, or the curved semicircular piece of the hitch attached to your trailer, into which the hitch ball inserts

**Hookups** – not the popular meaning, but in the RV world attachments for your water, power, or sewer hose; known as "full hookups" when all are available

**Hygrometer** – device to measure humidity within your RV

**Inverter** – converts DC power to AC power

**Jack** – device for lifting a vehicle or trailer; in the verb form (jacked up) can also mean really messed up

**Leveling Blocks** – may look like giant Legos or curved swooshes of plastic or even pieces of wood used under the jack or stabilizers when deployed to make sure an RV is relatively level

**Lithium Batteries** – batteries that cost a lot, have a longer life, and are lighter than AGM batteries

**LP** – liquid propane

**Moochdocking** – staying at a friend's property for free; customary to leave a small house gift

**Power Pedestal** – not what you stand on to reach your fuse box, but a vertical post at your campsite containing electric sockets for 50-amp, 30-amp, and sometimes 20-amp power

**Rally** – in the camping sense, camping a lot closer than you normally would, with many people who share similar interests, for example the Airstream International Rally or a maintenance rally

**RV** – recreational vehicle, inclusive of trailers, fifth wheels, motorhomes, Skoolies, and camper vans

**Setup** – your plate, cup, drink, and utensils (as in, "bring your own setup") for a campfire or potluck or buffet with other RVers

**Skoolies** – school buses modified to live in with kitchen, dining, sleeping, and bathroom facilities of some type

**SOB** – not an expletive, but the somewhat snarky way Airstreamers refer to "some other brand" of RV

**Soft start** – not what you do when you are trying to leave without your neighbors noticing, but a device that reduces the amps needed to start or cycle your air conditioner

**Stabilizers** – not for bearing weight, these retractable legs keep your RV steady when you walk around in it; use them to minimize "bounce" when camping, but never for leveling

**Stealth camping** – doesn't work with an Airstream; refers to parking a vehicle in which you sleep in an area that doesn't allow overnight parking

**Sticks and Bricks** – the kind of house most people live in

**Stinky Slinky** – the accordion-pleated black hose for dumping black water (see above)

**Surge Suppressor** – also called surge protector, this device protects electrical devices from voltage spikes

**Sway Bars** – often referred to as anti-sway bars, these may be a separate bar or bars or built into the weight distribution bars; they reduce sideways motion of the trailer at the hitch

**Tongue Weight** – how much weight sits on the ball of your tow vehicle's hitch when you hitch up your trailer; normally this should be 10–15 percent of GVWR

**Travel Trailer** – pulled by a tow vehicle attached to the trailer by a hitch; you can unhitch and drive the tow vehicle once trailer is parked at campsite

**Volt** – a unit of electromagnetic force, analogous to water pressure

**Watts** – a measurement of how much power is produced; amps multiplied by volts equals watts

**Weight Distribution Bars** – heavy bars on a hitch that distribute weight from the back axle to the front axle of the tow vehicle and may also have anti-sway capacity

**Wet Batteries** – what you have when your flashlight accidentally pops opens while you're looking inside your black tank; more commonly, a battery that contains liquid sulfuric acid and water that periodically must be replenished

# RESOURCES

These are materials that I've found helpful. It is not a comprehensive list, but a starting point for those who want to delve more deeply. Many of the websites have links to podcasts.

## Books

**RV Life**

*Nomadland: Surviving America in the Twenty-First Century,* Jessica Bruder (W. W. Norton & Company, Inc., 2018)

*Tales from the Black Tank,* Debra Benton, The Virtual Campground

*The (nearly) Complete Guide to Airstream Maintenance,* Rich Luhr (Church Street Publishing, Inc., 2015)

*The Newbies Guide to Airstreaming,* 4th Edition, Rich Luhr (Church Street Publishing, Inc., 2017)

*The Airstream That Ran Away with the Spoon: Discovering a New Home and a New Life with Chronic Fatigue,* Mary K. D. D'Rozario (Write Way Publishing Company, 2019)

*A Beginner's Guide to Living in an RV: Everything I Wish I Knew Before Full-Time RVing Across America,* Alyssa Padgett (independently published, 2017)

**Faith**

*Do Something Beautiful for God: The Essential Teachings of Mother Teresa* (Blue Sparrow, 2019)

*Catholicism: A Journey to the Heart of the Faith*, Robert Barron (Image, 2014)

*Nudging Conversions: A Practical Guide to Bringing Those You Love Back to the Church*, Carrie Gress (Beacon Publishing, 2015)

*Mere Christianity*, Revised Edition, C.S. Lewis (HarperOne, 2015)

*Rome Sweet Home: Our Journey to Catholicism*, Scott and Kimberly Hahn (Ignatius Press, 1993)

*What Catholics Really Believe*, Karl Keating (Ignatius Press, 1995)

*Fundamentals of the Faith: Essays in Christian Apologetics*, Peter Kreeft (Ignatius Press, 1998)

*The Catechism of the Catholic Church*, Second Edition (USCCB, 2020)

*The Bible*, NAB Revised Edition (American Bible Society)

*The Navarre Bible, Texts and Commentaries* (Scepter Publishers)

# Websites

**RV Life**

https://www.heathandalyssa.com

https://www.longlonghoneymoon.com

https://www.mortonsonthemove.com

https://www.livinginbeauty.net

https://www.homesonwheelsalliance.org

https://www.cheaprvliving.com

https://www.tincanpilgrim.com

https://thevirtualcampground.com

**Faith**

https://www.usccb.org
https://www.catholic.org
https://www.ewtn.com
https://www.aleteia.org
https://www.wordonfire.org
https://www.opusdei.org
https://www.dynamiccatholic.com
https://www.catholicherald.com
https://www.stphillipinstitute.org
https://www.saintjosemariainstitute.org
https://www.media.ascensionpress.com/all-bible-in-a-year-episodes

# THANKS

This book is a gift to God and would not be possible without His love and support. I wrote and edited much of it in my journals at church in front of the Blessed Sacrament. Also, many people prayed for me during this process as I was recovering from early-stage breast cancer while writing the book. I thank all of them and all the friends and neighbors I met throughout my journeys whether mentioned in these pages or not. May God bless you and may your lives be full of joy and peace.

Sincere thanks to the team at st. john's press, especially my editors, Torund Bryhn and Richard Willett, for their unwavering guidance, expertise, and encouragement. I wrote the rough draft of this book as part of taking the Bestseller Mastermind class offered by Torund in 2021. I literally had a draft in sixty days. All the members of that class have my affection and gratitude for how they helped me stay on track and overcome doubts in the process of birthing this book: Michelle Gil, Michaelle Gocko, Phoenix West Devereux, Lisa Geraci Rigoni, and Kim Radke. I look forward to reading all their forthcoming books.

I'm very grateful to the Reverend Father Jerry A. Wooton of Holy Spirit Parish and Coleen MacKay for their detailed reading, editing, and comments on the book, as well as their friendship. A big thank you goes to all my other beta readers who read and commented on portions of the various drafts: Amy Bilyeau, Laura Klucik, Karen Cassidy, Hank and Joanne DiToro, Peggy and Marshall Hendrickson, Ellen Pinker, Cara Yocum, the Reverend Father Thomas Tuan Nguyen of Saint Leo the Great Catholic Church, Michelle Gil, Bill Young, and Julia Taylor. My daughters also helped me with their comments and support during this process. I especially appreciate the prayerful support and encouragement of my pastor the Reverend Father David A. Whitestone and Deacon Marques Silva of Saint Leo the Great Catholic Church; the Reverend Father Robert J. Wagner of Saint Andrew the Apostle Catholic Church; as well as that of friends, priests, and retreat leaders in Opus Dei, who helped me keep seeing this work as prayer integrated into the daily tasks of life.

My friend Renata deserves special mention. On very short notice, Renata Grzan Wieczorek shared the gift of her artistry with me by photographing me for the book's back cover. Renata is a talented creator whose work is featured on her blog, For the Love of Beauty (https://www.FortheLoveofBeauty.com). She dedicates her art to elevating the everyday and sensitizing the soul to God's Divine beauty. Not only is Renata an amazing photographer, she writes compelling and lovely icons. For the Love of Beauty offers sacred and allegorical artworks, guidance on praying with art, spiritual bouquet and prayer cards, prayer beads, and inspirational jewelry.

The book's illustrator and cover artist, Hege Terese Fjaera, instantly understood the essence of Tin Can Pilgrim's journeys. Her lovely and charming art captures the spirit of joy and caring that I hope you have found within the pages of this book.

Thanks as well to all the wanderers, nomads, and adventurers who let me share portions of their lives as colleagues and friends, including (but not limited to!) Laural, Mary, Nan, Keith, Suzanne, Lindy, Nancy, Stacey, Christine, Marie, John, Ellen, Melia, Millie, Lisa, Brett, Matt, Beth, Heath, Alyssa, Jeremy, Jimmie, Britt, Josh, Brian, Teresa, Ken, Theresa, Larry, Scott, Renetta, Susan, Barry, Debra, Nick, Julie, Debbie, Maria, Robert, Joy, Bruce, Melinda, Kelsey, Joe, Ken, Cliff, Jes, Chris, and too many others to name. See you all down the road!

www.ingramcontent.com/pod-product-compliance
Lightning Source LLC
Chambersburg PA
CBHW071411070526
44578CB00003B/553